IFIP Advances in Information and Communication Technology 500

Editor-in-Chief

Kai Rannenberg, Goethe University Frankfurt, Germany

Editorial Board Members

IFIP – The International Federation for Information Processing

IFIP was founded in 1960 under the auspices of UNESCO, following the first World Computer Congress held in Paris the previous year. A federation for societies working in information processing, IFIP's aim is two-fold: to support information processing in the countries of its members and to encourage technology transfer to developing nations. As its mission statement clearly states:

> IFIP is the global non-profit federation of societies of ICT professionals that aims at achieving a worldwide professional and socially responsible development and application of information and communication technologies.

IFIP is a non-profit-making organization, run almost solely by 2500 volunteers. It operates through a number of technical committees and working groups, which organize events and publications. IFIP's events range from large international open conferences to working conferences and local seminars.

The flagship event is the IFIP World Computer Congress, at which both invited and contributed papers are presented. Contributed papers are rigorously refereed and the rejection rate is high.

As with the Congress, participation in the open conferences is open to all and papers may be invited or submitted. Again, submitted papers are stringently refereed.

The working conferences are structured differently. They are usually run by a working group and attendance is generally smaller and occasionally by invitation only. Their purpose is to create an atmosphere conducive to innovation and development. Refereeing is also rigorous and papers are subjected to extensive group discussion.

Publications arising from IFIP events vary. The papers presented at the IFIP World Computer Congress and at open conferences are published as conference proceedings, while the results of the working conferences are often published as collections of selected and edited papers.

IFIP distinguishes three types of institutional membership: Country Representative Members, Members at Large, and Associate Members. The type of organization that can apply for membership is a wide variety and includes national or international societies of individual computer scientists/ICT professionals, associations or federations of such societies, government institutions/government related organizations, national or international research institutes or consortia, universities, academies of sciences, companies, national or international associations or federations of companies.

More information about this series at http://www.springer.com/series/6102

Michail Maniatakos · Ibrahim (Abe) M. Elfadel ·
Matteo Sonza Reorda · H. Fatih Ugurdag ·
José Monteiro · Ricardo Reis (Eds.)

VLSI-SoC: Opportunities and Challenges Beyond the Internet of Things

25th IFIP WG 10.5/IEEE International Conference
on Very Large Scale Integration, VLSI-SoC 2017
Abu Dhabi, United Arab Emirates, October 23–25, 2017
Revised and Extended Selected Papers

 Springer

Editors
Michail Maniatakos (ID)
New York University Abu Dhabi
Abu Dhabi, United Arab Emirates

Ibrahim (Abe) M. Elfadel (ID)
Khalifa University
Abu Dhabi, United Arab Emirates

Matteo Sonza Reorda (ID)
Politecnico di Torino
Turin, Italy

H. Fatih Ugurdag (ID)
Ozyegin University
Istanbul, Turkey

José Monteiro (ID)
INESC-ID
Lisbon, Portugal

Ricardo Reis (ID)
Federal University of Rio Grande do Sul
Porto Alegre, Brazil

ISSN 1868-4238   ISSN 1868-422X   (electronic)
IFIP Advances in Information and Communication Technology
ISBN 978-3-030-15665-7   ISBN 978-3-030-15663-3   (eBook)
https://doi.org/10.1007/978-3-030-15663-3

This Springer imprint is published by the registered company Springer Nature Switzerland AG
The registered company address is: Gewerbestrasse 11, 6330 Cham, Switzerland

Preface

This book contains extended and revised versions of the highest quality papers that were presented during the 25th edition of the IFIP/IEEE WG10.5 International Conference on Very Large Scale Integration (VLSI-SoC), a global System-on-Chip Design and CAD conference. The 25th edition (Silver Jubilee Edition) of the conference was held in the period of October 23–25, 2017, at the Yas Viceroy Hotel, Yas Island, Abu Dhabi, United Arab Emirates. Previous conferences have taken place in Edinburgh, Scotland (1981); Trondheim, Norway (1983); Tokyo, Japan (1985); Vancouver, Canada (1987); Munich, Germany (1989); Edinburgh, Scotland (1991); Grenoble, France (1993); Chiba, Japan (1995); Gramado, Brazil (1997); Lisbon, Portugal (1999); Montpellier, France (2001); Darmstadt, Germany (2003); Perth, Australia (2005); Nice, France (2006); Atlanta, GA, USA (2007); Rhodes Island, Greece (2008); Florianopolis, Brazil (2009); Madrid, Spain (2010); Kowloon, Hong Kong (2011), Santa Cruz, CA, USA (2012); Istanbul, Turkey (2013); Playa del Carmen, Mexico (2014); Daejeon, South Korea (2015); and Tallin, Estonia (2016).

The purpose of this conference, which was sponsored by IFIP TC 10 Working Group 10.5, the IEEE Council on Electronic Design Automation (CEDA), and the IEEE Circuits and Systems Society, with the In-Cooperation of ACM SIGDA, is to provide a forum for the presentation and discussion of the latest academic and industrial results and developments as well as the future trends in the field of system-on-chip (SoC) design, considering the challenges of nano-scale, state-of-the-art, and emerging manufacturing technologies. The down-scaling of feature sizes of modern semiconductor technologies imposes numerous new challenges on the physical and system-level design of SoCs. In particular, growing reliability challenges demand new concepts in fault-tolerant SoC design and testing. In the post-IoT era, these challenges are complicated by more pressure to reduce cost so as to achieve edge-node ubiquity and further reduce power to extend edge-node lifetime. The chapters by Copetti et al., Garwal and Kapoor, and Thiele et al. relate to the post-IoT reliability concerns, while the chapters by Kimiyoshi et al., Nautiyal et al., and Rizzo et al. address low-power concerns. Other pressures include tighter integration of analog, communication, and signal processing functions within edge nodes. They are addressed in the chapters by Saadeh and Bin Altaf, Muzaffar and Elfadel, and Aldgheri and Bombieri. Finally, system-level thermal management and security concerns are taken up in the chapters by Cesairini et al. and Wamser and Sigl. The chapters of this new book in the VLSI-SoC series continue its tradition of providing an internationally acknowledged platform for scientific contributions and industrial progress on this field.

For the VLSI-SoC 2017 conference, 33 papers out of 112 submissions were selected for presentation, and out of these 33 full papers presented at the conference, 11 papers were chosen by a special selection committee to have an extended and revised version included in this book. The selection process of these papers considered the evaluation scores during the review process as well as the review forms provided by members of the Technical Program Committee and session chairs as a result of the presentations.

The chapters of this book have authors from Brazil, China, Germany, India, Italy, Japan, Pakistan, Switzerland, United Arab Emirates and USA. The Technical Program Committee for the regular tracks comprised 107 members from 25 countries.

This book also includes a special chapter that presents the history of the VLSI-SoC series of conferences and its relation with VLSI-SoC evolution since the early 1980s up to the present.

VLSI-SoC 2017 was the culmination of the work of many dedicated volunteers: authors, reviewers, session chairs, invited speakers, and various committee chairs. We thank them all for their contributions.

This book is intended for the VLSI community at large, and in particular the many colleagues who did not have the chance to attend the conference. We hope you enjoy reading this book and that you will find it useful in your professional life and for the development of the VLSI community as a whole.

October 2018

Michail Maniatakos
Ibrahim (Abe) M. Elfadel
Matteo Sonza Reorda
H. Fatih Ugurdag
José Monteiro
Ricardo Reis

Organization

The IFIP/IEEE International Conference on Very Large Scale Integration System-on-Chip (VLSI-SoC) 2017 took place during October 23–25, 2017, at the Yas Viceroy, Yas Island, Abu Dhabi, United Arab Emirates. VLSI-SoC 2017 was the 25th in a series of international conferences, sponsored by IFIP TC 10 Working Group 10.5 (VLSI), IEEE CEDA and ACM SIGDA.

General Chairs

Ibrahim (Abe) M. Elfadel   Khalifa University, UAE
H. Fatih Ugurdag   Ozyegin University, Turkey

Technical Program Chairs

Mihalis Maniatakos   NYU Abu Dhabi, UAE
Matteo Sonza-Reorda   Politecnico di Torino, Italy

Special Sessions Chairs

Mehdi Tahoori   Karlsruhe Institute of Technology, Germany
Youngsoo Shin   Korea Advanced Institute of Science and Technology, South Korea

PhD Forum Chairs

Soha Hassoun   Tufts University, USA
Leila Ismail   UAE University, UAE

Finance/Local Arrangements Chair

Ibrahim (Abe) M. Elfadel   Khalifa University, UAE

Academia Liaison

Mohammed Ismail   Wayne State University, USA

Industry Liaisons

Rafic Makki   Mubadala, UAE
Yervant Zorian   Synopsys, USA

Government Liaison

Hazem Al Assaly   Abu Dhabi Education Council, UAE

International Liaisons

Hazem ElTahawy   Mentor Graphics, Egypt
Anton Klotz   Cadence, Germany
Vazgen Melikyan   Synopsys, Armenia

Publicity Chairs

Ricardo Reis   UFRGS, Brazil
Masahiro Fujita   Tokyo University, Japan

VLSI-SoC Steering Committee

Manfred Glesner   TU Darmstadt, Germany
Salvador Mir   TIMA, France
Michel Robert   University of Montpellier, France
Chi-Ying Tsui   HKUST, Hong Kong, SAR China
Matthew Guthaus   UC Santa Cruz, USA
Ricardo Reis   UFRGS, Brazil
Luis Miguel Silveira   INESC ID, Portugal
Fatih Ugurdag   Ozyegin University, Turkey

Publication Chairs

Jerald Yoo   National University of Singapore, Singapore
José Monteiro   INESC, Portugal

Registration Chair

Mihai Sanduleanu   Khalifa University, UAE

Web Chair

Andreas Henschel   Khalifa University, UAE

Technical Program Committee

Analog, Mixed-Signal, and Sensor Architectures

Chairs

Jerzy Dabrowski   Linköping University, Sweden
Mihai Sanduleanu   Masdar Institute, UAE

Members

Kenichi Okada	Tokyo Institute of Technology, Japan
Jacob Wikner	Linköping University, Sweden
Rashad Ramzan	National University of Computer and Emerging Sciences-FAST-NU, Pakistan
Pawel Sniatala	Poznan University of Technology, Poland
Robert Szczygiel	AGH University of Science and Technology, Poland
Witold Machowski	AGH University of Science and Technology, Poland
Saul Rodriguez	Royal Institute of Technology KTH, Sweden
Tomas Golonek	Silesian University of Technology, Poland

Digital Architectures: NoC, Multi-core, and Reconfigurable

Chairs

Michael Hübner	Ruhr-Universität Bochum, Germany
Haris Javaid	Google, USA

Members

Jiang Xu	Hong Kong University of Science and Technology, SAR China
Farhad Medipour	Kyushu University, Japan
Catalin Bogdan Ciobanu	University of Amsterdam, The Netherlands
Rehan Hafiz	SEECS – NUST, Pakistan
Syed Waqar Nabi	University of Glasgow, Scotland
Diana Goehringer	TU Dresden, Germany
João Cardoso	FEUP/Universidade do Porto, Portugal

CAD, Synthesis and Analysis

Chairs

Matthew Guthaus	University of California Santa Cruz, USA
Ricardo Reis	UFRGS, Brazil

Members

Masahiro Fujita	University of Tokyo, Japan
Takashi Kambe	Kinki University, Japan
Bei Yu	Chinese University of Hong Kong, SAR China
Tiziano Villa	University of Verona, Italy
Srinivas Katkoori	University of South Florida, USA
Gustavo Wilke	Synopsys, USA
Renato Hentschke	Intel, USA

Prototyping, Verification, Modeling and Simulation

Chairs

Graziano Pravadelli   University of Verona, Italy
Sameh Asaad   IBM, USA

Members

Anupam Chattopadhyay   Nanyang Technological University, Singapore
Nicola Bombieri   University of Verona, Italy
Philip Kindt   Technical University of Munich, Germany
Thomas Roewer   IBM, USA
Geert Janssen   IBM, USA
Daniel Grosse   University of Bremen and DFKI, Germany
Laurence Pierre   Université de Grenoble, France

Circuits and Systems for Signal Processing and Communications

Chairs

Tobias Noll   RWTH Aachen, Germany
Luc Claesen   Hasselt University, Belgium

Members

Dajiang Zhou   Waseda University, Japan
Hm Bae   KAIST, South Korea
Per Larsson-Edefors   Chalmers University of Technology, Sweden
Oscar Gustafsson   Linköping University, Sweden
Chris Papachristou   Case Western Reserve University, USA
Peng Liu   Zhejiang University, China
Christoph Studer   Cornell University, USA
Nam Pham Ngoc   Hanoi University of Science and Technology, Vietnam
Chun-Jen Tsai   National Chiao Tung University, Taiwan

Embedded Systems: Architectures, Design and Software

Chairs

Zebo Peng   Linköping University, Sweden
Vijaykrishnan Narayanan   Pennsylvania State University, USA

Members

Lars Bauer   Karlsruhe Institute of Technology - KIT, Germany
Ing-Chao Lin   National Cheng Kung University, Taiwan
Zili Shao   Hong Kong Polytechnic University, SAR China
Yu Wang   Tsinghua University, China
Paul Pop   Technical University of Denmark

Jason Xue   City University of Hong Kong, SAR China
Theocharis Theocharidis   University of Cyprus, Cyprus
Soheil Samii   General Motors, USA

Low-Power and Thermal-Aware IC Design

Chairs

Sherief Reda   Brown University, USA
Alberto Macii   Politecnico di Torino, Italy

Members

Nadine Azemard   LIRMM/CNRS, France
Mirko Loghi   Università di Udine, Italy
Marina Zapater   Universidad Politécnica de Madrid, Spain
Martha Johanna Sepulveda   Technical University of Munich, Germany
Muhammad Shafique   Vienna University of Technology, Austria
Francesco Paterna   Intel, USA
Toufik Sadi   University of Glasgow, Scotland
Andrea Bartolini   University of Bologna, Italy

Emerging Semiconductor Technologies

Chairs

Andrea Calimera   Politecnino di Torino, Italy
Aida Todri-Sanial   CNRS-LIRMM, France

Members

Jingtong Hu   Oklahoma State University, USA
Wujie Wen   Florida International University, USA
Elena Ioana Vatajelu   Politecnico di Torino, Italy
Weisheng Zhao   Spintronics Interdisciplinary Center, Beihang
                                University, China
Danghui Wang   NorthWestern Polytechnical University, China
Jean-Michel Portal   Ecole Polytech' Marseille, France
Serge Bernard   CNRS-LIRMM, France
Valerio Tenace   Politecnico di Torino, Italy
Jean-Michel Portal   IM2NP, France

Variability, Reliability and Test

Chairs

Bernd Becker   University of Freiburg, Germany
Erik Larsson   Lund University, Sweden

Members

Tony Kim	Nanyang Technological University, Singapore
Stephan Eggersglüß	University of Bremen, Germany
Stefano Dicarlo	Politecnico di Torino, Italy
Emil Gizdarski	SYNOPSYS, USA
Maksim Jenihhin	Tallin University of Technology, Estonia
Satoshi Ohtake	Oita University, Japan

Hardware Security

Chairs

Jeyavijayan Rajendran	University of Texas at Dallas, USA
Georg Sigl	Technical University of Munich, Germany

Members

Debdeep Mukhopadhyay	IIT Kharagpur, India
Lilian Bossuet	University of Lyon, France
Thomas Eisenbarth	Worcester Polytechnic Institute, USA
Lejla Batina	Radboud University, The Netherlands
Valdimir Rozic	Katholieke Universiteit Leuven, Belgium
Salvador Manich	Universitat Politecnica de Catalunya, Spain
Tim Guneysu	University of Bremen, Germany
Patrick Schaumont	Virginia Tech, USA
Ilia Polian	University of Passau, Germany
Jens-Peter Kaps	George Mason University, USA
Stefan Mangard	TU Graz, Austria
Chip Hong Chang	Nanyang Technological University, Singapore

Contents

Level-Shifter-Less Approach for Multi-V_{DD} SoC Design to Employ Body Bias Control in FD-SOI

Kimiyoshi Usami[1(✉)], Shunsuke Kogure[1], Yusuke Yoshida[1], Ryo Magasaki[1], and Hideharu Amano[2]

[1] Shibaura Institute of Technology, 3-7-5 Toyosu, Koto-ku, Tokyo, Japan
usami@shibaura-it.ac.jp
[2] Keio University, 3-14-1 Hiyoshi, Kohoku-ku, Yokohama, Japan
hunga@am.ics.keio.ac.jp

Abstract. Level shifters to convert signal swings from low-voltage (VDDL) to high-voltage (VDDH) are required at the boundary of voltage domains in SoC employing multiple supply voltages. However, they cost delay, power and area in addition to increasing the complexity of physical design. This paper proposes a level-shifter-less (LSL) approach to use a reverse body bias (RBB) at pMOS transistors in the VDDH domain and superior threshold-voltage modulation capability of FD-SOI devices. Simulation results and measurements of a fabricated chip showed that the chip applying the LSL approach correctly operates at VDDL = 0.6 V and VDDH = 1.2 V under 2 V pMOS RBB while suppressing the static dc current in the VDDH domain. We also demonstrate that adaptive RBB control for pMOS can maintain effectiveness of this approach under process and temperature variations.

Keywords: Level shifter · Multi-VDD design · Body bias control · FD-SOI · Low power · Variations

1 Introduction

Multi-V_{DD} design to include multiple voltage domains within a chip is one of the key techniques in low-power oriented SoCs [1]. Lowering the supply voltage (V_{DD}) contributes to power reduction but it is likely that some circuits within a SoC cannot be made to operate at lower voltage. One reason is that lowering the supply voltage degrades the performance of MOS transistors, leading to degradation of circuit speed. If the circuit is required to operate at high clock frequency or is on the critical path, the voltage cannot be lowered. Another reason is that memory circuits provided as SRAM or ROM macros usually do not work at low voltage. To enjoy power reduction by lowering the supply voltage, multi-V_{DD} design is essential which allows the reduced V_{DD} domain and the nominal V_{DD} domain to coexist in a SoC.

Realizing multi-V_{DD} design comes with several overheads. In particular, when an output signal of a lower-V_{DD} (VDDL) circuit is connected to the input of a higher-V_{DD} (VDDH) circuit, a level shifter (LS) circuit needs to be inserted at the interface.

M. Maniatakos et al. (Eds.): VLSI-SoC 2017, IFIP AICT 500, pp. 1–21, 2019.
https://doi.org/10.1007/978-3-030-15663-3_1

The conventional cross-coupled LS [2] and the conventional current-mirror LS [3] are depicted in Fig. 1(a) and (b), respectively. LS converts the voltage swing VDDL to the voltage swing VDDH but its delay and power dissipation become a critical overhead. In addition, LS requires both VDDH and VDDL as the power supply. This makes the physical design using the standard P&R flow significantly complicated [4], and thereby increases design effort. Authors of [5] proposed another LS circuit which requires only one supply (VDDH). This eliminates the layout constraint that both VDDH and VDDL supplies must be connected to LS and hence mitigates the complexity in physical design. However, the overheads in delay, power and area remain as problems.

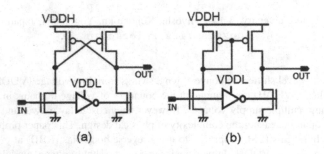

Fig. 1.   (a) Cross-coupled LS [2] and (b) Current-mirror LS [3].

In this paper, we propose a novel technique to make LS insertion unnecessary in the multi-V_{DD} design by the combination of body-bias control and threshold-voltage modulation capability of FD-SOI devices. We augmented the original conference paper [6] with the following contents:

- Impact by process variation

Process variation is one of the serious concerns in modern scaled devices. We investigated how much the process variation affects effectiveness of the proposed LSL approach through simulations. We also studied how much the approach can adaptively deal with the impact of the variation.

- Impact by temperature variation

The temperature of a chip varies during the operation by its own heat dissipation. Since effective threshold voltage of MOS transistors changes with the temperature [1], we investigated how much the temperature variation impacts on the proposed approach. This evaluation was conducted through real chip measurements.

- Influence of gate types in receivers

In the proposed LSL approach, a VDDH receiver gate with reverse-body-biasing receives the VDDL signal at the VDDL/VDDH interface. The paper [6] demonstrated that the gate types (e.g. NAND/NOR/inverter) of the receiver affect the delay. We newly added detailed simulation results in this paper showing that the receiver gate types also affect the lowest VDDL voltage to ensure the receiver's operation. We added description about underlying common mechanisms on how the receiver gate types relate to the delay and the lowest VDDL voltage.

• More detailed analysis on delay in cascaded gates influenced by RBB

RBB is applied to the whole pMOS transistors in the VDDH domain in the proposed LSL approach. We added more detailed analysis on how pMOS RBB influences the gate delay and demonstrated that only half of the gates in cascaded gates were made slower whereas others were made slightly faster.

We presented a part of the results for the process variation at another conference [18] but we have included new results to this paper. The rest of this paper is organized as follows: Sect. 2 describes the background and Sect. 3 presents the LSL approach that we propose. Section 4 presents simulation results and Sect. 5 presents measured results for a fabricated microprocessor test chip. Section 6 describes conclusions and the future work.

2 Background

First, we briefly describe the reason why LS is required when an output signal of a VDDL circuit is connected to the input of a VDDH circuit. As shown in Fig. 2, when the output of the VDDL circuit (INV1) is logical "1", the voltage of the node N1 is raised to VDDL. However, if VDDL < VDDH-|Vt,p|, the pMOS transistor M1 is not turned off, where Vt,p is the threshold voltage of M1. Since the nMOS transistor M2 is ON at this time, the static dc current flows from VDDH to the ground in INV2, dissipating static power. This is caused by the fact that the voltage at the node N1 is not raised higher than VDDL. Conventionally, this problem has been solved by inserting LS to N1 to convert the voltage swing from VDDL to VDDH. Notice that LS is not needed when a VDDH circuit drives a VDDL circuit. This is because the gate voltage of a pMOS transistor in VDDL circuit is raised to VDDH and thereby it is completely turned off.

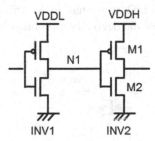

Fig. 2. VDDH gate driven by VDDL gate.

As described in Sect. 1, LS insertion has critical overheads in delay, power, design complexity and area. To reduce the number of required LSs, a clustered voltage scaling (CVS) approach was proposed [2]. In CVS, low voltage clusters are built in the circuit in such a way that there is no VDDL gate driving a VDDH gate. This is done by assigning VDDL to the gates starting from the circuit outputs depending on their slack in the path delay, eliminating the use of LS in the combinational logic. LS insertion is required only at the primary outputs of the circuits. Various algorithms were studied for cluster construction to maximize the power reduction [7, 8]. When the primary outputs of the combinational logic are connected to flip-flops (FFs), use of level-shifting FF circuits [9, 10] can eliminate the LS insertion. The level-shifting FF receives the data input with VDDL swing and produces the Q output with VDDH swing. These CVS based approaches basically try to minimize the number of required LSs by restricting the level-shifting points to the primary outputs of the combinational logic or FFs. Hence, they cannot be applied to a general SoC design in which the output signal of a pre-designed logic module operating at VDDL needs to be connected to the input of another pre-designed module operating at VDDH. In this case, LSs need to be inserted at the module boundary. Thus, the CVS based approaches cannot completely eliminate the required LSs at the entire chip level.

Diril et al. [11, 12] proposed a level-shifter free approach to use an additional threshold voltage. The concept is that they achieve VDDL > VDDH-|Vt,p| by employing larger |Vt,p|. As shown in Fig. 3, the second threshold voltage Vt,p2 whose magnitude is larger than the original Vt,p is used in the pMOS transistors of VDDH gates driven by VDDL gates. This approach reduces the static dc current flowing through the transistor when the gate voltage is VDDL. An approach similar to this idea was addressed in [13]. There is a performance penalty due to the increase of the rise time. The biggest advantage is the fact that it has no energy or area penalties. However, this approach has two critical problems: one is the requirement for the manufacturing. Although the multi-Vt process is available in a modern technology, the magnitude of Vt,p2 for this approach may not be the same as the High-Vt (HVT) which is regularly provided by the semiconductor vendors. Even if it is possible to add a special Vt for this purpose, there will be an extra cost. The other problem of this approach is the robustness for the process variation. Even though we determine the optimum value for Vt,p2 at the design stage, the threshold voltage varies in real chips [1]. When Vt,p2 is varied to smaller magnitude, the static dc current would not be reduced sufficiently. To deal with this, much larger Vt,p2 value has to be chosen considering the process variation but it further increases the delay. This problem becomes more serious as the device is scaled.

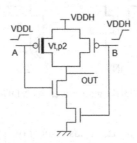

Fig. 3. Level shifting NAND [11].

The problems described above motivated us to study an approach for variation-tolerant multi-VDD design that requires no level-shifter insertion and no addition of extra threshold voltage.

3   Proposed Approach

First, we describe an approach we propose which employs body-bias control. Next we present the feature of an SOTB (Silicon on Thin BOX) device that maximizes effectiveness of the proposed approach.

3.1   Body-Bias Control to PMOS Transistors in VDDH Domain

We propose an approach to reduce the static dc current by raising the threshold voltage of pMOS transistors through the body bias control to the VDDH domain. This approach does not require any addition of extra Vt at the manufacturing. Moreover, the magnitude of Vt to minimize the static dc current can be adjusted adaptively in accordance with the process and temperature variations by varying the body bias. However, it is necessary to separate the body bias to pMOS transistors in the VDDH domain from that in the VDDL domain, and to apply a reverse body bias (RBB) to pMOS in the VDDH domain. To implement this, there are two possible approaches: one is a fine-grained approach to apply RBB only to the gates receiving the VDDL signal (i.e. the receiver gates), and the other is a coarse-grained approach to apply RBB to pMOS transistors in the entire VDDH domain. The fine-grained approach may be ideal to minimize the delay penalty due to the raised Vt in pMOS. However, it suffers from significant increase in area and the complexity of physical layout. This is because a triple-well process technology is required to separate the n-well (and hence the deep n-well) for the receiver gates from that for non-receiver gates. Different deep n-wells must be placed apart from each other with larger space in between as compared to the inter p-well separation. This incurs significant area penalty. Another difficulty in the fine-grained approach is that only the receiver gates need to be extracted from the VDDH domain and placed in a different domain to apply RBB. This is because zero body bias (ZBB) is applied to the non-receiver gates in the original VDDH domain. This requirement clearly increases the complexity of physical design. Considering these problems, we think that the fine-grained approach will not be realistic in real SoCs.

Our proposal is the coarse-grained approach. Since it applies RBB to pMOS transistors in the entire VDDH domain, there is no penalty in area and in the design complexity. However, the rise delay increases at all gates in the VDDH domain because RBB is applied to all pMOS transistors. The good news is that in a gate chain the rise operation typically occurs every other gate and hence delay penalty is incurred only at half of the gates at a time. In addition, the fall delay slightly reduces when applying RBB to pMOS transistors. This is because the pMOS transistor with raised Vt is turned off earlier than that of the non-RBB case at the fall transition. We will quantitatively discuss the delay penalty of our approach in Sect. 4. The n-well for the VDDH domain needs to be separated from the n-well for the VDDL domain so independent body bias control can be performed at both voltage domains.

3.2   SOTB Device

SOTB is a FD-SOI (Fully Depleted Silicon on Insulator) device with ultra-thin (10 nm) BOX layer [14]. Figure 4 depicts a schematic of SOTB MOS transistors. Vt can be controlled by changing the voltage of underlying n-well or p-well, which has the same effect as changing the body bias in a bulk-MOS device. Thanks to the ultra-thin BOX, SOTB has a large body-bias coefficient. It is reported that Vt shift is more than 0.15 V by the RBB voltage of 1 V [15]. Moreover, since the body bias is applied from below the insulating BOX layer, we do not have to concern about the junction leakage between the source/drain and the body. Inter-well leakage between the deep n-well and p-well is negligible within the voltage range considering the BOX reliability for RBB. Authors of [15] reported that they applied RBB of 2.0 V, observing that Vt of a pMOS transistor is shifted from 0.2 V to approximately 0.5 V. The features of SOTB described above enhance the capability of body-bias control for threshold-voltage modulation as compared to the bulk counterpart. By combining this capability with the coarse-grained body-bias control for pMOS transistors, we suppress static dc current in a LSL multi-V_{DD} design.

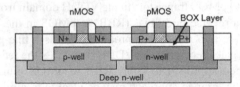

Fig. 4.   Schematic cross section of SOTB MOS transistors.

4   Results from Simulation

4.1   Simulation Setup

We conducted simulation analyses for delay, static current and active energy by using a HSPICE simulator and the 65 nm SOTB MOS transistor models. The nominal supply voltage (i.e. VDDH) is 1.2 V. In comparative evaluations with the conventional approach using LS, we used a LS circuit shown in Fig. 5 [16], instead of LSs depicted in Fig. 1. This is because evaluations for the wide range of VDDL require a LS circuit that converts the corresponding input voltage (i.e. VDDL).

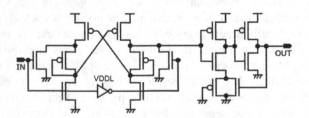

Fig. 5.   LS circuit [16].

In [16], it is reported that the delay of the cross-coupled LS shown in Fig. 1(a) increases significantly as the input voltage is reduced, and the delay is more than 10 ns even for the 0.6 V input in the 65 nm SOTB technology. Considering that the inverter delay is approximately 30 ps in the same technology, the cross-coupled LS is too slow. The current-mirror LS depicted in Fig. 1(b) gives the delay of ~200 ps for the same input voltage but consumes 100X energy. In contrast, LS shown in Fig. 5 gives the delay of 200 ps for the 0.6 V input at almost the same energy dissipation as the cross-coupled LS. Circuits of inverter, NAND and NOR gates used in the simulation are those of the standard cells provided in the 65 nm SOTB library.

In the LSL approach, logic gates in the VDDH domain receiving the VDDL input (i.e. receiver gates) are most affected in delay and static current. Logic gates receiving the outputs of the receiver gates are affected next, because output signals of the receiver gates may not necessarily produce the full swing between 0 V and VDDH. Since LS shown in Fig. 5 produces a non-inverted output, we define an equivalent receiver as two cascaded logic gates consisting of "a front-end (FE) NAND/NOR/inverter gate receiving the VDDL input" plus "a back-end (BE) inverter gate operating at VDDH", as depicted in Fig. 6. Notice that RBB to pMOS transistors (referred to as pRBB) is applied to both the FE receiver and the BE inverter in the LSL approach, unlike the approach with LS. We discuss electrical characteristics of LS-based and LSL approaches by focusing on LS and the equivalent receivers.

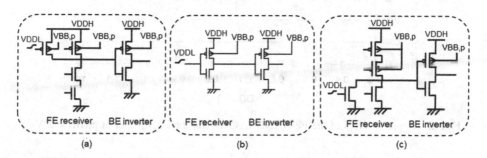

Fig. 6. Equivalent receivers: (a) NAND-type, (b) inverter-type and (c) NOR-type.

4.2 Voltage Limit for VDDL

Before discussing the delay or energy, we discuss how much we can reduce the VDDL voltage for the stable operation and understand the mechanism that determines the lowest VDDL voltage. We investigated VDDL$_{LIMIT}$ which is the lowest operable input voltage of the equivalent receivers while changing the pRBB voltage. Figure 7 shows the output voltage of the FE NAND receiver and the output voltage of the BE inverter at ZBB as a function of the VDDL voltage. We assumed the input voltage transition from 0 V to VDDL. For the VDDL voltage range from 1.2 V to 0.75 V, the correct output voltage of the BE inverter (i.e. 1.2 V) can be obtained. However, for the VDDL voltage below 0.75 V, the BE inverter produces incorrect output voltage 0 V because the FE NAND receiver does not produce sufficient low output voltage. In contrast, as shown in Fig. 8, by applying pRBB of 2 V the BE inverter produces the correct output voltage even at 0.6 V. This is because the output voltage of the FE NAND receiver is suppressed to low voltage even below 0.75 V. Thus, VDDL$_{LIMIT}$ reduces from 0.75 V to 0.6 V by applying pRBB of 2 V. The mechanism of this can be explained as follows.

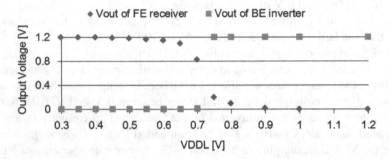

Fig. 7. Output voltages of the FE NAND receiver and the BE inverter at ZBB.

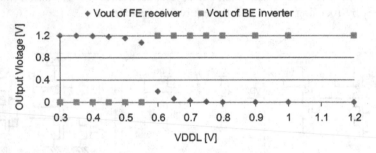

Fig. 8. Output voltages of the FE NAND receiver and the BE inverter at pRBB = 2 V.

As depicted in Fig. 6(a), when the input voltage is VDDL, the contention occurs between the current flowing incompletely turned-off pMOS transistors and the current flowing turned-on nMOS transistors in the FE NAND receiver. As reducing the VDDL voltage, the current flowing incompletely turned-off pMOS increases. This raises the output voltage of the FE NAND receiver, resulting in producing the incorrect output voltage at the BE inverter. By applying pRBB, the current flowing incompletely turned-off pMOS at the FE receiver is reduced and thereby the contention is reduced. As a result, the FE receiver produces the sufficiently low output voltage even for lower VDDL input, leading to the correct operation at the BE inverter.

Next, we investigated VDDL$_{LIMIT}$ of other types of equivalent receivers such as inverter-type or NOR-type while changing the pRBB voltage. Figure 9 shows the results. It is demonstrated that VDDL$_{LIMIT}$ reduces as we increase pRBB at any type of equivalent receivers. Another important observation is that for any pRBB voltage, VDDL$_{LIMIT}$ of the NAND-type is the highest among three, followed by the inverter-type and that of the NOR-type is the lowest. This reason can be explained by the contention occurring in the FE receiver as well. As depicted in Fig. 6(a) and (c), pMOS pull-up transistors are in parallel in the NAND-type receiver and are in series in the NOR-type. Hence, the combined conductance of incompletely turned-off pMOS pull-up transistors in the NAND-type is larger than that of the NOR-type, leading to larger contention in the NAND-type than the NOR-type. Since the inverter-type receiver has no parallel or series pMOS pull-up transistors, the degree of the contention is in the middle.

Since we aim to investigate the potential of RBB in the proposed LSL approach, we choose the pRBB voltage as 2 V which is close to the allowable maximum RBB voltage in this study. As seen in Fig. 9, $VDDL_{LIMIT}$ is lowered to or below 0.6 V at any type of the receivers among NAND/NOR/inverter for pRBB of 2 V. This indicates that the circuit in the VDDH domain could work for the VDDL voltage of as low as 1/2 of the VDDH voltage in the proposed LSL approach.

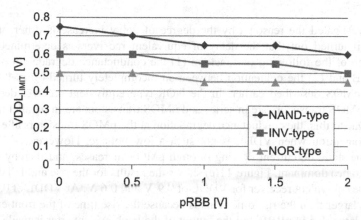

Fig. 9. $VDDL_{LIMIT}$ of equivalent receivers as a function of pRBB voltage.

4.3 Delay

We compared the delay of LS and the equivalent receiver circuits in the LSL approach, assuming that they drive 4 inverter cells as the load capacitance. We analyzed rise and fall delays and found that the fall delays are shorter than the rise delays when applying pRBB of 2 V. The reason is described later.

Figure 10 shows the rise delay of LS and the equivalent receivers as a function of the VDDL voltage. For the VDDL voltage of 0.65 V and higher, any equivalent receivers give smaller delay than LS. In contrast, at VDDL of 0.6 V, the delay of a NAND-type equivalent receiver excesses that of LS but both NOR-type and inverter-type receivers still 2X faster than LS. While the inverter-type receiver becomes slower than LS at VDDL of 0.5 V, the NOR-type receiver remains faster than LS even at VDDL of 0.45 V.

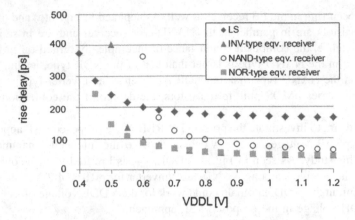

Fig. 10. Rise delay of LS and equivalent receivers.

We investigated the reason why the degree of delay increase is different among receivers. It turned out that the delay of equivalent receivers is determined by the combination of the following two factors: (1) the conductance degradation of pMOS due to RBB and (2) the contention between an incompletely turned-off pMOS and a turned-on nMOS described earlier. In the NOR-type equivalent receiver depicted in Fig. 6(c), pMOS transistors are in series and nMOS transistors are in parallel in the FE receiver. Due to this, the conductance degradation at the pMOS transistors affects more than the contention when VDDL is not such a low voltage. However, as VDDL is lowered, the static dc current flowing through pMOS increases, and thereby the contention becomes dominant. Figure 11(c) shows the results for the rise and fall delays of a NOR-type equivalent receiver for VDDL of 0.9 V and 0.6 V. At VDDL of 0.9 V, the fall time is larger than the rise time. This is because the rise time of the front-end NOR receiver is large due to pRBB and the output of the back-end inverter is made slow. In contrast, at VDDL of 0.6 V, the rise time becomes larger than the fall time. Since the increased dc current flowing through pMOS hinders the discharging of nMOS transistors (i.e. contention), the fall operation at the front-end receiver becomes slower.

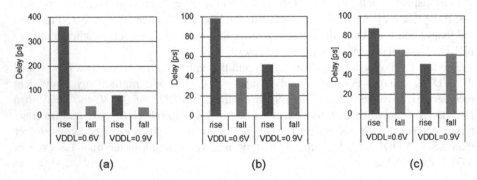

Fig. 11. Rise and fall delays of equivalent receivers: (a) NAND-type, (b) inverter-type and (c) NOR-type.

Furthermore, the rise operation at the back-end inverter gets slower due to pRBB. As a result, the magnitude relation between the rise and fall times gets inverted.

In the NAND-type and inverter-type equivalent receivers, the rise times are larger than the fall times both at 0.9 V and 0.6 V for VDDL, as shown in Fig. 11(a) and (b). Since there are no series pMOS transistors in those circuits, the influence of the contention is dominant over that of the conductance degradation.

In the LSL approach, we also need to consider the delay degradation due to pRBB at the gates that follow the equivalent receiver. We analyzed the path delay for gate chains with 30 stages, in which LS or an inverter-type equivalent receiver is followed by cascaded inverters. We assumed that the cascaded inverters are minimum sized cells provided in the library and each gate in a path drives 4 inverter cells as the load capacitance. Figure 12 shows the results for the total delay of the gate chain as a function of the number of stages N at VDDL = 0.6 V and VDDH = 1.2 V. We assumed the pRBB voltage as 2 V for the LSL approach. For comparison, we also analyzed the path delay for the LSL approach with ZBB.

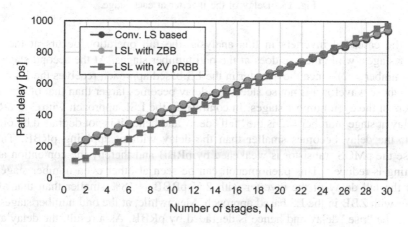

Fig. 12. Path delay for gate chains as a function of the number of stages.

The delay values for N = 1 correspond to the rise delays of LS or the equivalent receivers. In "LSL with ZBB", since no pRBB is applied to the equivalent receiver, the fall operation at the FE inverter in the equivalent receiver gets slower due to the contention and thereby the rise operation at the BE inverter becomes slower. As a result, the rise delay for the equivalent receiver with ZBB becomes larger than the rise delays of LS and the equivalent receiver with 2 V pRBB. In the conventional LS based technique and the LSL approach with ZBB, their cascaded inverters in the second and subsequent stages are both the inverters with ZBB and hence their path delays almost match. In contrast, in the LSL approach with 2 V pRBB, the delay at N = 1 is approximately 100 ps smaller than that of the LS based approach. As the number of stages increases, the path-delay difference between "LS based" and "LSL with 2 V pRBB" gradually reduces due to the performance degradation by pRBB. Interestingly, the path-delay difference is not reduced constantly at each stage. To investigate the reason, we analyzed the delay of the inverter at each stage. Figure 13 shows the results.

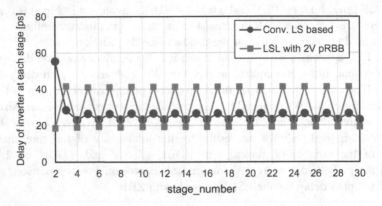

Fig. 13. Delay of the inverter at each stage.

In the cascaded inverters in this analysis, the fall operation occurs at the even number stages, while the rise does at the odd number stages. At the second stage (i.e. stage_number = 2), since the inverter in the LS based approach receives the LS output signal whose waveform is not so steep, the delay becomes larger than that of any other inverters at the even number stages. In contrast, in the LSL approach with 2 V pRBB, the delay at stage_number = 2 is the "fall" delay and hence it is not degraded by pRBB. Rather, the delay becomes smaller than the delay without applying pRBB. This is because the pMOS transistor is weakened by pRBB and thereby the contention at the switching is reduced. This phenomenon can be seen at other even number stages, in which the fall delay of the inverter with 2 V pRBB is 18% smaller than that of the inverter with ZBB in the LS based approach. Meanwhile, at the odd number stages, the delay is the "rise" delay and hence is degraded by pRBB. As a result, the delay at the odd number stage becomes 55% larger than that in the conventional LS based approach.

Thus, in the LSL approach with 2 V pRBB, performance degradation caused by applying RBB does not occur at all gates but instead occurs only at half of the gates. In the remaining half gates, the delay rather reduces. As demonstrated in Fig. 12, the path delay for the LSL approach with 2 V pRBB is smaller than that for the conventional LS-based technique if the number of stages is less than 23.

Another strong point of the proposed LSL approach is the fact that pRBB is always applied to the circuits in the VDDH domain. Although applying RBB at lower voltage degrades the circuit performance significantly, we do not need to be concerned about it in the proposed LSL approach.

4.4 Static Current

Figure 14 shows the results for static current in LS and equivalent receivers. When VDDL is 1.2 V, the static current of the equivalent receivers is smaller than that of LS, because there is no contention and applying pRBB reduces leakage of the equivalent receivers. As we reduce VDDL, the static current of the equivalent receivers drastically increases even with pRBB. It should be noted that for VDDL of 0.9 V, the static current for pRBB = 0.5 V is more than 50X as compared to that for pRBB = 2 V. For VDDL of 0.6 V, this difference reduces, but even only a receiver draws static current of as much as 50 μA when pRBB is 0.5 V. The largest pRBB voltage allowed in the technology should be applied as long as the maximum delay constraint is met. Difference in the static current among equivalent receivers is due to the difference in the dc current flowing through the pMOS transistors. Compared with the NAND-type and the inverter-type equivalent receivers, the NOR-type counterpart draws less dc current for the same pRBB voltage because pMOS transistors are in series.

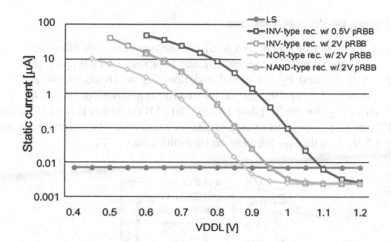

Fig. 14. Static current in LS and equivalent receivers.

4.5 Active Energy

Figure 15 shows the results for active energy of LS and equivalent receivers with pRBB of 2 V. This energy includes both the dynamic energy for charging and discharging the output capacitance and the static energy. For the VDDL voltage higher than 0.8 V, energy dissipation of the equivalent receivers is only 60% of that of LS. As we reduce VDDL, the energy of the equivalent receivers goes up due to the increased static dc current. When the VDDL voltage is 0.6 V, the NAND-type and the inverter-type equivalent receivers consume 1.5X energy as compared to LS. In contrast, the NOR-type equivalent receiver dissipates less energy than LS until VDDL is lowered to ~0.5 V. The difference in active energy dissipation among equivalent receivers results from the difference in the static energy component.

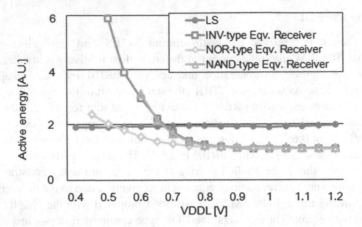

Fig. 15. Active energy of LS and equivalent receivers.

4.6 Influence by Process Variation

We studied an impact of global and local process variations on effectiveness of the proposed LSL approach. First, we investigated how much $VDDL_{LIMIT}$ of the equivalent receiver is affected by the global variation. Figure 16 shows the results from SPICE simulations for $VDDL_{LIMIT}$ of an inverter-type receiver at the five process corners. $VDDL_{LIMIT}$ for the SF (slow nMOS, fast pMOS) corner is 0.02 V higher than that of TT due to higher conductance of pMOS transistors. By adaptively increasing pRBB to 2.5 V, $VDDL_{LIMIT}$ becomes equal to the value at TT.

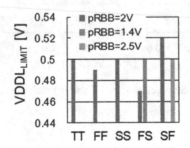

Fig. 16. $VDDL_{LIMIT}$ of an inverter-type receiver at the five process corners.

We also investigated an impact of local variations. Generally, designers should pay attention to the stability of a memory cell under local variations, because the conductance of individual nMOS and pMOS transistors within a memory cell varies. In particular, since RBB is applied only to pMOS transistors in the proposed LSL approach, the balance between nMOS and pMOS in the conductance becomes worse as compared to ZBB. We evaluated the static noise margin (SNM) of a flip-flop cell under the local process variation. SNM is determined by the butterfly curves for cross-coupled inverters [1] in a master or slave latch of a flip-flop cell. Unlike an SRAM cell, we do not need to be concerned about the "read SNM" in a flip-flop because there is no structure to share the bit line in the flip-flop. We do not need to care about the "write SNM" in a flip-flop because the inverter-loop in a latch is electrically cut off at the write operation. Hence, we only investigated the "hold SNM" of master and slave latches in a flip-flop cell.

Assuming a design in which a flip-flop does not become a receiver but pRBB of 2 V is applied to all internal pMOS transistors, we conducted Monte Carlo simulations for Vt variation for 1,000 times under the condition of ±0.1 V at 5σ at the five process corners. Since RBB is applied only to pMOS in the proposed approach, the balance between nMOS and pMOS becomes worst at the FS corner. As shown in Fig. 16, applying 2 V pRBB is required to achieve VDDL$_{LIMIT}$ = 0.5 V at TT, whereas only 1.4 V pRBB is just enough for achieving the same VDDL$_{LIMIT}$ at the FS corner. Hence, we investigated influence of local variations at the FS corner for a flip-flop with 1.4 V pRBB and without it (i.e. ZBB). Figure 17 shows the butterfly curves and the histogram of SNM for the hold operation in a master latch for the FS corner with pRBB = 1.4 V.

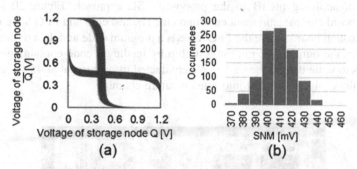

(a)   (b)

Fig. 17. (a) Butterfly curves of master latch of a flip-flop in the hold operation for the FS corner with pRBB = 1.4 V; (b) Distribution of SNM.

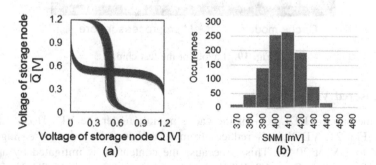

(a)   (b)

Fig. 18. (a) Butterfly curves of master latch of a flip-flop in the hold operation for the FS corner with ZBB; (b) Distribution of SNM.

The mean value of SNM was 403 mV for pRBB = 1.4 V. We compared these results with those for ZBB (Fig. 18). The mean value of SNM for ZBB was 402 mV. Thus, the hold SNM of a master latch did not change so much even if we apply RBB to pMOS for the FS corner. This means that the proposed LSL approach does not impair robustness of the latch operation under the local variation. We also evaluated SNM of the slave latch as well, but it was almost the same as that of the master latch.

5 Results from Chip Measurements

5.1 Test Chip Design and Measurement Environment

We designed and fabricated a test chip consisting of a 32-bit MIPS based microprocessor core and 8 KB caches for instruction and data in a 65 nm SOTB technology. The caches were implemented only with standard cell flip-flops and logic gates. Figure 19 shows the layout of the test chip. We separated the power supply of the cache module from that of the microprocessor core so the microprocessor core and the cache module are made to operate at VDDL and VDDH, respectively. The cache module is the target of applying pRBB in the proposed LSL approach. Figure 20 shows an evaluation board and measurement environment. The test chip and FPGA are equipped on the evaluation board where the FPGA feeds a program code and data to the test chip and monitors the output. We ran the test chip by feeding a code containing a loop of instructions to write data to the cache. We conducted measurement at 45 °C and 65 °C by setting the evaluation board into a temperature chamber.

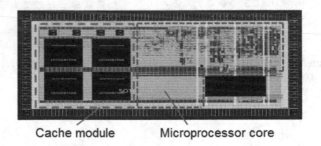

Cache module   Microprocessor core

Fig. 19. Layout of the test chip.

5.2 Measured VDDL$_{\text{LIMIT}}$

First we measured VDDL$_{\text{LIMIT}}$ of the cache module under the VDDH of 1.2 V. As shown in Fig. 21, VDDL$_{\text{LIMIT}}$ reduces from 0.58 V to 0.48 V by increasing pRBB from 0 V to 2 V at 20 °C. This is because the contention is mitigated by applying pRBB as described in Sect. 4.2. When the temperature goes up to 65 °C, VDDL$_{\text{LIMIT}}$ increases by 0.02 V at pRBB = 2 V. By increasing pRBB to 2.5 V, VDDL$_{\text{LIMIT}}$ returns to the value at 20 °C (i.e. 0.48 V). These phenomena can be interpreted as follows. First, as the temperature goes up, |Vt,p| reduces [1] and thereby the current flowing through the incompletely turned-off pMOS increases at the receiver gate. This leads to the increase of the contention and hence raising VDDL$_{LIMIT}$. Increasing pRBB from 2 V to 2.5 V further increases |Vt,p| and reduces the contention, resulting in lowering VDDL$_{LIMIT}$.

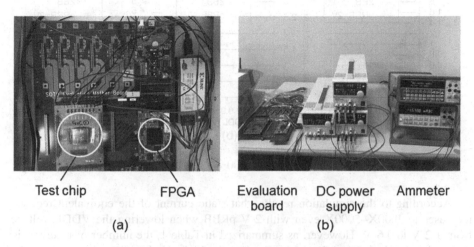

Test chip   FPGA   Evaluation   DC power   Ammeter
                                    board   supply
          (a)   (b)

Fig. 20. (a) Evaluation board; (b) Measurement environment.

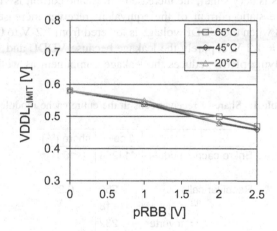

Fig. 21. Measured VDDL$_{LIMIT}$.

5.3 Measured Static Current and Power Dissipation

Figure 22(a) shows the measured results for the static current flowing through the cache module at 20 °C. We measured the static current by stopping the clock after executing above described program for the sufficient time. In ZBB, as we lower the VDDL voltage, the static current starts to increase at 0.9 V and reaches 1.6 mA at 0.6 V.

When we apply pRBB of 2 V, the static current keeps constant until 0.8 V and slightly increases for the lower VDDL voltage. It should be noted that for the VDDL voltage of 0.6 V the static current is only 1/5 of that of the ZBB case.

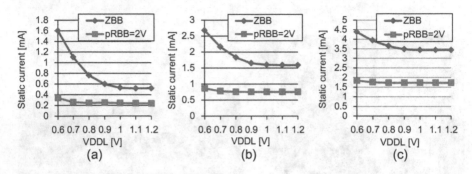

Fig. 22. Measured static current at (a) 20 °C, (b) 45 °C and (c) 65 °C.

According to the simulation results, that static current of the equivalent receiver increases to 1000X–5000X even with 2 V pRBB when lowering the VDDL voltage from 1.2 V to 0.6 V. However, as summarized in Table 1, the number of receivers in this design is only 0.2% of the total cells. As a result, the total static current of the cache module does not increase so much when we apply pRBB of 2 V. Even though the number of receivers is very small, the increase of the static current is visible with ZBB. This is because the static current of the equivalent receiver increases to more than 20,000X with ZBB when the VDDL voltage is lowered from 1.2 V to 0.6 V. The static current for VDDL = 1.2 V is purely the leakage because VDDL and VDDH voltages are the same. Applying pRBB reduces the leakage component as well.

Table 1. Share of receiver cells in the entire cache module

	# cells	share (%)
Entire cache module	114264	100
Receiver cells	250	0.2
├ NOR	18	
├ inverter	232	
├ NAND	0	
└ others	0	

Figure 22(b) and (c) show the measured results for the static current at 45 °C and 65 °C, respectively. By applying pRBB = 2 V for VDDL = 0.6 V, the static current was reduced to 1/3 at 45 °C and to 2/5 at 65 °C. Thus, the proposed LSL approach effectively reduced the static current increasing with lowering VDDL for a wide range of the temperature.

We also evaluated the impact of the proposed approach on the entire power dissipation. We measured power dissipation of the cache module at 20 °C. As described in Sect. 5.1, the VDDL supply was connected to the microprocessor core and the VDDH supply was to the cache module. Since we reduced the VDDL voltage to 0.6 V, the microprocessor core was made to operate at 0.6 V. Due to this, we chose 8 MHz as the clock frequency to ensure the correct operation of the microprocessor core. Figure 23 (a) and (b) show the results for the measured power dissipation. It is demonstrated that the share of the static power component increases as we lower the VDDL voltage.

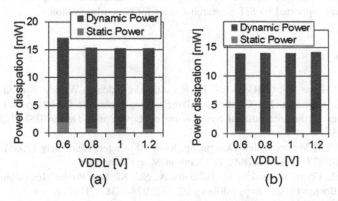

Fig. 23. Share of static power component (meas.) for (a) ZBB and (b) pRBB = 2 V at 20 °C.

Although the share of the static power component is 11% at VDDL of 0.6 V for ZBB, it is reduced to 3% by applying pRBB of 2 V. Thus, the measured results at real silicon demonstrated that the proposed LSL approach enabled us to suppress the static current and thereby effectively reduce the static power component in the entire power dissipation.

6 Conclusions and Future Work

We proposed an LSL approach to employ body-bias control to pMOS transistors in a SOTB device for suppressing the static dc current in the multi-V$_{DD}$ design. Results from simulations and measurements at a microprocessor test chip demonstrated effectiveness of the proposed approach under process and temperature variations.

As the future work, delay evaluation at real silicon is required. This time the objective of the chip measurement was to demonstrate the feasibility of the proposed LSL approach. Hence, we applied it to an existing design of a microprocessor [17] and showed that it works at VDDL = 0.6 V and VDDH = 1.2 V. Meanwhile, this application imposed a constraint for the Fmax-based delay measurement. Since the PLL we used only produces a clock signal with 0.5 MHz increment, the delay difference less than 8 ns could not be detected at the measurement around 8 MHz. This is because the clock periods are 125 ns at 8 MHz and 133 ns at 7.5 MHz, respectively, leading to the difference of 8 ns. To measure the delay difference less than 1 ns, we need to design a special circuit to which the proposed LSL approach is applied. Furthermore, to enhance the capability of this LSL approach, combination with other approaches such as an increased-L (increased transistor length) technique should be explored. Since it also increases $|Vt,p|$ and can be used locally, an optimized combination may produce better results and hence is the future work.

Acknowledgment. This work was partially supported by JSPS KAKENHI S Grant Number 25220002. This work was supported by VLSI Design and Education Center (VDEC), the University of Tokyo in collaboration with Synopsys, Inc. and Cadence Design Systems, Inc. This presentation was supported by SIT Research Center for Green Innovation.

References

1. Weste, N., Harris, D.: CMOS VLSI Design, 4th edn. Addison-Wesley, Boston (2011)
2. Usami, K., Horowitz, M.: Clustered voltage scaling technique for low-power design. In: Proceedings of the International Symposium on Low Power Design (ISLPED), pp. 3–8, April 1995
3. Itoh, K.: VLSI Memory Chip Design, pp. 84–87. Springer, Heidelberg (2001). https://doi.org/10.1007/978-3-662-04478-0. The Current-Mirror Amplifier
4. Keating, M., Flynn, D., Aitken, R., Gibbons, A., Shi, K.: Low Power Methodology Manual. Springer, Boston (2007). https://doi.org/10.1007/978-0-387-71819-4
5. Puri, R., et al.: Pushing ASIC performance in a power envelope. In: Proceedings of the 40th Design Automation Conference (DAC), pp. 788–793, June 2003
6. Usami, K., Kogure, S., Yoshida, Y., Magasaki, R., Amano, H.: Level-shifter-less approach for multi-V_{DD} design to use body bias control in FD-SOI. In: Proceedings of the 25th IFIP/IEEE International Conference on Very Large Scale Integration (VLSI-SoC), October 2017
7. Chen, C., Srivastava, A., Sarrafzadeh, M.: On gate level power optimization using dual-supply voltages. IEEE Trans. Very Large Scale Integr. (VLSI) Syst. **9**(5), 616–629 (2001)
8. Donno, M., Macchiarulo, L., Macii, A., Macii, E., Poncino, M.: Enhanced clustered voltage scaling for low power. In: Proceedings of the 12th ACM Great Lakes Symposium on VLSI (GLSVLSI), pp. 18–23, April 2002
9. Hamada, M., et al.: A top-down low power design technique using clustered voltage scaling with variable supply-voltage scheme. In: Proceedings of the IEEE Custom Integrated Circuits Conference (CICC), pp. 495–498, May 1998
10. Ishihara, F., Sheikh, F., Nikolic, B.: Level conversion for dual-supply systems. IEEE Trans. Very Large Scale Integr. (VLSI) Syst. **12**(2), 185–195 (2004)
11. Diril, A., Dhillon, Y., Chatterjee, A., Singh, A.: Level-shifter free design of low power dual supply voltage CMOS circuits using dual threshold voltages. In: Proceedings of the 18th International Conference on VLSI Design (VLSID), January 2005
12. Diril, A., Dhillon, Y., Chatterjee, A., Singh, A.: Level-shifter free design of low power dual supply voltage CMOS circuits using dual threshold voltages. IEEE Trans. Very Large Scale Integr. (VLSI) Syst. **13**(9), 1103–1107 (2005)

13. Tawfik, S., Kursun, V.: Low power and high speed multi threshold voltage interface circuits. IEEE Trans. Very Large Scale Integr. (VLSI) Syst. **17**(5), 638–645 (2009)
14. Tsuchiya, R., et al.: Silicon on thin BOX: a new paradigm of the CMOSFET for low-power and high-performance application featuring wide-range back-bias control. In: IEEE International Electron Devices Meeting (IEDM) Technical Digest, December 2004
15. Yamamoto, Y., et al.: Ultralow-voltage operation of Silicon-on-Thin-BOX (SOTB) 2Mbit SRAM down to 0.37V utilizing adaptive back bias. In: Symposium on VLSI Technology, June 2013
16. Nakamura, S., Usami, K.: Level converter design for ultra-low voltage operation in FDSOI devices. In: Proceedings of the 28th International Technical Conference on Circuits/Systems, Computers and Communications (ITC-CSCC), July 2014
17. Usami, K., et al.: Design and control methodology for fine grain power gating based on energy characterization and code profiling of microprocessors. In: Proceedings of the 19th Asia and South Pacific Design Automation Conference (ASP-DAC), pp. 843–848, January 2014
18. Usami, K., Kogure, S., Yoshida, Y., Magasaki, R., Amano, H.: Level-shifter free approach for multi-V$_{DD}$ SOTB employing adaptive Vt modulation for pMOSFET. In: Proceedings of the IEEE SOI-3D-Subthreshold Microelectronics Technology Unified Conference (S3S), October 2017

Evaluating the Impact of Resistive Defects on FinFET-Based SRAMs

Thiago S. Copetti[1], Guilherme C. Medeiros[2],
Letícia M. B. Poehls[2(✉)], and Tiago R. Balen[1]

[1] Graduate Program on Microelectronics – PGMICRO,
Federal University of Rio Grande do Sul, Porto Alegre, RS, Brazil
{thiago.copetti,tiago.balen}@ufrgs.br
[2] Graduate Program on Electrical Engineering,
Pontifical Catholic University of Rio Grande do Sul, Porto Alegre, RS, Brazil
leticia@poehls.com

Abstract. The development of FinFET technology has made possible the continuous scaling-down of CMOS technological nodes. In parallel, the increasing need to store more information has resulted in the fact that Static Random Access Memories (SRAMs) occupy great part of Systems-on-Chip (SoCs). The manufacturing process variation has introduced several types of defects that directly affect the SRAM's reliability, causing different faults. Thus, it remains unknown if the fault models used in CMOS memory circuits are sufficiently accurate to represent the faulty behavior of FinFET-based memories. In this context, a study of manufacturing's functional implications regarding resistive defects in FinFET-based SRAMs is presented. In more detail, a complete analysis of static and dynamic fault behavior for FinFET-based SRAMs is described. The proposed analysis has been performed through SPICE simulations, adopting a compact Predictive Technology Model (PTM) of FinFET transistors, considering different technological nodes. Faults have been categorized as single or coupling, static or dynamic.

Keywords: FinFET · SRAM · Resistive defects · SPICE · PTM

1 Introduction

During the last decades, important advances in nano-scale technology have allowed to miniaturize and integrate hundred million transistors in a small silicon area. Since the development of the first commercial Integrated Circuit (IC), miniaturization and integration have been carried out following Moore's Law. Every two years, new circuits designed with smaller technological nodes were announced by the industry. However, significant changes to the paradigms of digital and analog circuit design were required throughout this technological progression of the Metal-Oxide Semiconductor Field Effect Transistors (MOSFETs) technology.

In technological nodes below 20 nm, the gate terminal begins to lose control over the potential distribution and current flow of the transistor's channel region. This causes a phenomenon denominated Short-Channel Effect (SCE), which occurs due to the

M. Maniatakos et al. (Eds.): VLSI-SoC 2017, IFIP AICT 500, pp. 22–45, 2019.
https://doi.org/10.1007/978-3-030-15663-3_2

proximity between source and drain [1]. In the face of this adversity, new types of transistors have been designed to address the challenges caused by the scaling of CMOS transistors. Two technologies are widely adopted: Silicon-On-Insulator (SOI) MOSFET and FinFET. In fact, FinFET technology is already replacing CMOS transistors in state-of-the-art ICs – major electronics companies such as Intel [2] and Samsung [3] have already migrated to FinFET technology owing to its reduced short channel effects, electrostatic characteristics [4–6], and its compatibility with standard CMOS manufacturing process [1, 7].

As a result of this changes in technological paradigms caused by the introduction of the FinFET technology, several circuit devices needed to be redesigned, tested, and evaluated. One special kind of circuit that can be cited in this context are Static Random Access Memories (SRAM), the focus of this research. Due to the always-increasing need to store more and more information on chip, SRAMs have become the main contributor to the overall area of Systems-on-Chips (SoCs) [8]. Thus, the overall performance of the chip can be improved significantly by optimizing these memory circuits.

As explained in [9], SRAMs are designed with high density and produced at the limit of the technological process. Hence, they are very susceptible to manufacturing defects. The resistive defect model, which can be modeled as resistive-open or resistive-bridge, is a well-accepted defect model studied in bulk CMOS technology. A resistive-open defect is defined as a resistor between two circuit nodes that share a connection [10], while a resistive-bridge is defined as a resistor between two circuit nodes that should not be connected [11, 12]. Open defects have traditionally been a concern in the CMOS technology test scenario. More recently, this concern shifted towards weak resistive-open and weak resistive-bridge defects as their probability of occurrence may increase in nanometer technologies due to the ever-growing number of interconnections between layers [10].

While the influence of resistive defects in circuit parameters (e.g. voltage, current) is irrefutable, it is easier to evaluate their impact by analyzing what faulty behaviors they lead to. Functional faults are deviations from expected behavior of the memory under a set of operations [13]. Faults can be static (whose occurrence happens with one operation) and dynamic, in which at least two consecutive operations are required to sensitize the fault. These faults generally cause timing dependent faults, meaning that at least a 2-pattern sequence is necessary to sensitize them [14]. Moreover, the number of dynamic faults is directly correlated to the presence of weak resistive defects [15].

With the scaling down of technological nodes, weak resistive defects are likely to be one of the main reliability challenges in IC design [16]. This can be partially attributed to the difficulty of detecting these defects, and therefore the dynamic faults they cause. Indeed, open/resistive vias are the most common origin of test escapes in deep-submicron technologies [17]. Many of the standard March algorithms fail to detect dynamic faults [10, 15, 18] or present certain limitations by limiting the number of consecutive operations required to sensitize the fault by no more than two [19–21]. Recently, a new March test designed for FinFET-based memories was proposed in [22]. The authors formulated this new test algorithm based on reports from their previous works in which they observed dynamic faults sensitized by up to eight consecutive read operations [23, 24].

Traditionally, characterization of fault behavior observed in defective SRAM cells has been performed following a well stablished methodology based on SPICE electrical simulations. Many works focused on evaluating the resistance in which a certain defect starts to sensitize faults. This resistance, known as critical resistance, is the threshold between a fault-free and faulty behavior [25]. Critical resistances of resistive-open defects were investigated in [10, 18, 26, 27] adopting technological nodes of 130 nm down to 40 nm, while critical resistances of resistive-bridge defects were investigated in [28, 29] adopting technological nodes of 90 nm down to 40 nm.

However, all these previous researches were conducted using planar CMOS technology. So far, little research has been conducted considering resistive defects in FinFET memories. In [24], the authors modeled resistive open and bridge defects taking into account the physical structure of 28 nm FinFET devices aiming to observe possible unique faults of this technology. An analysis of faults in FinFET SRAM cells affected by resistive defects was presented in [30]. Simulations were carried out using a 20 nm technology model. No further works have been proposed focusing on smaller nodes. This is especially worrisome since 14 nm FinFET devices are currently in production [31, 32].

This work presents a study on the behavior of FinFET-based SRAM cells affected by resistive defects. In particular, this study intends to map and determine how manufacturing defects, specifically resistive-open and resistive-bridge defects, impact in the behavior of FinFET SRAM cells. Resistive defects with different magnitudes were injected in memory bitcells aiming to sensitize static and dynamic faults. The analysis was performed through electrical simulation using HSPICE^{TM} software and adopting Predictive Technology Models (PTM) [33] of multi-gate transistors based on 20 nm, 16 nm, 14 nm, 10 nm, and 7 nm bulk FinFET. These analyses demonstrated that smaller FinFET technologies will be more prone to weak resistive defects and therefore dynamic faults, proving the need for specific test methodologies for this unique technology.

The rest of the work is organized as follows. Section 2 explains the concepts related to the design of FinFET SRAMs and the set of fault models adopted in this work. Next, Sect. 3 describes the simulation setup and the set of resistive defects injected into the SRAM cells. Section 4 discusses the results obtained from simulations and compares the different technological nodes. Finally, Sect. 5 presents this work's final considerations.

2 Background

FinFET circuits have been adopted as a way to continue the scaling of ICs and fulfill the performance requirements established by the miniaturization-oriented goals of More Moore. Thus, it is of vital importance to understand the aspects of FinFET-based SRAM arrays and the faults related to this new technology in order to identify discrepancies caused by resistive defects. In this Section, main characteristics of FinFET technology and FinFET SRAM design are discussed, followed by the background on the fault models associated to resistive-open and resistive-bridge defects.

2.1 FinFET Characteristics

FinFET transistors are quasi-planar, multi-gate devices consisting of vertical silicon islands, denominated "fins", with metal wrapped around the gate and placed on top of the oxide. The first fabricated structure alike FinFETs was the DELTA [34], a double-gate MOS transistor manufactured in 1989. Afterward, other transistor structures were proposed aiming to surpass the scalability limitations of the CMOS technology [1]. It is possible to design different FinFET structures based on the way the transistors are fabricated. In Silicon-On-Insulator (SOI) FinFETs, fins are built over Buried Oxide (BOX) and are isolated from the substrate. In Bulk FinFETs, the fin is connected directly to the substrate through the oxide layer, and a Shallow Trench Isolation (STI) of oxide is formed on the side.

FinFETs can also be classified based on their gate configuration. In Shorted-Gate (SG) FinFETs, all three sides of the gate are physically shorted in order to create a single terminal, allowing a higher on-current and lower off-current. In Independent-Gate (IG) FinFETs, the top part of the gate is etched in order to create two independent gate terminals. This offers the possibility of applying different signals in each terminal, enabling the modulation of V_{TH} of the front-gate by biasing the back-gate. However, this also implies in a certain area penalty due to the necessity of two separate gate contacts [7].

The fundamental design parameters of a FinFET transistor are its fin's height (H_{FIN}), its thickness (T_{FIN}), and channel length (L_g). Other parameters, such as Gate Oxide Thickness (T_{OX}), Gate Work Function, Body Doping, Source/Drain Doping, and Supply Voltage complete the typical parameters [35]. Figure 1 depicts the architecture of a Bulk FinFET transistor and its main parameters. In this work, the bulk-FinFET technology is studied.

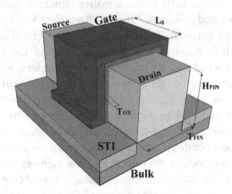

Fig. 1. Structure of bulk-FinFET transistors

The main advantage of this technology is to minimize the Short-Channel Effect (SCE), allowing the continuity of the downscaling of integrated circuits. This is possible due the improved control of gates over the conduction channel, bringing other benefits such as high density and low operational voltage.

2.2   Static Random Access Memories

A standard 6T SRAM cell is composed of six transistors; four of them form two cross-coupled inverters (M1 & M2, M3 & M4), while the other two act as Pass Gates (PG, M5 and M6), providing read and write access to the cell. The word line (*WL*) controls the two PG nMOS transistors that are each connected to their respective bit lines (*BL* and $\overline{BL}$). The value stored in the cell corresponds to the digital representation of the voltage on Q ('1' for V_{DD}, '0' for 0 V). Figure 2 shows a schematic of an 6T SRAM cell designed with SG-FinFET transistors.

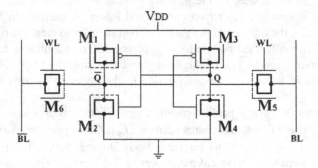

Fig. 2. FinFET-based SRAM-cell

Jointly, a group of SRAM cells forms a matrix structure, allowing data storage in any combination of rows and columns. All cells share electrical connections: vertically, through the bit line, and horizontally, through the word line. Each cell has a unique position (address), so it is possible to access each one of them individually by the appropriate selection of word and bit lines. Address decoders, write drivers, registers, and sense amplifiers complete the set of peripheral circuitry working to guarantee the proper operation of the memory. Figure 3 depicts an example of this architecture. This structure is well known and a more detailed explanation can be found in literature.

Memories can operate in three distinct modes: hold mode, read mode, and write mode. In hold mode, no operations are being performed on the cell. The word line is off, and the cell has no connection with the rest of the memory array. In read mode, bit lines are pre-charged to V_{DD} and word line is turned on, enabling the cell to discharge BL or $\overline{BL}$ based on the stored value. During write mode, word lines are turned on and bit lines are kept in opposite voltage levels in order to force the new value into the cell.

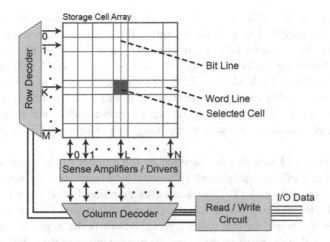

Fig. 3. Architecture of an SRAM memory.

2.3 FinFET SRAM

Technology scaling of conventional CMOS SRAMs are limited due to the random variations of threshold voltage (V_{TH}) caused by Random Dopant Fluctuation. As high doping is not required in FinFETs due to their enhanced SCE, Random Dopant Fluctuation is expressively reduced, which diminishes V_{TH} variations and allows V_{DD} to be scaled down. Furthermore, reduced Random Dopant Fluctuation also improves the Static Noise Margin (SNM) and consequently enhances the cell's robustness [7]. Moreover, improved sub-threshold swing allows not only lower V_{TH} for a given off-state leakage current, but also enhances the on-state current per device width. Such improvements shorten the read and write access times on SRAM cells. Thus, the FinFET technology can bring many specific advantages to SRAM memories' performance and stability.

The SRAM cell's structure is divided into three parts, with the proper notation of (PU:PG:PD) to describe its configuration, where PU, PG and PD stand for: Pull-Up, composed of the two pMOS transistors of the inverters; Pass Gate, consisting of the two pass-through nMOS transistors; and Pull-Down, which are the two nMOS transistors of the inverters, respectively. One of the drawbacks of designing SRAM cells with FinFET technology is the discrete nature of fins limited to a quantized number. Distinct configurations using different numbers of fins have been proposed for FinFET-based SRAM cell designs [36–38]. For this work, the High-Density configuration presented in [38] of (1:1:1) was adopted.

2.4 Fault Models Associated to Resistive Defects

Due to imperfections on the manufacturing process, memory cells may be affected by manufacturing defects such as resistive-open and/or resistive-bridge defects that can compromise the correct behavior of the device. These defects can be characterized as strong or weak defects based on the nature of the fault they sensitize: strong defects are related to static faults, while weak defects are associated to dynamic faults. Faulty behaviors can be specified using Fault Primitive (FP), which characterizes the sensitizing sequence (S), the faulty behavior observed (F), and the output of read operations (R) [13, 21], following the notation <$S/F/R$>. A non-empty set of fault primitives is known as a Functional Fault Model (FFM). FPs can be classified as static or dynamic according to the number of required operations in order to sensitize the fault. Furthermore, the number of necessary operations to sensitize the fault may depend on many factors, such as defect resistance, operating temperature, process corner, among others [10].

Furthermore, an FP can also be classified by the number of cells involved: single-cell and multi-cell FP. In a single-cell FP, faulty behaviors are only observed in the defective cell. In multi-cell FP (also known as coupling-faults), two cells (or two groups of cells) interact to produce a fault. The cell that suffers the faulty behavior is the victim (v-cell), while the cell that triggers the fault is the aggressor (a-cell). It is important to note that the resistive defect can be present either in the a-cell and/or in the v-cell [13, 21].

Since an FFM is defined as a set of FPs, FFM will assume their characteristics, resulting in the follow classifications: static and dynamic FFM; single-cell and multi-cell FFM. In more details, FFMs can represent the following fault space that was considered in this work, and described in [11] and [13]:

- *Stuck-at Fault* (SAF): A cell is said to have a SAF (even know State Fault) when the cell is stuck and stores only one logic value '0' or '1';
- *No Store Fault* (NSF): This fault is the opposite to SAF, where a cell with NSF cannot retain any logic value in their nodes;
- *Transition Fault* (TF): A cell is said to have a TF if it fails to undergo a transition from '0' to '1' or vice versa when it is written;
- *Write Disturb Fault* (WDF): A cell is said to have a WDF if a non-transition write operation causes a transition in it;
- *Read Destructive Fault* (RDF): A cell is said to have an RDF if a read operation performed on the cell changes the data in the cell and returns the incorrect value to the output. This type of fault can also have a dynamic behavior classified as dRDF;
- *Deceptive Read Destructive Fault* (DRDF): A cell is said to have a DRDF if a read operation performed on the cell returns the correct logic value, but changes the contents of the cell. This type of fault can also have a dynamic behavior classified as dDRDF;
- *Incorrect Read Fault* (IRF): A cell is said to have an IRF if a read operation performed on the cell returns an incorrect logic value, even though the correct value is still stored in the cell. This type of fault can also have a dynamic behavior classified as dIFR;
- *Weak Read Fault* (WRF): A cell is said to have a WRF when, during the read operation, the sense amplifier cannot produce the correct logic output due to the small voltage difference between bit lines;
- *Disturb Coupling Fault* (CFds): This fault occurs in groups of at least two cells, called aggressor (a-cell) and victim (v-cell), and is sensitized when a read or write operation in an a-cell affects a v-cell or a group of v-cells, forcing them to change

their stored values. This type of fault can also have a dynamic behavior classified as dCFds;

- *Transition Coupling Fault* (CFtr): This fault occurs when a transition write operation performed on the v-cell fails due to a given logic value stored in the a-cell. Thus, the fault is sensitized by a write operation on the v-cell and setting the a-cell into a given state.
- *Read Disturb Coupling Fault* (CFrd): This fault occurs when a read operation performed on a v-cell changes the data in the cell and returns the incorrect value on the output if a given value is present in the a-cell. This type of fault can also have a dynamic behavior classified as dCFrd.
- *Incorrect Read Coupling Fault* (CFir): This fault occurs when a read operation performed on a v-cell returns an incorrect value on the output when a given value is present in the a-cell. This type of fault can also have a dynamic behavior classified as dCFir.

Table 1. Functional fault models and their respective fault primitives.

FFM	FPs
SAF	<0/1/->; <1/0/->
NSF	<0/-/->; <1/-/->
TF	<0w1/0/->; <1w0/1/->
WDF	<0w0/1/->; <1w1/0/->
RDF	<0r0/1/1>; <1r1/0/0>
dRDF	<0w0r0/1/1>; <0w1r1/0/0>; <1w0r0/1/1>; <1w1r1/0/0>
DRDF	<0r0/1/0>; <1r1/0/1>
dDRDF	<0w0r0/1/0>; <0w1r1/0/1>; <1w0r0/1/0>; <1w1r1/0/1>
IRF	<0r0/0/1>; <1r1/1/0>
dIRF	<0w0r0/0/1>; <0w1r1/1/0>; <1w0r0/0/1>; <1w1r1/1/0>
WRF	<0r0/0/?>; <1r1/1/?>
CFds	<x;0/1/->; <x;1/0/->
dCFds	<xx;0/1/->; <xx;1/0/->
CFtr	<x;0w1/0/->; <x;1w0/1/->
CFrd	<x;0r0/1/1>; <x;1r1/0/0>
dCFrd	<x;0w0r0/1/1>; <x;0w1r1/0/0>; <x;1w0r0/1/1>; <x;1w1r1/0/0>
CFir	<x;0r0/1/0>; <x;1r1/0/1>
dCFir	<x;0w0r0/1/0>; <x;0w1r1/0/1>; <x;1w0r0/1/0>; <x;1w1r1/0/1>

Table 1 shows the FFMs observed in this work and their respective FPs. As previously mentioned, an FFM is composed by a set of FPs represented by *<S/F/R>*. On single-cell faults, *S* may assume none or one operation of read or write for a static FFM, and two or more operations for dynamic FFM.

For simplification purposes, FPs of dynamic FFMs are represented with only two operations. *F* represents the faulty behavior of the cell, and is represented by a logic '1' or '0'. *R* is the output of a read operation, represented by a logic '0' or '1'. In case no read operation is performed, '-' is adopted, while '?' is used when it is not possible to determine the output value. For coupling faults, S assumes the form of $x; y$, in which x is the operation in the a-cell and y is for v-cell. Furthermore, xx is used to represent a dynamic behavior of more than one operation. It's important to note that in this work, dynamic FPs are comprised of a write operation followed by consecutive n read operations. Thus, it's necessary to repeatedly read a cell and evaluate the retrieved value [13].

3   Simulation Setup

In order to provide the proposed analysis, electrical simulations have been performed on HSPICE adopting a FinFET SRAM block composed of 1024 lines and 1024 columns each, connected to functional blocks, using a 20 nm low-power PTM compact model and considering temperatures of −40 °C, 27 °C, and 125 °C. Furthermore, this work analyzes the impact of resistive defects on SRAM blocks designed in smaller technological nodes, such as 16 nm, 14 nm, 10 nm, and 7 nm. Table 2 presents the supply voltage adopted for each node. The operational clock signal frequency chosen is set to 1 GHz. In order to simplify and fasten the simulations, only 8 lines consisting of 8 columns each were implemented, while the remaining cells were emulated by capacitances.

Table 2. Supply voltage of the analysed technological nodes.

Technological node	V_{DD}
20 nm	0.90 V
16 nm	0.85 V
14 nm	0.80 V
10 nm	0.75 V
7 nm	0.70 V

To recreate an SRAM block as genuine as possible, auxiliary circuitry was used. A differential sense amplifier was adopted for read operations, while write operations were assisted by write buffers. Pre-charge circuits, row-decoders, and registers complete the setup. All circuits, including memory cells, were designed using the low power technological library. As stated before, the SRAM cell was designed using only one fin in each transistor to achieve higher densities.

3.1   Modeled Defects

In this work, a set of 12 defects was modeled and injected into a memory cell, one at a time. Six of them are classic resistive-open defects, previously studied for bulk CMOS technology [14]. In summary, resistive-open defects are non-designed resistances between two nodes that have a connection. Figure 4 depicts the scheme adopted to model the resistive-open defects.

The other six defects analyzed are considered resistive-bridge defects, which are resistive connections between nodes that, upon design, were not connected [10]. Figure 5 shows the set of resistive-bridge defects analyzed in this work. DFB1-DFB5 are classic resistive-bridge defects that have been previously analyzed in CMOS technology [11]. DFB6 is a new defect that, considering FinFET architecture, may create a bridge between drain and source of transistors [39]. Due to cell's symmetry, only one instance of each defect is necessary to analyze their impact on the cell's behavior.

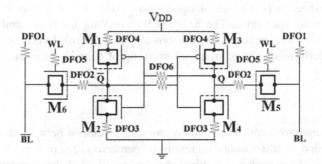

Fig. 4. Resistive-open defects injected into a SRAM cell.

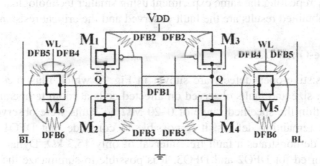

Fig. 5. Resistive defects injected into a SRAM cell.

3.2 Evaluation of Defect Size on Fault Behavior

To analyze the impact of each defect on the behavior of memory cells, an automated tool was developed. For each defect, simulations were performed while varying the resistance value of modeled defects up to a maximum of 20 MΩ, or until the occurrence of a static fault. The resistance on this iteration is defined as "upper limit" and, based on this resistance value, the tool simulated the circuit again using increasingly weaker resistances in order to observe either dynamic faults or fault-free behavior.

Applying this procedure, it is possible to observe three distinct cases: the defect is too weak to sensitize any type of fault at logic level; the defect is weak, but great enough to sensitize dynamic faults; and the defect is great enough to sensitize static faults. The output of read operations and internal nodes of the cell are analyzed in order to identify faults.

To evaluate defects that result in single static faults, simple verification of the value is performed after the defect is injected. Single write and read operations ($0r0$, $1r1$, $0w0$, $0w1$, $1w0$ and $1w1$) are executed to analyze static faults. To evaluate dynamic faults, a write followed by n read operations were performed ($0w0r0^n$, $0w1r1^n$, $1w0r0^n$ and $1w1r1^n$, where n is number of operations). Note that n was defined to be at maximum 50 read operations. The analysis for coupling faults is similar, with the exception that for this type of fault, operations may be performed in certain cells, while evaluation is performed in a different cell or group of cells in the array.

4 Results

This Section summarizes the results and discusses the relation between defect size and cell behavior. First, results obtained for resistive-open defects and resistive-bridge defects considering the 20 nm node in a nominal temperature of 27 °C are presented. Next, an evaluation comparing the behavior of this same node in temperatures of −40 °C and 125 °C is presented. These analyses were first presented in [30], and are further extended in this work by repeating the same experiment using smaller technological nodes. In all analyses, the obtained results are the fault observed and the critical resistance.

4.1   Resistive-Open Defects

Results for resistive-open defects are shown in Fig. 6, which illustrates the relation between defect size and faults observed on affected cells at room temperature (27 °C). For DFO4, within the specified range of 0–20 MΩ no faults were observed at 27 °C. Observing the remaining defects, it is possible to conclude that DFO1 is the most critical one; it demonstrates a fault free interval of only 15.3 kΩ. Dynamic behaviors were only reported for DFO2 and DFO3. It is possible to summarize the results: TFs can be observed for defects DFO1, DFO5, and DFO6. RDF and dRDF can be observed injecting RODF3. Finally, DRDF and dDRDF are observed when injecting DFO2 and DFO3.

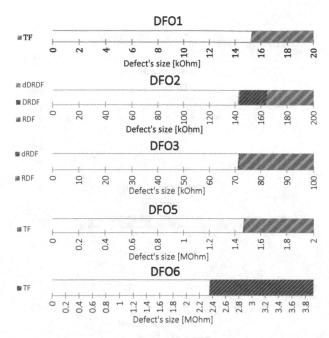

Fig. 6. Faults observed during simulations of SRAM cells affected by resistive-open defects of different magnitudes.

4.2 Resistive-Bridge Defects

As previously mentioned, resistive-bridge defects create connections between nodes that were not planned upon design. Therefore, depending on the defect size, such defects may actively unbalance the cell and cause faults such as NSF and SAF. The full relation between defect size and observed faults is depicted in Fig. 7. From the obtained results, it is possible to conclude that the most critical resistive-bridge defect is DFB3 as it creates the greatest faulty behavior interval (from 0 to 46 kΩ).

However, there is a different aspect of resistive-bridge defects the results draw special attention to: as such defects create connections, a resistive-bridge defect affecting one cell may have an impact in other fault-free neighbor cells, causing Coupling Faults (CF). In Fig. 7, this was defined as "Array Impact", and observed in DFB5 and DFB6. It is important to mention that these "Array Impact" faults affected fault-free cells. Figure 8 depicts this behavior. It shows the simulation of a cell that is located at row 0 and is affected by a resistive-bridge defect (DFB5) that creates a connection between the word line 0 (WL0) and $\overline{BL}$ of magnitude 11.5 kΩ. This defect size does not sensitize any fault in a-cell, as shown in Fig. 7. A write '0' operation is successfully performed on the cell, followed by three consecutive read operations in the same cell on row 0. The faulty behavior is observed in a v-cell in row 1, as a dynamic CFrd, and in a v-cell in row 2 as a CFrd.

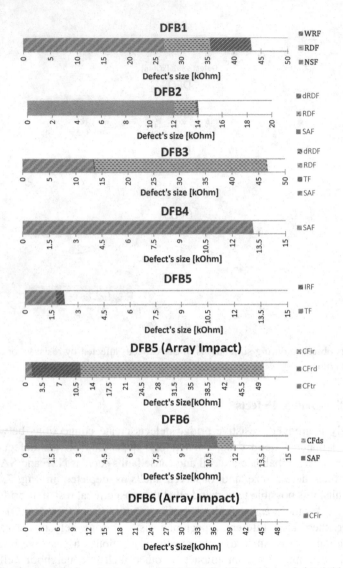

Fig. 7. Faults observed during simulations of SRAM cells affected by resistive-bridge defects of different magnitudes.

By performing a read operation on row 1 (Fig. 8), $\overline{BL}$ is not able to charge as it is being drained by the WL0. This results in an IRF, as can be seen in the *Out* signal. As all of the three analyzed cells are located on the same column, they all share the same output signal. A subsequent read operation has a bigger impact, causing a dynamic CFrd on the cell. The same destructive behavior is observed when performing subsequently read operations in another fault-free cell from a different row, this time a static CFrd can be observed.

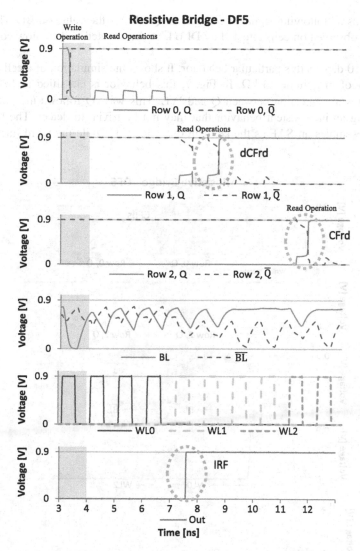

Fig. 8. Simulation output of a cell affected by a resistive-bridge causing faults on other cells of the array.

Additionally, operations performed on fault-free cells can affect defective cells as long as they are in the same column. This way, the fault-free cell is the aggressor and the faulty cell is the victim. Figure 9 illustrates this fault behavior on a cell affected by DFB6, which creates a resistive-bridge between source and drain of transistor M5, connecting $\overline{BL}$ and $\overline{Q}$. As the fault-free cell on row 2 is written, the value on the defective cell on row 1 is flipped. This happens due to the shared connection between $\overline{BL}$ and $\overline{Q}$. As $\overline{BL}$ is discharged due to a write '0' operation, $\overline{Q}$ discharges as well, causing a misbalancing, and eventually a flip on the stored value. This can also be considered as a "following-signal" behavior, as Q̄ follows the value on B̄L̄. The same behavior is observed on cells affected by DFB4, as the affected node is now connected to WL.

Figure 10 depicts this particular behavior. It shows the simulation of a cell affected by a DFB4 of magnitude 13 kΩ. In Fig. 7, this behavior is classified as SAF. This defect creates a connection between Q̄ and WL. This way, Q̄ follows the voltage on WL, causing an inconsistent behavior that may not be trivial to detect. The behavior observed resembles an SAF as the cell can only store '1' while the word line is off.

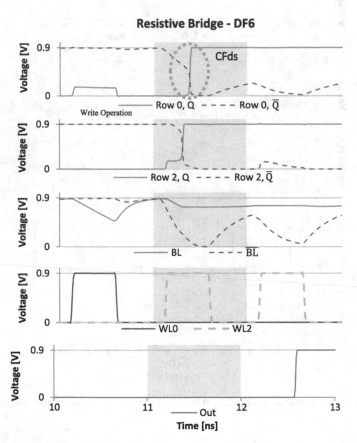

Fig. 9. Simulation output of a cell affected by a resistive-bridge defect suffering a destruction fault caused by an operation in a neighbor cell.

4.3   Analysis Considering Different Operating Temperatures

Table 3 shows the comparison between the critical resistances for resistive-open and resistive-bridge defects considering three different temperatures, −40 °C, 27 °C, and 127 °C. Analyzing the results obtained throughout simulations, it is possible to observe that for each defect, a similar relation between critical resistances and temperature exists. In DFO1, DFO2, DFO3, DFO4, DFO6, DFB2, and DFB5 (register) an increased temperature worsens the critical resistance. On the contrary, DFO5, DFB1, DFB3, DFB4, DFB5 (cell and array) and DFB6 are more prominent in lower temperatures.

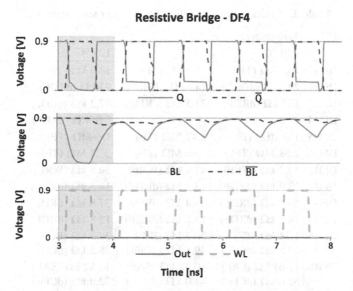

Fig. 10. Simulation output of a cell affected by a resistive-bridge defect connecting $\bar{Q}$ to the word line.

The operating temperature affects the critical resistances, since the current capabilities of the transistors are also affected. In this manner, the process of charging and discharging the nodes and the resistive-open and bridge defect's value are affected by temperature.

On the one hand, for resistive-open defects, the high temperature facilitates the occurrence of faults, because it lowers the critical resistance. However, for DFO5, low resistance slightly moved the cell's operational window to a more convenient period within higher temperatures, resulting in an improvement of operation in this design. Further, it is interesting to note, that DF4 only causes faults at the highest temperature setting.

On the other hand, resistive-bridge defects are more likely to sensitize faults considering lower temperature. Note that the critical resistance value necessary to cause RDFs decreases with temperature for DFB2 and DFB3, because the resistance alters the discharge characteristics of nodes. Note that for resistive-bridge defects a smaller resistance value represents a stronger defect. Considering DFB5, it is possible to observe that the TF occurs with a smaller resistance value when simulating the memory cell operating at −40 °C. Finally, coupling faults are more prominent in low temperature, since a weaker defect is necessary to cause the fault.

The presented analysis considering different operating temperatures demonstrates a pattern for FinFET-based SRAMs and will further assist in future researches on evaluating weak resistive defects' impact on memory cells.

Table 3. Critical resistance values for different temperatures.

DF	Temperature		
	−40 °C	27 °C	125 °C
DFO1	16.9 kΩ (TF)	15.3 kΩ (TF)	13.6 kΩ (TF)
DFO2	297 kΩ (dDRDF)	144 kΩ (dDRDF)	73 kΩ (dRDF)
DFO3	137 kΩ (dRDF)	71.5 kΩ (dRDF)	37.2 kΩ (dRDF)
DFO4	–	–	6.6 MΩ (dRDF)
DFO5	1.4 MΩ (TF)	1.47 MΩ (TF)	1.6 MΩ (TF)
DFO6	2.58 MΩ (TF)	2.46 MΩ (TF)	2.23 MΩ (TF)
DFB1	54.4 kΩ (WRF)	41.6 kΩ (WRF)	30.8 kΩ (WRF)
DFB2	13.9 kΩ (dRDF)	13.8 kΩ (dRDF)	14.8 kΩ (dRDF)
DFB3	54.6 kΩ (dRDF)	46.4 kΩ (dRDF)	37.8 kΩ (dRDF)
DFB4	14.1 kΩ (dRDF)	13.2 kΩ (dRDF)	12.8 kΩ (dRDF)
DFB5	1.74 kΩ (TF)	2.13 kΩ (IRF)	3.53 kΩ (IRF)
	57.5 kΩ (dCFir)	49.5 kΩ (dCFir)	38.2 kΩ (dCFir)
DFB6	11.61 kΩ (SAF)	10.92 kΩ (SAF)	10.52 kΩ (SAF)
	52.6 kΩ (dCFir)	44.0 kΩ (dCFir)	32.0 kΩ (dCFir)

4.4   Analysis Considering Different Nodes

In order to evaluate critical resistances for smaller nodes, an extensive fault mapping process was carried out, adopting different technological nodes: 16 nm, 14 nm, 10 nm, and 7 nm. Tables 4, 5, 6, 7, 8 and 9 present the faults observed in each simulation setup, including the 20 nm node as reference. The resistance values shown represent the critical resistance responsible to sensitize a fault at logic level.

The tables are grouped in two sets according to the kind of defect. In the first set, the critical resistance associated to resistive-open defects is analyzed considering three different operating temperatures. The second set presents the results for bridge defects. Table 4 presents the results obtained for resistive-open defects considering the temperature of 27 °C. Analyzing the summarized results, it is possible to observe a significant change in critical resistance for the same defect in different technological nodes. The only exception is DFO1, whose critical resistance remained around 14 kΩ. Note that with DFO4 no faults have been observed for the considered temperature range. For all other resistive-open defects, the scale-down of technological nodes made them less relevant as only stronger defects are now necessary to sensitize faults. In fact, the critical resistance for DFO2 in a 20 nm node is more than 30 times smaller when compared to its critical resistance in 7 nm technology.

Table 4. Critical resistances for resistive-open defects at 27 °C.

Defect	Fault	Critical resistance [kΩ]				
		20 nm	16 nm	14 nm	10 nm	7 nm
DFO1	TF	15.3	13.8	12.2	13.7	16.6
DFO2	DRDF	144.3	225.2	463.9	937.4	4500.0
	RDF	165.4	232.2	505.4	–	–
	dDRDF	144.2	224.5	461.0	923.8	4041.2
DFO3	RDF	71.6	103.4	190.1	357.9	1345.9
	dRDF	71.5	103.3	189.5	356.3	1324.8
DFO5	TF	1471.1	1858.0	2385.6	2778.4	3137.5
DFO6	TF	2457.5	3665.9	5105.0	6055.0	7685.0

A similar behavior can be observed in the results shown in Tables 5 and 6, which present the results obtained for the simulations injecting resistive-open defects with operating temperature set to 125 °C and −40 °C, respectively. Once again, all defects presented a significant increase in critical resistance, except for DFO1. Note also that DFO4 only caused faults when considering a temperature of 125 °C and the range of resistance used in the executed simulations.

Table 5. Critical resistances for resistive-open defects at 125 °C.

Defect	Fault	Critical resistance [kΩ]				
		20 nm	16 nm	14 nm	10 nm	7 nm
DFO1	TF	13.6	11.5	9.5	10.1	11.2
DFO2	RDF	73.1	93.0	137.7	206.3	420.3
	dRDF	73.0	92.8	137.4	205.9	420.0
DFO3	RDF	37.3	46.2	64.9	92.8	182.3
	dRDF	37.2	46.1	64.8	92.7	182.1
DFO4	dDRDF	6598.7	17662.9	–	–	–
DFO5	TF	1566.9	1947.0	2440.5	2851.4	3145.8
DFO6	TF	2231.5	3384.4	4671.6	5485.2	6225.0

Table 6. Critical resistances for resistive-open defects at −40 °C.

Defect	Fault	Critical resistance [kΩ]				
		20 nm	16 nm	14 nm	10 nm	7 nm
DFO1	TF	16.9	16.0	14.9	17.4	21.7
DFO2	DRDF	297.4	694.6	–	–	–
	dDRDF	296.7	680.2	7414.0	–	–
DFO3	RDF	136.7	261.3	1301.3	–	–
	dRDF	136.6	260.4	1285.0	9187.6	–
DFO5	TF	1393.5	1764.7	2278.1	2713.3	3060.8
DFO6	TF	2575.3	3830.4	5345.0	6360.0	7985.0

In Tables 7, 8, and 9, the results obtained from the analysis of faults caused by resistive-bridge defects in the temperatures of 27 °C, 125 °C and −40 °C are shown, respectively. Analyzing the results obtained in Table 7, it is possible to observe a significant change in critical resistance (increasing 84%) for the defect DFB1, when moving from 20 nm to 7 nm technology. Reducing the technology node also causes some variation to the value of critical resistance for the remaining defects. The lowest values tend to appear for the 14 nm technology, while for 7 nm the value increases when compared to any other technology node simulated.

Table 7. Critical resistance values for DFB at 27 °C.

Defect	Fault		Critical resistance [kΩ]				
			20 nm	16 nm	14 nm	10 nm	7 nm
DFB1	NSF		26.67	32.93	49.14	58.70	75.78
	WRF		43.11	45.38	49.14	58.70	75.78
	RDF		35.21	37.85	49.14	58.70	75.78
	dRDF		35.39	43.73	50.04	59.80	76.88
DFB2	SAF1		11.98	11.09	10.58	11.38	13.40
	TF		11.98	11.09	10.60	11.42	13.92
	RDF		13.80	12.18	11.36	12.34	14.40
	dRDF		14.04	12.20	11.44	14.62	15.56
DFB3	SAF0		13.22	12.82	12.56	12.55	15.04
	TF		13.46	13.42	13.10	13.14	17.60
	RDF		46.41	45.48	45.42	53.03	66.92
	dRDF		46.42	45.49	45.44	53.04	67.00
DFB4	SAF0		13.20	12.32	11.54	12.56	15.02
	RDF		13.20	12.82	12.64	13.80	16.26
DFB5	Cell	TF	1.65	1.66	1.36	1.37	2.29
		IRF	2.12	2.02	1.24	1.26	2.34
	Array	CFtr	1.67	1.67	1.36	1.37	2.32
		CFrd	11.36	10.68	9.40	10.34	12.24
		CFir	50.19	26.31	24.29	27.50	38.98
		dCFrd	11.92	10.86	9.61	10.66	12.36
		dCFir	50.20	10.87	24.40	27.66	39.01
DFB6	Cell	SAF0	10.92	10.02	9.67	10.26	11.16
	Array	CFds	11.86	10.02	9.67	10.26	11.16
		CFir	44.00	22.83	20.81	24.02	35.50
		dCFir	44.01	22.88	20.88	24.12	35.65

It is important to mention that some faults are masked by others. This happens to TF in DFB1, which is masked by NSF and SAF. This also occurs with WRF in DFB2 and DFB3. In older technologies, a well-defined range for such behavior is encountered, while FinFET's technology range of transitions is comparably diffuse, since the critical resistance values often differ by less than 1 kΩ. There are presented some faults with the same value, because this faults are noted for some nodes, but are masked for another. For example, in DFB1 for the 7 nm technology, WRF and RDF are masked by NSF.

Observing some faults, the SAF can be notice that the value stuck-at could be different, according how the resistance is presented in the cell. For example, in defect DFB2, SAF is stuck-at '1', however this would be '0' if the resistance are connected to $\bar{Q}$. Fr the CFir array faults of DFB5 and DFB6, the value of critical resistance keep the higher in all cases; this event occurs due the variations in the register's sensibility in the set of V_{DD} and frequency operation used.

Analyzing the data of Tables 8 and 9, it is observed that the effect of temperature variation is more prominent in the 7 nm node, whose the critical resistance in Table 8 is lower than the 20 nm node. However, in Table 9 the situation is inversed and the critical resistance of the 7 nm node is higher. It may be noted that the dynamic fault occurrence rate is higher when compared to open defects for all nodes.

Table 8. Critical resistance values for DFB at 125 °C.

Defect	Fault		Critical Resistance [kΩ]				
			20 nm	16 nm	14 nm	10 nm	7 nm
DFB1	NSF		18.70	18.52	20.16	27.27	43.88
	WRF		32.09	29.55	30.31	35.69	44.06
	RDF		21.88	20.04	21.26	27.63	43.80
	dRDF		21.97	20.14	21.36	28.07	44.06
DFB2	SAF1		11.60	10.12	9.21	9.61	10.78
	TF		11.60	10.12	9.21	9.61	10.80
	RDF		14.78	12.14	10.44	10.56	11.50
	dRDF		14.95	12.20	10.68	10.68	11.60
DFB3	SAF0		12.86	11.20	9.88	10.38	11.80
	TF		12.86	12.22	9.96	10.42	12.84
	RDF		37.81	34.63	32.66	36.25	42.77
	dRDF		37.82	34.64	32.68	36.26	42.79
DFB4	SAF0		12.84	11.18	9.86	10.36	11.80
	RDF		12.84	11.18	10.22	10.36	12.16
	dRDF		12.85	11.19	10.41	10.53	12.17
DFB5	Cell	TF	1.57	157	1.24	1.20	2.00
		IRF	3.48	3.54	2.77	2.83	3.06
	Array	CFtr	1.57	1.57	1.24	1.21	2.02
		CFrd	10.74	9.19	7.60	8.11	9.20
		CFir	38.74	16.12	14.96	17.76	23.36
		dCFrd	10.78	9.21	7.67	8.19	9.25
DFB6	Cell	SAF0	10.52	9.09	8.44	8.84	9.55
	Array	CFir	10.52	9.09	8.44	8.84	9.56
		dCFir	31.99	12.25	11.09	13.89	19.49

Table 9. Critical resistance values for DFB at −40 °C.

Defect	Fault		Critical Resistance [kΩ]				
			20 nm	16 nm	14 nm	10 nm	7 nm
DFB1	NSF		47.35	60.60	66.90	83.08	113.81
	WRF		55.74	60.60	66.91	83.08	113.81
	RDF		55.05	60.60	66.90	83.08	113.81
	dRDF		56.14	61.02	67.12	85.45	114.74
DFB2	SAF1		12.76	12.34	12.20	13.38	16.22
	TF		12.76	12.40	12.46	13.92	18.48
	RDF		13.86	12.92	12.44	13.38	16.28
	dRDF		14.04	13.73	14.03	16.17	20.14
DFB3	SAF0		14.08	13.78	13.56	15.20	18.92
	TF		14.99	15.34	14.02	15.70	22.96
	RDF		54.62	55.99	58.51	71.21	96.33
	dRDF		54.63	56.00	58.52	71.29	97.02
DFB4	SAF0		14.06	13.76	13.54	15.20	18.92
	RDF		14.08	13.76	13.54	15.20	18.92
DFB5	Cell	TF	1.74	1.84	1.51	1.55	2.89
		IRF	0.64	0.58	0.81	0.87	3.16
		dRDF	0.65	1.81	1.52	1.58	2.66
	Array	CFtr	1.74	1.84	1.52	1.54	2.85
		CFrd	11.88	12.04	11.12	12.64	15.44
		CFir	57.61	33.07	31.38	38.05	49.53
		dCFrd	13.12	12.05	11.44	12.65	15.82
		dCFir	57.62	33.08	31.39	38.06	49.54
FB6	Cell	SAF0	11.62	11.00	10.60	10.96	12.96
	Array	CFds	12.86	12.92	12.86	14.30	12.96
		CFir	52.58	28.04	24.25	30.92	42.40
		dCFir	52.59	28.06	24.27	30.94	42.42

5 Final Remarks

This work presents an analysis of the behavior of FinFET-based SRAMs affected by resistive defects. The range of analyzed defects is vast and includes weak resistive-open and weak resistive-bridge defects that may escape manufacturing tests. Faulty behaviors detected by an automated tool were mapped and categorized in different kinds of faults. Further, the impact of defects on other cells of the array was evaluated, showing that defects that do not sensitize faults in the defective cell may still compromise the behavior of other cells. The fault models categorized comprise single and couple, static and dynamic faults. Finally, each defect was further characterized considering three different operating temperatures (−40 °C, 27 °C, and 125 °C) and five technological nodes (20 nm, 16 nm, 14 nm, 10 nm, and 7 nm). Except for DFO5, increasing the temperature amplify the impact of resistive-open defects on memory cells. Moreover, a significant increase in critical resistance was observed when mapping faults in smaller technologies, especially for DFO4. Thus, it is possible to conclude that only stronger defects will sensitize faults in further scaled memories.

As for resistive-bridge defects, each defect showed a particular behavior when considering different operating temperatures, mainly the 7 nm that suffers great variations for temperature variation. Besides some exceptions, lower temperatures increase the critical resistance. Coupling faults were observed in cells affected by DFB5 and DFB6.

Dynamic faults will increase their range of appearance with the reduction of technology, to the open defects consequently the 7 nm technology presents a high dynamic fault rate. Considering bridge defect the occurrence of dynamic faults is variable. It is important to mention that weak defects, that do not cause any faulty behavior, may become a reliability concern over lifetime. Under these circumstances, the necessity to adopt defect-oriented test methodologies for performing the manufacturing test procedures increases.

It is important to highlight that weak defects, that do not cause any faulty behavior, may become a reliability concern over lifetime. Under these circumstances, the necessity to adopt defect-oriented test methodologies for performing the manufacturing test procedures increases.

Finally, with this mapping and characterization of different resistive defects, it is possible to start analyzing the impact of these defects when considering memory block's in combination with other reliability issues, such as aging and/or noise tolerance.

References

1. Colinge, J.-P.: FinFETs and Other Multi-Gate Transistors. Springer, Boston (2008). https://doi.org/10.1007/978-0-387-71752-4
2. Intel: Intel® 22 nm Technology. http://www.intel.com/content/www/us/en/silicon-innovations/intel-22nm-technology.html
3. Samsung: Strong 14 nm FinFET Logic Process and Design Infrastructure for Advanced Mobile SOC Applications (2013)
4. Tang, S.H., et al.: FinFET-a quasi-planar double-gate MOSFET. In: 2001 IEEE International Solid-State Circuits Conference. Digest of Technical Papers. ISSCC (Cat. No.01CH37177), pp. 118–119. IEEE (2001)
5. Yu, B., et al.: FinFET scaling to 10 nm gate length. In: Digest. International Electron Devices Meeting, pp. 251–254. IEEE (2002)
6. Chang, J.B., et al.: Scaling of SOI FinFETs down to fin width of 4 nm for the 10 nm technology node. In: 2011 Symposium on VLSI Technology - Digest of Technical Papers (2011)
7. Bhattacharya, D., Jha, N.K.: FinFETs: from devices to architectures. Adv. Electron. **2014**, 1–21 (2014)
8. International Technology Roadmap for Semiconductors: Executive Summary - 2013 Edition (2013)
9. Bosio, A., Dilillo, L., Girard, P., Pravossoudovitch, S., Virazel, A.: Advanced test methods for SRAMs. In: Proceedings of the IEEE VLSI Test Symposium, pp. 300–301 (2012)

10. Dilillo, L., Girard, P., Pravossoudovitch, S., Virazel, A., Borri, S., Hage-Hassan, M.: Resistive-open defects in embedded-SRAM core cells: analysis and March test solution. In: 13th Asian Test Symposium, pp. 266–271 (2004)
11. Fonseca, R.A., et al.: Analysis of resistive-bridging defects in SRAM core-cells: a comparative study from 90 nm down to 40 nm technology nodes. In: 2010 15th IEEE European Test Symposium, ETS 2010, vol. 1, pp. 132–137 (2010)
12. Li, J.C.M., Tseng, C.-W., McCluskey, E.J.: Testing for resistive opens and stuck opens. In: Proceedings International Test Conference 2001 (Cat. No. 01CH37260), pp. 1049–1058. IEEE (2001)
13. Van de Goor, A.J., Al-Ars, Z.: Functional memory faults: a formal notation and a taxonomy. In: Proceedings of the 18th IEEE VLSI Test Symposium, pp. 281–289 (2000)
14. Borri, S., Hage-Hassan, M., Dilillo, L., Girard, P., Pravossoudovitch, S., Virazel, A.: Analysis of dynamic faults in embedded-SRAMs: implications for memory test. J. Electron. Test. 21, 169–179 (2005)
15. Dubey, P., Garg, A., Mahajan, S.: Study of read recovery dynamic faults in 6T SRAMS and method to improve test time. J. Electron. Test. 26, 659–666 (2010)
16. Harutyunyan, G., Shoukourian, S., Vardanian, V., Zorian, Y.: Impact of process variations on read failures in SRAMs. In: East-West Design & Test Symposium (EWDTS 2013), pp. 1–4. IEEE (2013)
17. Needham, W., Prunty, C., Yeoh, E.H.: High volume microprocessor test escapes, an analysis of defects our tests are missing. In: Proceedings International Test Conference 1998 (IEEE Cat. No. 98CH36270), pp. 25–34 (1998). Int. Test Conference
18. Borri, S., Hage-Hassan, M., Dilillo, L., Girard, P., Pravossoudovitch, S., Virazel, A.: Analysis of dynamic faults in embedded-SRAMs: implications for memory test. J. Electron. Test. Theory Appl. 21, 169–179 (2005)
19. Benso, A., Bosio, A., Di Carlo, S., Di Natale, G., Prinetto, P.: March AB, March AB1: new March tests for unlinked dynamic memory faults. In: Proceedings of the - International Test Conference 2005, pp. 834–841 (2005)
20. Bosio, A., Di Carlo, S., Di Natale, G., Prinetto, P.: March AB, a state-of-the-art March test for realistic static linked faults and dynamic faults in SRAMs. IET Comput. Digit. Tech. 1, 237–245 (2007)
21. Hamdioui, S., Al-Ars, Z., Van De Goor, A.J.: Testing static and dynamic faults in random access memories. In: Proceedings of the IEEE VLSI Test Symposium 2002, January, pp. 395–400 (2002)
22. Harutyunyan, G., Martirosyan, S., Shoukourian, S., Zorian, Y.: Memory physical aware multi-level fault diagnosis flow. IEEE Trans. Emerg. Top. Comput. 1 (2018)
23. Harutyunyan, G., Tshagharyan, G., Zorian, Y.: Test and repair methodology for FinFET-based memories. IEEE Trans. Device Mater. Reliab. 15, 3–9 (2015)
24. Harutyunyan, G., Tshagharyan, G., Vardanian, V., Zorian, Y.: Fault modeling and test algorithm creation strategy for FinFET-based memories. In: 2014 IEEE 32nd VLSI Test Symposium (VTS), pp. 1–6. IEEE (2014)
25. Segura, J.A., Champac, V.H., Rodríguez-Montañés, R., Figueras, J., Rubio, J.A.: Quiescent current analysis and experimentation of defective CMOS circuits. J. Electron. Test. 3, 337–348 (1992)
26. Dilillo, L., Girard, P., Pravossoudovitch, S., Virazel, A., Bastian, M.: Resistive-open defect injection in SRAM core-cell. In: Proceedings of the 42nd Annual Conference on Design Automation - DAC 2005, p. 857. ACM Press, New York (2005)
27. Vatajelu, E.I., et al.: Analyzing resistive-open defects in SRAM core-cell under the effect of process variability. In: 2013 18th IEEE European Test Symposium (ETS), pp. 1–6. IEEE (2013)

28. Fonseca, R.A., et al.: Analysis of resistive-bridging defects in SRAM core-cells: a comparative study from 90 nm down to 40 nm technology nodes. In: 2010 15th IEEE European Test Symposium, ETS 2010, pp. 132–137 (2010)
29. Fonseca, R.A., et al.: Impact of resistive-bridging defects in SRAM core-cell. In: 2010 Fifth IEEE International Symposium on Electronic Design, Test & Applications, pp. 265–269. IEEE (2010)
30. Copetti, T.S., Medeiros, G.C., Poehls, L.M.B., Balen, T.R.: Analyzing the behavior of FinFET SRAMs with resistive defects. In: 2017 IFIP/IEEE International Conference on Very Large Scale Integration (VLSI-SoC), Abu Dhabi, pp. 1–6 (2017)
31. Intel: Intel's 14 nm Technology: Delivering Ultrafast, Energy-Sipping Products (2017)
32. Samsung: Samsung Mass Produces 14-Nanometer Exynos Processor with Full Connectivity Integration (2016)
33. Nanoscale Integration and Modeling (NIMO): Predictive Technology Model (PTM). http://ptm.asu.edu/
34. Hisamoto, D., Kaga, T., Kawamoto, Y., Takeda, E.: A fully depleted lean-channel transistor (DELTA)-a novel vertical ultra thin SOI MOSFET. In: International Technical Digest on Electron Devices Meeting, pp. 833–836. IEEE (1989)
35. Simsir, M.O., Bhoj, A., Jha, N.K.: Fault modeling for FinFET circuits. In: 2010 IEEE/ACM International Symposium on Nanoscale Architectures, pp. 41–46. IEEE (2010)
36. Karl, E., et al.: A 4.6 GHz 162 Mb SRAM design in 22 nm tri-gate CMOS technology with integrated read and write assist circuitry. IEEE J. Solid-State Circ. **48**, 150–158 (2013)
37. Jan, C.H., et al.: A 22 nm SoC platform technology featuring 3-D tri-gate and high-k/metal gate, optimized for ultra low power, high performance and high density SoC applications. Tech. Dig. - Int. Electron Devices Meet. IEDM. 44–47 (2012)
38. Burnett, D., Parihar, S., Ramamurthy, H., Balasubramanian, S.: FinFET SRAM design challenges. In: 2014 IEEE International Conference on IC Design & Technology, pp. 1–4. IEEE (2014)
39. Liu, Y., Xu, Q.: On modeling faults in FinFET logic circuits In: 2012 IEEE International Test Conference, pp. 1 9. IEEE (2012)

Lifetime Enhancement of Non-Volatile Caches by Exploiting Dynamic Associativity Management Techniques

Sukarn Agarwal$^{(\boxtimes)}$ and Hemangee K. Kapoor

Department of Computer Science and Engineering,
Indian Institute of Technology Guwahati,
Guwahati 781039, Assam, India
{sukarn,hemangee}@iitg.ac.in

Abstract. By showcasing the attractive features like high density and low static power, the emerging Non-Volatile Memories (NVMs) have recently being accepted act as a prominent choice in the memory hierarchy, including caches. However, the limited write endurance with the write variation introduced by the applications and the existing cache management policies leads to an early breakdown of NVM cells, thus reducing the effective lifetime.

This chapter presents efficient techniques to improve the lifetime by mitigating inter-set write variation. Our first technique: FSSRP partitions the cache into groups of sets called fellow groups. Each set has two logical parts: Normal and Reserve. Sets within the fellow group can use the reserve part of its fellow sets to distribute the uneven writes. The second technique: FSDRP, based on FSSRP, partitions the cache vertically into equal-sized windows and use a different window one at a time as a reserve part during the execution to disperse the writes uniformly. Experimental results using full system simulation show a significant reduction in inter-set write variation over the baseline and existing technique.

Keywords: Cache memory · Non-Volatile Memory ·
Inter-set write variation · Lifetime · Fellow sets ·
Dynamic Associativity Management

1 Introduction

With the large processing and data demands by the next generation applications, many cores and large-sized Last Level Caches (LLCs) are integrated on-chip. Traditional caches made up of SRAM fail to fulfill the application demands in the context of performance, power, and area. Previous studies [17] have shown that the majority of the LLC power consumption is due to leakage (almost 80%) which alarmingly raises circuit reliability issues. Hence, in the recent days, the emergence of Non-volatile Memory (NVM) technologies is motivating the

© IFIP International Federation for Information Processing 2019
Published by Springer Nature Switzerland AG 2019
M. Maniatakos et al. (Eds.): VLSI-SoC 2017, IFIP AICT 500, pp. 46–71, 2019.
https://doi.org/10.1007/978-3-030-15663-3_3

researchers to look beyond for alternative technologies in the memory hierarchy [19–22]. These emerging NVM technologies include Spin Transfer Torque Random Access Memory (STT-RAM), Phase Change Random Access Memory (PCRAM) and, Resistive Random Access Memory (ReRAM). The benefits of using these NVMs in the memory hierarchy are high density, low static power consumption and, good scalability. However, the major limitations of using NVM technologies in the cache hierarchy are costly write operations (such as latency and energy) and, weak write endurance. The write endurance value of the NVMs are: 10^{11} writes for ReRAM [6], 10^8 writes for PCRAM [5] and, for STT-RAM the predicted write endurance value is around 10^{15} writes, but the value tested so far is $4 * 10^{12}$ write operations [7,23]. In contrast, the write endurance value for the charge based traditional memory technologies such as SRAM/DRAM is more than 10^{15} writes. This shows that the compared to NVM caches, the lifetime of the conventional caches are at-most 1000 times better.

With the limited write endurance, the lifetime of NVM cache is further affected by the write variations generated by the applications running on multiple cores. Because of the write variations, the running applications create certain hot-spots in a cache to better utilize the temporal locality. In a cache, the write variations are categorized into two types: *Inter-set* and *Intra-set* write variations. Intra-set write variation actually takes place inside a single cache set. Specifically, the intra-set write variation occurs due to distinct write counts of the blocks inside a set. In particular, some of the blocks inside the set experience more number of writes as compared to other blocks, which implies that the heavily written blocks inside the set wear out faster than the other blocks. Inter-set write variation, on the other hand, implies non-uniform write count values across the cache sets. This non-uniform write distribution between the cache sets clearly indicates that some of the cache sets face much more writes compared to other sets inside the bank, which results into the breakdown of the some of the (heavily written) sets faster than the other ones.

This chapter proposes effective techniques to reduce the inter-set write variation with the improvement in the lifetime for the NVM cache. Our first technique: Fellow Set with Static Reserve Part (FSSRP) logically partitions the cache sets into groups of sets called fellow groups. Every group has two logical parts: Normal Part and Reserve Part (NP and RP). The working of NP in the group is same as the conventional cache. While the RP of the group is used to handle the non-uniform write distribution of the heavily written sets in the group. In other words, sets within a fellow group can use the reserve parts from their fellow sets to distribute the writes uniformly. However, the major hurdle with the employment of the FSSRP is the limited lifetime improvement due to large number of writes in the static or fixed RP section of the cache which in turn contributes to the intra-set write variation. To overcome this, our second technique: Fellow Set with Dynamic Reserve Part (FSDRP) based on FSSRP, logically divides the cache into multiple equal-sized windows. During the execution, a different window of the cache is used as RP section for a certain predefined interval in order to distribute the writes. By this way, the FSDRP disperses the redirected writes over the cache.

We implemented our proposed schemes on STT-RAM [4] based non-volatile cache. However, the techniques can be easily extended to other non-volatile caches such as PCRAM and ReRAM based caches. The main contributions of this chapter are as follows:

- We present the efficient techniques to reduce the inter-set write variation that helps to improve the lifetime of non-volatile caches.
- Our first technique: Fellow Set with Static Reserve Part (FSSRP) [18] partitions the cache sets into groups called fellow groups. Each set in the group has two parts: Normal and Reserve. Sets within the fellow group can use the reserve parts from their fellow sets to distribute the writes uniformly.
- Our second technique: Fellow set with Dynamic Reserve Part (FSDRP) uses fellow groups as same as FSSRP. In addition, it further partitions the cache vertically into multiple windows. During execution, a different window is used as reserve part over a certain interval in order to distribute the writes uniformly.
- We use full system simulator GEM-5 [1] for experimental evaluation. Results are compared with the existing technique: Swap Shift [8] and the baseline STT-RAM based cache with no support of wear leveling. We also provide a detailed analysis with different configurations of the LLC and, by varying the parameters of the techniques.

The rest of the chapter is organized as follows: Background and Motivation are discussed in Sect. 2. Section 3 reports the related works. Section 4 presents the proposed wear leveling techniques. Experimental Setup is discussed in Sect. 5. Results and Analysis are presented in Sect. 6. Finally, Sect. 7 concludes the chapter.

2   Background and Motivation

2.1   STT-RAM

We applied our schemes on an STT-RAM [4] based non-volatile cache. This subsection gives the brief overview of STT-RAM cell. Figure 1 depicts the schematic view of STT-RAM cell.

The STT-RAM cell contains an Access transistor and a Magnetic Tunnel Junction (MTJ). An MTJ is constructed from two ferromagnetic layers viz. reference and the free layer and the tunnel barrier (made up of MgO). The use of tunnel barrier in the MTJ is to provide an insulation between the ferromagnetic layers. The magnetization direction of the reference layer is fixed whereas, the magnetization direction of the free layer is changed according to the spin-polarized current. These magnetization directions are actually used to represent the data bit stored in the cell. The anti-parallel magnetization direction resembles high resistance that represents a logical '1', while the parallel magnetization direction represents the logical '0' having low resistance.

The read and write operations in the STT-RAM cell are performed with the help of source and a bit-line. The SET operation or writing '1' in the STT cell

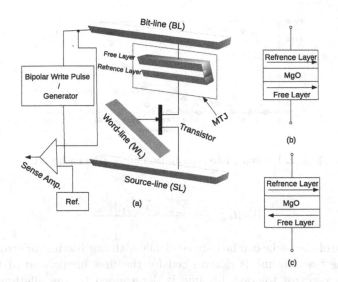

Fig. 1. (a) Representational View of STT-RAM cell (b) Parallel low resistance, representing '0' state (c) Anti-parallel high resistance, representing '1' state.

is completed by applying a large negative voltage between the source and bit-line. On the other hand, the RESET operation or writing '0' in the STT cell is achieved by a large positive voltage. In order to perform the read operation or to detect the state of STT cell, a small voltage is applied between the lines which in turn generates the current. The generated current is compared with the reference current to detect the state of a cell.

2.2   Coefficients of Write Variation and Lifetime

The chapter gives wear leveling policies to reduce the inter-set write variation present in the cache. The write variations inside the cache are measured with the help of coefficients. Equations (1) and (2) represent these coefficients [8]: (i) $InterV$, that measures the average coefficient of variation across cache sets, and (ii) $IntraV$ measures the average coefficient of variation inside a cache set.

$$InterV = \frac{1}{Write_{avg}} \sqrt{\frac{\sum_{k=1}^{S}\left(\sum_{l=1}^{A}\frac{W_{k,l}}{A} - Write_{avg}\right)^2}{N-1}} \qquad (1)$$

$$IntraV = \frac{1}{S.Write_{avg}} \sum_{k=1}^{S} \sqrt{\frac{\sum_{l=1}^{A}\left(W_{k,l} - \sum_{m=1}^{A}\frac{W_{k,m}}{A}\right)^2}{A-1}} \qquad (2)$$

In Eqs. (1) and (2), S is the number of cache sets, A implies cache associativity, $W_{k,l}$ is the write count in set k and way l and, $Write_{avg}$ is the average write count in a cache bank. Following equation represents the average write count:

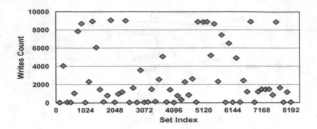

Fig. 2. Uneven write distribution across the cache set.

$$Write_{avg} = \frac{\sum_{k=1}^{S} \sum_{l=1}^{A} W_{k,l}}{S.A} \tag{3}$$

The Lifetime of the cache can be defined either with raw lifetime or error tolerant lifetime. The raw lifetime is determined by the first breakdown of the cache block, whereas, error tolerant lifetime is determined by raw lifetime and the error recovery methods. In this work, we focus on the raw lifetime which is the base of an error-tolerant lifetime. We assume that by integrating other existing error recovery methods with our techniques the lifetime can be further improved. To measure the raw lifetime, it is important to consider three factors: average write count ($Write_{avg}$), the coefficient of Inter-set write variation ($InterV$) and, the coefficient of Intra-set write variation ($IntraV$). To measure the Lifetime Improvement [8] (LI), we use the following equation:

$$LI = \frac{Write_{avg\_base} * (1 + InterV_{base} + IntraV_{base})}{Write_{avg\_pt} * (1 + InterV_{pt} + IntraV_{pt})} - 1 \tag{4}$$

Here $Write_{avg\_base}$, $InterV_{base}$ and $IntraV_{base}$ represent average write count, coefficient of Inter-set write variation and coefficient of Intra-set write variation, respectively of the baseline scheme against which the lifetime is computed. Correspondingly, $Write_{avg\_pt}$, $InterV_{pt}$ and $IntraV_{pt}$ are the average write count, the coefficient of Inter-set write variation and coefficient of Intra-set write variation of the proposed technique, respectively.

2.3 Motivation

Our proposed schemes are dealing with the inter-set write variation present in the cache. To measure the effect of inter-set write variation, we conducted an experiment with 8MB 16-way set associative L2 cache as LLC (details about the experimental setup is discussed in Sect. 5) on *dedup* workload. Figure 2 shows the write distributions across the cache sets inside a cache bank. The conclusion that can be drawn from Fig. 2 is the non-uniform write distribution across the cache sets which in turn indicates the inter-set write variation inside the cache bank. This write variation is of concern as it not only reduces the lifetime but also shrinks the cache capacity eventually over the period of time.

3   Related Works

In the existing state of the art, previously many inter-set wear leveling techniques have been proposed. This section gives a brief insight about such policies. We also discuss the other existing inter-set wear leveling policies and the Dynamic Associativity Management (DAM) based approaches in the cache.

Wang et al. [8] presented a technique called *iiwap* to reduce both inter-set and intra-set write variation inside the cache. The first technique to reduce the inter-set write variation is Swap Shift where the two cache sets of a bank interchange their mapping by invalidating their data after a certain number of writes represented by the variable $SwapTh$. The second technique to reduce the intra-set write variation is Probabilistic Set Line Flush (PoLF) that invalidates the data block after a fixed number of writes called Flush Threshold (FT). Another inter-set wear leveling technique proposed by Chen et al. [13] that changes the cache set mapping at regular intervals by performing XOR operation between the content of register (called remap register) and the set index of the block. At the end of each interval, the content of remap register is changed. Jokar et al. [9] reports an inter-set wear leveling approach that changes the set mapping between the heavily written set and lightly written set with the help of counters. Partitioning the cache into multiple clusters and dynamically changing their mapping according to their write intensity, history and the number of clean/invalid blocks are proposed by Soltani et al. [15]. Wang et al. [14] presented a word and partition level write variation reduction scheme that explores the narrow width data for the word, and software and hardware partitions for the different running applications. Here, the write variation is balanced by swapping the data in the word and across the partitions. A software controlled cache coloring page mapping approach presented by Mittal et al. [16] changes the mapping of the two colors according to their write traffic. Unlike the previously presented approaches, our technique neither changes the set mapping nor swaps the data, rather it uses the same set mapping by exploiting the Dynamic Associativity Management (DAM) towards balancing the write variation across the set.

Qureshi et al. [10] proposed V-way, a DAM-based approach, where the associativity is managed by decoupling the data and tag array. Another approach based on skew associative cache, called Z-cache was reported in [11]. Here, the associativity is increased by increasing the replacement candidates. A DAM based victim retention approach is reported by Das and Kapoor [12]. Our work is inspired by [12].

4   Proposed Wear Leveling Techniques

In this section, we will illustrate both of our proposed techniques: (i) Fellow Sets with Static Reserve Part and (ii) Fellow Sets with Dynamic Reserve Part. Note that, former one, Fellow Sets with Static Reserve Part is from our prior work [18] and it is demonstrated and examined extensively in this chapter.

4.1 Fellow Sets with Static Reserve Part (FSSRP)

Architecture: The main idea of FSSRP is to exploit Dynamic Associativity Management (DAM) towards the inter-set wear leveling. The scheme partitions the cache into groups of sets, called fellow groups. To empower DAM for a set, we further partition each set into two parts: Normal Part (NP) and Reserve Part (RP). The NP simply replicates the conventional cache, whereas, RP of all sets within a fellow group are shared and thus can be used by the sets belonging to the same group. This phenomenon enables the heavily written set in the fellow group to use the RP section of a lightly written set in the same group in order to store its blocks. By this way, we can dynamically manage the associativity towards the inter-set wear leveling. Note that, our intention is not to increase the associativity, rather to use the RP section and fellow sets towards the inter-set wear leveling. Particularly, a set having heavy write usage can avoid the additional writes by redirecting the writes to the RP section of a lightly written set in its fellow group. The write redirection is initiated with the help of a counter associated with each set.

One critical issue with the architecture of FSSRP is to search the relocated blocks that are moved to the sets other than their home set. To deal with this, an additional mapping table, called TaG Storage (TGS) is used. Basically, TGS is a two-dimensional table where each entry contains the tag address and a valid-bit for the blocks that belong to the RP section. In particular, each entry of TGS has one to one mapping with every block in the RP.

Let there be a set associative cache with associativity A and S number of cache sets. The total number of ways reserved for the RP section be r with the size of the fellow group m. Note that all the sets in the fellow group are statically grouped. With this information, the fellow group in the cache has the following properties:

- Total number of fellow groups in the cache: S/m.
- Distance between any two sets of the fellow group in the cache: $S/m - 1$.

The architecture of TGS has the following characteristics:

- TGS Associativity: $A_{tgs} = r * m$.
- Number of sets in TGS: $S_{tgs} = S/m$.
- Total number of blocks in TGS: $B_{tgs} = r * S$.

As mentioned previously, each entry in the RP section of the cache has one to one mapping with each entry of the TGS. For a given TGS set (S_{tgs_i}) and TGS associativity (A_{tgs_j}), the respective cache set (S_k) and cache associativity (A_l) can be easily mapped with the help of following equations:

$$A_l = (A - r) + (A_{tgs_j} \% r) \tag{5}$$

$$S_k = ((A_{tgs_j}/r) * S_{tgs}) + S_{tgs_i} \tag{6}$$

Similarly, for a given cache associativity (A_v) and cache set (S_u), the respective TGS set (S_{tgs_n}) and TGS way (A_{tgs_m}) can be simply mapped with the help of following equation:

$$A_{tgs_m} = (S_u/S_{tgs}) * r + (A_v - (A - r)), \quad (A - r) \le A_v \le A \qquad (7)$$

$$S_{tgs_n} = S_u \% S_{tgs} \qquad (8)$$

In addition to TGS, we add a write counter with each cache set and a write bit with each block belonging to the NP section of the cache. The use of the write counter is to count the number of writes performed in the set. Detailed use of the write counter and the write bit is explained in the next subsection.

The example of our proposed architecture: FSSRP is shown in the Fig. 3. In the example, an L2 cache or LLC with 16-way associativity and 8 cache sets, partitioned into two parts: NP and RP. The number of ways allocated to NP and RP section is 12 and 4 $(r = 4)$ respectively. Let the fellow group size to be 2 $(m = 2)$. With these given values, the distance between two sets in the fellow group is $S/m - 1 = 3$ and the total number of the groups formed in the cache is $S/m = 4$. As shown in the Fig. 3, these four groups are labeled with $G0, G1, G2$ and $G3$ respectively, with the corresponding distance between the two sets $S0$ and $S4$ in the group $G0$ is 3. Similarly, the TGS architecture has the following set of characteristics: $S_{tgs} = S/m = 4$, $A_{tgs} = r * m = 8$ and $B_{tgs} = r * S = 32$. Each set in the TGS resembles one fellow group of the cache. In our example, the set-0 of TGS contains an entry for the fellow group G0 i.e. way-12 to way-15 of cache set 0 and 4.

Operation: We demonstrate the operation of our proposed scheme through Algorithm 1. In the algorithm, the variable parameter I is used as a predefined interval (line 1). The variable W_i is used to represent the write counter associated with the cache set i (line 2). Similarly, the variable b_{ij} (set i and way j) resembles the write bit incorporated with each block in the NP section of cache (line 3). The lightly written set of the fellow group is represented by S_l. The decision of the lightly written set in the group is taken with the help of write counter associated with the set of the group. In particular, the set with the least value of the write counter in the group is treated as a lightly written set (S_l) of the group. For the initial I cycles of the process execution, the cache is treated as a normally available cache (line 4). During the interval, if any write happens to any block in the set, the write bit associated with the block b_{ij} is set and the respective write counter W_i is incremented (line 5 and 6).

Once the application crosses I cycles, for each request R coming from L1 cache to L2 cache, the tag lookup operation is performed in the NP section of the cache. Simultaneously, the tag of the requested block is also searched in the RP section of the cache through TGS. Note that in this case, the TGS set location is mapped by using Eq. (8). In case, the result of lookup operation is hit and if the requested block is present in the NP section of the cache, then it is a direct hit. Otherwise, it is an indirect hit. Note that for the block B present

Algorithm 1. FSSRP Wear Leveling Algorithm

```
1:  I : Predefined interval.
2:  W_i : Write counter associated with set i. 0 ≤ i ≤ S
3:  b_{ij} : Write bit associated with the block in set i and way j. 0 ≤ i ≤ S,
    0 ≤ j < (A − r)
4:  Run application for I cycles treating the cache as a normal cache.
5:  During I cycle, the write counter (W_i) is incremented with each write in set i.
6:  Similarly, the write bit(b_{ij}) is set with each write in the block.
7:  repeat
8:     for each request R coming from L1 cache to block B in L2 cache do
9:        if R == ReadHit then
10:           The Read operation is performed on the block B irrespective of its location.
11:        else if R == WriteHit then
12:           if Block B is found in NP part of cache  then
13:              if the write bit b_{ij} of the block B is set then
14:                 if there exist a light written set S_l in the group then
15:                    The write request for the block B is redirected to the location L in
                       the RP part of S_l. { Block B moved to RP on first write back}
16:                 else
17:                    The write operation is performed on Block B.
                       Increment the write counter (W_i) and keep the write bit set.
18:                 end if
19:              else
20:                 The write operation is performed on Block B.
                    Increment the write counter (W_i) and set the write bit b_{ij}.
21:              end if
22:           else
23:              The write operation is performed on block B.
                 Increment the write counter of the set in which the write
                 operation is performed. { Block B in RP part}
24:           end if
25:        else
26:           Forward the Request R to main memory. Keep the newly arrived block
              in NP part of cache. {cache miss}
27:        end if
28:     end for
29:  until the end of the execution
```

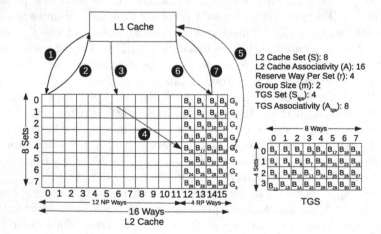

Fig. 3. Working example of FSSRP wear leveling policy

in the RP section of the cache, the respective cache set and cache associativity of the block can be easily mapped with the help of Eqs. (5) and (6).

Depending upon the result of the lookup operation, different operations are performed in the cache which can be explained as follows:

- **Read Hit:** The requested block B is served normally to the L1 cache irrespective of its location in the L2 cache (line 9 and 10).
- **Write Hit (PUTX or write-back) and block B in NP part of the cache:** If the requested block B is present in the NP section of the cache then we have two cases:
  - If there exist any lightly written set (S_l) other than the current set in the group with write bit b_{ij} of the requested block B set, the write request R from L1 cache is redirected to the RP section of S_l. In this case, if there is an invalid line in the RP section of the cache, the write request R from the L1 cache is simply redirected from the current set to the first invalid location. If there is no invalid line present in the RP section of S_l, the LRU victim line is picked from the RP section and the write-back operation is scheduled according to the status of the dirty bit and the corresponding TGS entry is invalidated. Thereafter, the write request R from the L1 cache is redirected to the generated location of the RP section in S_l. Once the request is served, the subsequent block B is invalidated from its corresponding location in the NP section of the cache. Subsequently, a new entry is created in TGS with the help of Eqs. (7) and (8) (line 14 to 16).
  - On the other end of the spectrum, if there is no lightly written set (S_l) existing in the group or if the associated write bit (b_{ij}) with the requested block B is not set, the write request R is served from the current set. Subsequently, the write bit b_{ij} of the block is set (line 17 to 21). Note that in this context, the unavailability of lightly written set implies that the current set itself is the lightly written set of the group.

  Once the write request is served, the write counter (W_i) of the cache set (in which the write operation is performed) is incremented.
- **Write Hit (PUTX or write-back) and block B in RP part of the cache:** If the requested block B is present in the RP section of the cache, the write request R from the L1 cache is served normally from the respective location of the block B in the L2 cache. Once the write request R is served, the write counter (W_i) of the cache set in which the write operation is performed is incremented (line 22 to 24).
- **Cache Miss:** In case, if requested block B is not present in the cache, the request R from the L1 cache will be forwarded to the next level of memory (i.e. main memory in our case). In this case, the incoming block from main memory is placed in NP section of the cache. Simultaneously, the write bit b_{ij} of the cache location in which the incoming block is placed will be reset (line 25 to 27).

The working methodology of an algorithm is presented in Fig. 3. Note that, the architecture of the cache and TGS have already been elaborated in the previous subsection.

Table 1. Percentage increase in coefficient of intra set write variation

Workloads	Swap	Dedup	Body	Fluid	Freq	Stream	X264	Mean
IntraV %	1.3%	45.8%	47.1%	−2.5%	7.1%	8.7%	1.2%	15.5%

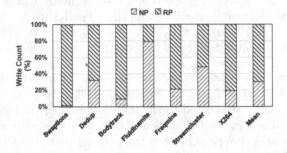

Fig. 4. Write count percentages in the different section of FSSRP

Example: To explain the methodology, three cases are considered with respect to set-0. In the first case, a read request R from L1 cache to the way-0 (shown by arrow 1) of L2 cache is served normally (shown by arrow-2) irrespective of the location (NP or RP) of requested block. In the second case, a write request R (shown by arrow 3) is coming from the L1 cache to the block in way-6 of L2 cache that implies the NP section of the cache. In this case, the write request is redirected to the RP section of the lightly written set (shown by arrow 4) of the fellow group, let say set-4 in our example. Once the request is scheduled in the RP section, the respective TGS entry is updated in the set-0 with the corresponding data attributes of the redirected blocks. Afterwards, the write-back acknowledgment is sent back to L1 cache (shown by arrow 5). In the third case, the write request R (arrow 6) from the L1 cache to the way-14 of L2 cache (RP section) is served normally with the write-back acknowledgment (arrow 7).

Limitation: The limitation of FSSRP is the extensive write accesses and redirections in the limited sized static RP section of the cache. Fig. 4 presents the write count percentages in the NP and RP sections of the cache for different benchmark applications (Details about the experimental setup over the selected value is given in Sect. 5). The conclusion that can be derived from Fig. 4 is that, on an average 69.6% of the write access is handled by the limited size static RP section which in turn generates the intra-set write variation as shown in the Table 1. This increment in Coefficient of intra-set write variation of 15.5% over the baseline limits the lifetime improvement (given in Eq. (4)) despite the reduction in inter-set write variation by the proposed approach: FSSRP. This motivates us to make RP section dynamic in the cache in an attempt to control intra-set write variation.

4.2 Fellow Sets with Dynamic Reserve Part (FSDRP)

Architecture. The architecture framework of FSDRP is based on FSSRP in that respect it also creates fellow groups. The main idea of FSDRP is to further logically partition the cache vertically into multiple uniformly sized windows (such that each window contains an equal number of ways) and over a certain period of execution a single window is used as an RP, exclusively. In other words, instead of partitioning the cache into two static parts: NP and RP, FSDRP partitions the cache into multiple equal-sized windows of size r ways and dynamically uses a different partition as RP for a certain period of time over the execution. However, during that time, the remaining ways behave as the NP section. By using different windows as RP over the execution, the writes are not concentrated on one part of the cache but get dispersed over the different ways of the sets in the fellow group. Note that our intention is not to reduce the intra-set write variation of the cache but to distributes the redirected writes of the RP section in the cache uniformly over the set.

The one to one static mapping between the TGS entry and relocatable blocks in the other sets of the fellow group has evolved as a major bottleneck towards the implementation of FSDRP. Practically, the dispersion of relocatable blocks in the fellow sets by the dynamic RP window destroys the static mapping setup by FSSRP. In order to deal with this, we add an additional field called win_num with each entry of TGS and a relocate bit (r_{ij}) is added to each entry of the cache along with the write bit (b_{ij}). The use of the win_num field is to store the partition or window number where the relocatable block resides in the cache. The use of relocate bit (r_{ij}) is to identify the normal block from the relocated block in the cache set since the RP window keeps moving.

The partition or window has the following characteristics:

- Size of the window or partition in the cache: r.
- Total number of window or partition in the cache (P): A/r.
- Partition or window number for a given way number (W) in the cache: $\lfloor W/r \rfloor$.

Similar to FSSRP, for a given TGS set (S_{tgs_i}) and TGS associativity (A_{tgs_j}), the corresponding cache set (S_k) can be easily mapped with Eq. (6). However, the corresponding cache way (A_l) is identified by the following search operation in the cache:

$$A_l = Search(TGS[S_{tgs_i}][A_{tgs_j}].win\_num, TGS[S_{tgs_i}][A_{tgs_j}].tag) \quad (9)$$

The $Search()$ used in Eq. (9) takes two arguments: win_num and tag address (tag) from the respective location of TGS and searches the corresponding block in the cache. Similarly, the respective TGS set (S_{tgs_n}) for the cache set (S_u) and cache way (A_v) is mapped from Eq. (8). On the other hand, the TGS associativity (A_{tgs_m}) is derived by the search operation:

$$A_{tgs_m} = Search(Cache[S_u][A_v].tag, A_{tgs_{st}}, A_{tgs_{st}} + r), \quad A_{tgs_{st}} = (S_u/S_{tgs}) * r \quad (10)$$

Here, the $Search()$ used in Eq. (10) takes three arguments: tag address of the cache block $(Cache[S_u][A_v].tag)$ and the range of the TGS way location as second and third argument $(A_{tgs_{st}}$ to $A_{tgs_{st}} + r)$ where the searching takes place for the respective cache block.

Example: The example of FSDRP architecture is depicted in Fig. 5. In the example, a 16-way $(A = 16)$ associative L2 cache having 8 sets is considered with the values of $m = 2$ and $r = 4$. With these given parameters, the cache is partitioned into four $(A/r = 4)$ equal-sized windows of size four ways each$(r = 4)$. As shown in the example, these four windows are labeled with Win_0, Win_1, Win_2 and Win_3 and the relocatable blocks from the different cache sets of the fellow groups are dispersed in these different windows. The lookup of these relocatable blocks is performed with the help of TGS through Eqs. (6) and (9). As shown in the example, the block B_{12} placed in window W_0 of the cache has an entry in TGS and it is searched with the help of win_num field (value 0) stored within the TGS entry. In order to distinguish these relocatable blocks, the corresponding relocate bit is set to one. For example, the write bit and the relocate bit for the relocatable block B_{31} are set to 0 and 1.

Operation: The operation of the FSDRP is elaborated through Algorithm 2. In this algorithm, the use of parameters I, W_i and b_{ij} is same as the FSSRP (line 1 to 3). In addition of these parameters, the parameter P acts as the total number of logical partitions or windows in the cache (line 4). The relocate bit associated with each block of the cache is represented by variable r_{ij} (line 5).

For the initial I cycles of the process execution, the cache is available as a normal cache. Meanwhile, during the interval (I), the write operation to any block in the set increments the write counter (W_i) of that cache set, and the respective write bit (b_{ij}) of the block is set (line 6 to 8).

Once the application crosses first I cycles, one window of the cache is selected and treated as RP section of the cache and the rest of the windows act as an NP section. Afterwards, periodically for every interval I, a new window is treated as RP by rotation (line 9 to 13). The process continues until the execution is over.

In the meantime, between the intervals, for each request R coming from L1 cache to L2 cache, the tag lookup operation is performed in the L2 cache simultaneously in both NP and RP (through TGS by Eq. (8)). Note that, in the case of an indirect hit, the respective cache set and the cache way is mapped through Eqs. (6) and (9). Depending upon the result of the lookup and the cache request, different operations are performed in the L2 cache:

- **Read Hit:**The read operation is same as the FSSRP, as given in Sect. 4.1 (line 16 and 17).
- **Write Hit (PUTX or write-back) and block B in NP section of the cache:** In case of write request R, if the requested block B belongs to the NP section of the cache then we have two cases:
  - In the first case, for the requested block B if the write bit (b_{ij}) is set and the relocate bit (r_{ij}) is zero. And, at the same time, if the lightly written set (other than the current set) (S_l) is present in the fellow group, the

Algorithm 2. FSDRP Wear Leveling Algorithm

1: I : Predefined interval.
2: W_i : Write counter associated with set i. $0 \le i \le S$
3: b_{ij} : Write bit associated with each cache block in set i and way j. $0 \le i < S$, $0 \le j < A$
4: P : Number of logical partition or windows.
5: r_{ij} : Relocate bit associated with each cache block in set i and way j. $0 \le i < S$, $0 \le j < A$
6: Run application for I cycles treating the whole cache as a normal available cache.
7: During I cycle, the write counter (W_i) is incremented with each write in set i.
8: Similarly, the write bit(b_{ij}) is set with each write in the block.
9: After I cycle, treat one window of the cache as a RP window and rotate window number in a round robin fashion.
10: **repeat**
11:    **for** every interval I **do**
12:       $i = (i+1)\%P$
13:       Window Win_i is selected as a RP section for the current interval I.
14:       Windows other than the W_i is treated as NP section of the cache.
15:       **for** each request R coming from L1 cache to block B in L2 cache **do**
16:          **if** $R == ReadHit$ **then**
17:             The Read operation is performed on the block B irrespective of its location.
18:          **else if** $R == WriteHit$ **then**
19:             **if** Block B is found in NP part of cache **then**
20:                **if** the write bit b_{ij} of the block B is set and the relocate bit r_{ij} is not set **then**
21:                   **if** there is any light written set S_l exist in the group **then**
22:                      The write request for the block B is redirected to the location L in the RP part of S_l. { **Block B move to RP after first write back**}
23:                      The relocate bit (r_{lm}) for the redirected block is set.
24:                   **else**
25:                      The write operation is performed on Block B. Increment the write counter (W_i) and keep the write bit set.
26:                   **end if**
27:                **else**
28:                   The write operation is performed on Block B. Increment the write counter (W_i) and set the write bit in set i and way j.
29:                **end if**
30:             **else**
31:                The write operation is performed on block B. Increment the write counter of the set in which the write operation is performed. { **Block B in RP part**}
32:                **if** r_{ij} is not set **then**
33:                   Set the write bit (b_{ij}) for the block B.
34:                **end if**
35:             **end if**
36:          **else**
37:             Forward the Request R to main memory. Keep the newly arrived block in NP part of cache (location other than Win_i). {**cache miss**}
38:          **end if**
39:       **end for**
40:    **end for**
41: **until** the end of the execution

write request R is redirected to the RP window (Win_i) of the S_l. In this case, if the invalid entries exist in the TGS (within the range $A_{tgs_{st}}$ to $A_{tgs_{st}} + r$) and the RP window, the write request (R) is simply redirected to the invalid location of the RP section by updating the TGS entry. On

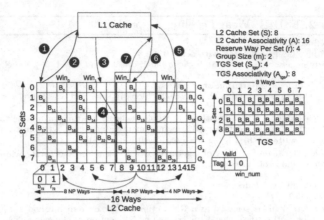

Fig. 5. Working example of FSDRP wear leveling policy

the other hand, if there is no invalid entry present in the RP window of
the cache or if there is no vacant entry present in the TGS, the respective
LRU victim entry is picked from the RP window or from the TGS and
the write-back operation is performed for either or both the entries of
the L2 cache. Note that, the cache location of the LRU TGS entry is
mapped by the Eqs. (6) and (9). Afterwards, the write request R from an
L1 cache is redirected to the newly generated entry in the RP window.
Simultaneously, the newly generated TGS entry is also updated with the
redirected data entry attributes. Once the write request R is redirected,
the subsequent block B is invalidated from the NP section and the relocate
bit (r_{lm}) is set for the redirected block in the RP window section for future
identification (line 21 to 23).

- In the second case, if the write bit (b_{ij}) is not set or if the relocate bit (r_{ij})
  is set or if there is no lightly written set other than the current set exist in
  the group, the write operation is performed in the current location of the
  block B by setting the write bit b_{ij} (line 24 to 28). Note that the setting
  of the relocate bit r_{ij} implies that the current block belongs to the other
  set of the fellow group.

Once the write operation is performed, the respective write counter (W_i) of
the cache set is incremented.

- **Write Hit (PUTX or write-back) and block B in RP section of
  the cache:** In this case, the write request R is performed normally from
  the current location of the block B. If the relocate bit (r_{ij}) of the block B
  is not set then the corresponding write bit (b_{ij}) is set. This implies that the
  block B is not yet redirected and currently belongs to the home set (line 30
  to 33).
- **Cache Miss:** In case of cache miss, the request R from L1 cache is forwarded to the next level of memory (main memory in our case). In this case,
  the incoming block from the main memory is placed into the window other
  than the RP window (Win_i). In particular, the block is placed in one of

Table 2. System parameters

Components	Parameters
Processor	2 Ghz, Quad Core, X86
L1 Cache	Private, 32 KB SRAM Split I/D caches, 4-way set associative cache, 64B block, 1-cycle latency, LRU, write-back policy
L2 Cache	Shared, 64B block, LRU, write-back policy
Protocol	MESI CMP Directory

that window which is currently treated as NP section of cache. The write bit (b_{ij}) and the relocate bit (r_{ij}) of the cache location in which the block is placed are reset (line 36 to 38).

Example: The working example of FSDRP is explained through Fig. 5. In this example, the window Win_2 is treated as an RP section and the rest of the windows (Win_0, Win_1, Win_3) act as an NP section of the cache. As same as FSSRP, three cases are considered to demonstrate the method with respect to set-0. In the first case, a read request (arrow 1) is served normally irrespective of the location (NP or RP) (arrow 2). In the second case, a write request (arrow 3) to the block (way-6) that belong to the NP section is redirected (arrow 4) to the RP section window (Win_2) of the lightly written set (set-4 in our case) of the fellow group. At the same time, the respective TGS entry of set-0 is updated with the respective data attributes. Once the write operation is performed, the write-back acknowledgment is sent back to L1 cache (arrow 5). In the last case, the write request (arrow 6) to the block B_3 in the RP section of the cache is served normally by the L2 cache with the write-back acknowledgment (arrow 7).

5   Experimental Setup

We implemented our proposed schemes on a full system simulator GEM-5 [1]. Table 2 shows the system parameters used in the simulations. In the simulator, the memory module is simulated with the help of Ruby memory module along with the MESI CMP based cache controller. We perform our experiments on a quad-core system with the different configuration of L2 or LLC. Table 3 reports the timing and energy parameters for these configurations. The timing and the energy parameters are obtained by using NVSIM [2] at 32 nm technology node.

We compared our proposed techniques with baseline STT-RAM cache that uses LRU as a replacement policy with no wear leveling strategy associated and, the existing technique: Swap Shift. Swap Shift invalidates the data of two sets after the certain number of writes called swap threshold $(SwapTh)$. In our experiment, the value of $SwapTh$ is set to 511. The rationale behind the large value of the $SwapTh$ is to restrict the frequent invalidation process of data sets

Table 3. Timing and energy parameters for STT-RAM L2 cache

	Leakage power (mW)	Hit energy (nJ)	Miss energy (nJ)	Write energy (nJ)	Hit latency (ns)	Miss latency (ns)	Write latency (ns)
16MB, 16way	15.674	0.367	0.096	4.322	78.453	11.854	271.035
8MB, 32way	8.116	0.366	0.185	6.454	74.792	8.259	270.981
8MB, 16way	8.030	0.273	0.093	4.387	78.497	11.964	270.981
8MB, 8way	7.983	0.227	0.047	3.221	74.454	7.921	270.981
4MB, 16way	7.960	0.217	0.093	4.228	23.876	5.575	126.585

in the cache. The frequent invalidation process in the Swap shift increases the accesses in the main memory that results in the extra performance and energy overhead.

In the proposed schemes, the searching of the block in the home set and the other sets of the fellow group (through TGS) will take place in parallel, so it does not affect the system performance. However, the write redirection of the blocks from the home set to the other set takes 3 extra cycles and an additional swap buffer to the transfer the tag. These 3 cycles are divided as follows: 1 cycle for tag transfer into the swap buffer, 1 cycle for writing the tag in swap buffer and, 1 cycle for transferring the tag to TGS and RP part of the cache. In addition to these cycles, an extra cycle is required in FSDRP for the searching of the block into the respective window of the other sets of the fellow group. We have considered all these overheads in our simulations. We also take into account the energy consumption due to accesses in the TGS. The energy overhead of TGS (made up of SRAM) is modeled by using NVSIM. There is some logic overhead associated with the Algorithms 1 and 2 which will consume extra area overhead.

We verified our proposed techniques with the help of PARSEC benchmarks suite [3]. Seven applications (Swaptions (Swap), Dedup, Bodytrack (Body), Fluidinamite (Fluid), Freqmine (Freq), Streamcluster (Stream), X264) with large input set are used in the simulation. These benchmarks are the multi-threaded real time applications such as animation, data mining, multimedia etc. We run each application for five billion instructions in the parallel region (i.e. Region Of Interest (ROI)).

6   Results and Analysis

We evaluate our proposed approaches on a quad-core system. Out of the different configurations of L2 cache, we conducted our experiment on 8MB, 16-way associative L2 cache. In the proposed schemes, we set the value for m, r and I to 4, 4 and 5 million cycles. Later in the section, we analyze the effects by changing these values. We present our results on the following metrics: reduction in coefficient of Inter-set write variation ($InterV$) calculated with the help of Eq. (1), percentage reduction in coefficient of Intra-set write variation over the previous proposed scheme: FSSRP and the baseline STT-RAM, lifetime improvement percentage calculated with the help of Eq. (4), speedup, energy overhead and the number of invalidation/flushes.

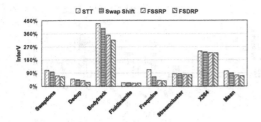

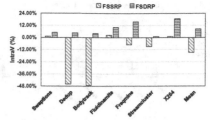

Fig. 6. Inter-set write variation of proposed schemes: FSSRP and FSDRP and, Swap Shift against baseline STT-RAM. (Lesser is better)

Fig. 7. Percentage reduction in intra-set write variation by FSSRP and FSDRP over baseline STT-RAM. (More is better)

6.1 Inter-set Write Variation

Figure 6 shows the inter-set write variation. Our proposed schemes reduce the inter-set write variation from 103.9% (STT), 91.4% (Swap Shift), 76.3% (FSSRP) to 69.9% (FSDRP). The reduction in the coefficient of inter-set write variation is due to uniform write distribution across the cache sets by redirecting the writes from the heavily written sets to the lightly written sets of the fellow groups. However, further improvement in the inter-set write variation for FSDRP over FSSRP is due to different RP window over the period of execution that restricts the write redirection of the blocks from their home sets. Note that, FSSRP redirects every block on the second write without considering its write intensity. While, this is not the case with FSDRP as it partially restricts the redirection of the block that belongs to the current RP window.

6.2 Reduction in Intra-set Write Variation

Figure 7 shows the percentage reduction in intra-set write variation by FSDRP. Compared to baseline and FSSRP, FSDRP reduces the intra-set write variation by 8.55% and 17.7%, respectively. The reduction in the intra-set write variation is mainly due to the dispersion of the relocatable blocks over the cache set by dynamic RP windows. This reduces the possibility of write concentration in the specific section/region of the cache.

6.3 Lifetime Improvement

Figure 8 presents the lifetime improvement percentage by the proposed schemes. Compared to STT-RAM, the improvement in the lifetime by FSSRP is 14.77% and by FSDRP is 20.77%. However, the respective values for the lifetime improvement over Swap Shift is 6.58% by FSSRP and 12.11% by FSDRP. These improvements by the proposed schemes are mainly due to the reduction

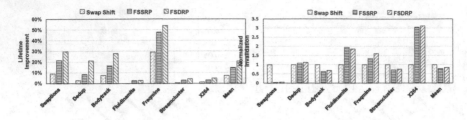

Fig. 8. Lifetime improvement by FSSRP, FSDRP and, Swap Shift with respect to baseline STT-RAM. (More is better)

Fig. 9. Normalized invalidations by the proposed techniques: FSSRP and FSDRP over Swap Shift. (Lesser is better)

in the coefficient of inter-set write variation. The improvement in the lifetime by FSDRP with respect to FSSRP is 3.03%. The reason for the further lifetime improvement by FSDRP is due to reduction in intra-set write variation in lieu of the dynamic RP window.

6.4 Invalidation/flushes

The invalidation/flushes by the proposed schemes with respect to Swap Shift is depicted in Fig. 9. Flushes take place due to the write redirection from heavily written sets to lightly written sets of the fellow group. Compared to swap shift, the proposed schemes reduce the invalidation by 21.59% (FSSRP) and 15.58% (FSDRP). However, as can be seen, FSDRP increases the invalidation against the FSSRP by 7.66%. This is because, in FSDRP, a block gets evicted: (i) from current RP to accommodate the redirected block and (ii) in order to make an entry in the TGS one would need to evict the relocatable block from the current NP or RP section. Note that in some of the cases (dedup, fluid, freqmine and x264) the number of invalidation by our techniques is large than the swap shift. This is because we set a larger value of threshold ($SwapTh$) in swap shift, in order to maintain the performance and energy consumption.

6.5 Energy Overhead

The energy overheads of the proposed schemes are shown in Fig. 10. Note that the negative values in the figure implies the energy savings. The energy overhead percentage over the baseline and the Swap Shift by the proposed schemes are 0.78% and 0.99% by FSSRP and, 0.84% and 1.05% by FSDRP. This marginal increment in the energy is basically due to the transfer of tag, invalidation/flushes, accesses in TGS and, the extra window search operation for the relocatable block in the cache by FSDRP.

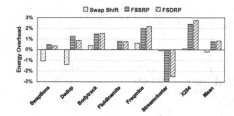
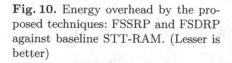

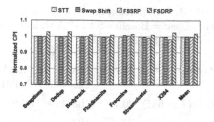

Fig. 10. Energy overhead by the proposed techniques: FSSRP and FSDRP against baseline STT-RAM. (Lesser is better)

Fig. 11. Normalized performance by the proposed techniques: FSSRP and FSDRP and Swap Shift with respect to baseline STT-RAM.

6.6 Performance

The proposed scheme: FSSRP maintains the same performance as in the baseline STT-RAM and Swap Shift as shown in Fig. 11. Performance is not affected in FSSRP because searching for the block in RP section (with the help of TGS) takes place in parallel with the lookup operation in the NP section, and the writing in TGS will be in parallel with the writing in the RP. However, a small degradation of 1% is observed in the CPI for FSDRP due to time taken by extra search operations in the dynamic RP windows.

6.7 Storage Overhead

In our proposed schemes, we use 12-bit write counter (W_i) to measure the write counts in the set. In addition, we add a relocate bit (r_{ij}) and a write bit (b_{ij}) with each block in the cache. Further, each entry of TGS is made up of 42-bit tag address (t), one valid bit (v) and $\log_2 A/r$ bits for window number (win_num) (used in case of FSDRP). We also add a 42-bit swap buffer to transfer the tag to the new location. Thus, the overhead of FSDRP and FSSRP are computed by using the following couple of equations:

$$FSDRP\_Overhead = \frac{S*W_i+S*A*(b_{ij}+r_{ij})+S*r*(t+v+win\_num)+42}{S*A*(B+t)} * 100 \quad (11)$$

$$FSSRP\_Overhead = \frac{S*W_i+S*(A-r)*b_{ij}+S*r*(t+v)+42}{S*A*(B+t)} * 100 \quad (12)$$

In the above Eqs. (11) and (12), B represents the block size. As an example, in our selected configuration: 8MB 16-way associative L2 cache with the following set of attributes: $m = 4$, $r = 4$ and $I = 5$ million cycles, the percentages of storage overhead in FSSRP and FSDRP are merely 2.21% and 2.52%.

Table 4. Comparison analysis for different interval values (I) (LI = Lifetime Improvement, Base = Baseline STT-RAM, EDP = Energy Delay Product) Ref.= 8MB, 16-way, $m = 4$, $r = 4$ and $I = 5M$

Param.	LI (%)	InterV Base	InterV FSDRP	IntraV Red. (%)	Norm. EDP	Invalidation (k)
Ref. ($I = 5M$)	20.7%	103.9	69.9	8.5%	1.02	173k
$I = 2M$	23.2%	103.9	68.2	9%	1.03	188k
$I = 10M$	19.3%	103.9	73.3	3.5%	1.01	155k

Table 5. Comparison analysis for different fellow group size (m)

Param.	Policy	LI (%)	InterV Base	InterV FS	IntraV Red. (%)	Norm. EDP	Invalidation (k)
Ref. ($m = 4$)	FSSRP	14.7%	103.9	76.3	−14.8%	1.01	161k
	FSDRP	20.7%	103.9	69.9	8.5%	1.02	173k
$m = 8$	FSSRP	15.5%	103.9	71.3	−17.6%	1.02	172k
	FSDRP	22.1%	103.9	68.9	2.2%	1.02	186k
$m = 2$	FSSRP	12.8%	103.9	78.5	−13.6%	1.00	119k
	FSDRP	19.8%	103.9	73.5	9.3%	1.01	157k

6.8 Parameter Comparison Analysis

In addition to the results presented in the previous subsections, we also performed experiments with different configurations of the cache and the parameters (m, r and I) for the algorithms. Here, we show the results for the reduction in inter-set write variation, the percentage reduction in the intra-set write variation over the baseline, lifetime improvement, EDP overhead and number of invalidations. This analysis is very useful to pick the optimal values (of the parameters) for the proposed approaches in different cache configurations.

Change in Interval (I): Table 4 reports the values over distinct intervals against the reference interval with $I = 5$ Million cycles in the case of FSDRP. Change in the interval-span affects the RP window rotation process. Smaller intervals increase the number of rotations of the RP window over the cache and number of rotations is reduced for the case of larger intervals. Small interval value reduces the inter-set write variation more compared to the large interval. This is because, the large interval value increases the residency of the block that belongs to the home set in the RP window. Such blocks residing in the RP window do not get redirected and thus increase the write count of the set and become eventually dead over the interval. In particular, the blocks belonging to the home set and the RP window incurs several writes before the RP window gets rotated to another location. Simultaneously, with large interval, the write concentration in the RP window region of the cache increases that in turn impacts (and increases) the intra-set write variation. However, in case of small interval values, due to increased invalidations and write redirections, the system performance is affected with more energy consumption which is further resulting into the increment in EDP.

Table 6. Comparison analysis for different window size or RP size (r)

Param.	Policy	LI (%)	InterV Base	InterV FS	IntraV Red. (%)	Norm. EDP	Invalidation (k)
Ref. ($r = 4$)	FSSRP	14.7%	103.9	76.3	−14.8%	1.01	161k
	FSDRP	20.7%	103.9	69.9	8.5%	1.02	173k
$r = 6$	FSSRP	12.7%	103.9	78.2	−18%	1.00	139k
$r = 8$	FSDRP	16.7%	103.9	73.8	2.1%	1.01	169k
$r = 2$	FSSRP	14.3%	103.9	75.8	−12.4%	1.02	201k
	FSDRP	19.3%	103.9	70.3	8.4%	1.03	187k

Table 7. Comparison analysis for different cache capacity (C)

Param.	Policy	LI (%)	InterV Base	InterV FS	IntraV Red. (%)	Norm. EDP	Invalidation (k)
Ref. ($C = 8$MB)	FSSRP	14.7%	103.9	76.3	−14.8%	1.01	161k
	FSDRP	20.7%	103.9	69.9	8.5%	1.02	173k
$C = 4$MB	FSSRP	4.2%	73.6	66	−18.4%	1.01	138k
	FSDRP	13.7%	73.6	53.6	4%	1.02	145k
$C = 16$MB	FSSRP	11.2%	169.5	141.2	−2.20%	1.01	153k
	FSDRP	13%	169.5	133.2	2%	1.03	198k

Change in Group Size (m): Table 5 presents the results for the different group size (m) in the proposed schemes. Note that, the negative values in the table implies the increment in the intra-set write variation. Change in group size affects the availability of the lightly written sets in the fellow group. In particular, the large group size increases the chance of finding the lightly written set(s) in the group compared to small group size. With the large availability of lightly written set, the chances of write redirection increases and this improves the lifetime and further reduce the inter-set write variation. However, due to increased invalidation and the write redirections, the system performance is marginally affected along with the energy consumption that in turn increases the EDP. Also, the increased number of redirections populates more data in the RP window over the interval, which further impacts the reduction in intra-set write variation as can be seen by the reduced reduction percentage in the Table 5 for both FSSRP and FSDRP.

Change in Window or RP size (r): Table 6 lists the result metrics for changing the window size (i.e. RP size (r)). Change in the window size affects the residency of the relocatable block in the different sets of the fellow group. An increment in window size increases the residency of the relocatable blocks. This, in turn, increases the write count of the lightly written set and it becomes heavily written set over the period of the time. This reduces the possibility of finding the lightly written set in the group and leads to more inter and intra-set write variation compared to small RP/window size. However, in these cases, the inter-set write variation is marginally affected compared to the reference case.

Table 8. Comparison analysis for different cache associativity (A)

Param.	Policy	LI (%)	InterV Base	InterV FS	IntraV Red. (%)	Norm. EDP	Invalidation (k)
Ref. (A = 16way)	FSSRP	14.7%	103.9	76.3	−14.8%	1.01	161k
	FSDRP	20.7%	103.9	69.9	8.5%	1.02	173k
A = 8way	FSSRP	8.8%	149.8	130.3	−11.4%	1.00	132k
	FSDRP	16.5%	149.8	110.8	12.9%	1.01	151k
A = 32way	FSSRP	5.4%	74.8	66.2	−4.9%	1.02	202k
	FSDRP	10.6%	74.8	58.3	1.6%	1.03	243k

Table 9. Recommended values of m, r and I

Cache configuration	FSSRP		FSDRP		
	m	r	m	r	I
Small Size, Small Assoc.	↑	↓	↑	↓	= /↑
Small Size, Large Assoc.	↓	↑	↓	↑	↓
Large Size, Small Assoc.	↑	↓	↑	↓	= /↑
Large Size, Large Assoc.	↑	↑	↑	↑	↓

Change in Capacity (C): Table 7 lists the change in metrics values for different cache capacities. The capacity of the cache impacts the number of sets in the cache. Larger caches suffer from large inter-set variation as compared to the smaller sized cache. This is because, in case of larger caches with fixed associativity, the number of cache sets are very large. With the large number of sets, there is a good possibility for the non-uniform write distribution across the cache set which in turn generates the inter-set write variation. However, in both the cases (for smaller and larger caches) our proposed schemes show considerable improvement in the coefficient of inter-set write variation and thus improves the lifetime.

Change in Associativity (A): Table 8 shows the behavior of the proposed schemes with different associativity of the cache. Caches with lower associativity suffers from large inter-set write variation as compared to cache with larger associativity. This is because the cache with the same size and lower associativity have a large number of sets compared to the cache with higher associativity. As same as previous case, the large number of cache sets introduces the uneven write distribution across the set. Although, in both the cases: cache with lower associativity and higher associativity, our proposed schemes efficiently reduce the inter-set write variation and improves the lifetime, accordingly.

Recommended Values: Based on the above analyses, we recommend the values to be used for the m, r (in case of FSSRP) and I (in case of FSDRP) with the different configurations of caches. The Table 9 lists these recommended values for the proposed schemes: FSSRP and FSDRP. Note that these recommended values are with respect to the reference values i.e. $m = 4$, $r = 4$ and $I = 5$ million cycles. The rationale behind the recommended values are presented below:

- **Interval** (I): To control the block residency, higher associativity needs small interval value. Whereas, the cache with lower associativity is not directly affected by I. Here, the value of I may be increased or kept same according to the requirement.
- **Reserve ways** (r): In case of larger associativity, to handle the large write redirections from the NP the value of r need to be increased. The value of r has to be decreased for lower associativity.
- **Fellow Group Size** (m): Large sized cache suffers from large variation. To control this, the value of m needs to be increased. However, in the case of smaller cache, the value of m is decided according to the associativity and the window size.

7 Conclusion

Write variation inside the cache are affected by the applied replacement policy and the access patterns of the next generation applications running on many cores. In NVM based cache, this large write variation not only curtails the life but also diminishes the capacity of the cache over the period of time. This chapter presented efficient techniques to reduce the write variation across the cache sets called the inter-set write variation. Our first technique: FSSRP partitions the cache into groups of sets called fellow groups. Further, each group is logically divided into two parts: Normal and Reserve. In order to distribute the writes uniformly across the set, the normal part of the set can use the reserve part of the other sets in a fellow group. However, the major concern with the architecture of FSSRP is the increment in write concentration in the reserve part of the cache which in turn increases the intra-set write variation thus limiting the lifetime improvement. To overcome this shortcoming, our second technique: FSDRP, based on FSSRP, partitions the cache vertically into multiple equal-sized windows. During the execution, a different window is selected exclusively as a reserve part for a certain predefined interval. This helps to disperses the redirected writes over the cache. We examine the efficacy of the proposed approaches against the baseline STT-RAM and an existing technique: Swap Shift. Experimental evaluation with a full system simulator shows significant reduction in the coefficient of inter-set write variation along with the lifetime improvement of 14.77% (FSSRP) and, 20.77% (FSDRP) respectively. Simultaneously, we also observe some reduction in intra-set write variation by FSDRP due to dispersion of redirected writes. Thus, minimizing write variation inside the limited endurance non-volatile caches can make the system even more reliable and efficient.

References

1. Binkert, N., et al.: The gem5 simulator. SIGARCH Comput. Archit. News **39**(2), 1–7 (2011)
2. Dong, X., Xu, C., Xie, Y., Jouppi, N.P.: NVSim: a circuit-level performance, energy, and area model for emerging nonvolatile memory. IEEE Trans. Comput.-Aided Des. Integr. Circ. Syst. **31**, 994–1007 (2012)
3. Bienia, C., Kumar, S., Singh, J.P., Li, K.: The PARSEC benchmark suite: characterization and architectural implications. In: International Conference on Parallel Architectures and Compilation Techniques (PACT), pp. 72–81 (2008)
4. Apalkov, D., et al.: Spin-transfer torque magnetic random access memory. J. Emerg. Technol. Comput. Syst. **9**(2), 13:1–13:35 (2013). Article 13
5. Qureshi, M.K., Gurumurthi, S., Rajendran, B.: Phase Change Memory: From Devices to Systems, 1st edn. Morgan & Claypool Publishers, San Rafael (2011)
6. Kim, Y.B., et al.: Bi-layered RRAM with unlimited endurance and extremely uniform switching. In: Symposium on VLSI Technology - Digest of Technical Papers, pp. 52–53 (2011)
7. Mittal, S., Vetter, J.S., Li, D.: A survey of architectural approaches for managing embedded DRAM and non-volatile on-chip caches. IEEE Trans. Parallel Distrib. Syst. **26**(6), 1524–1537 (2015)
8. Wang, J., Dong, X., Xie, Y., Jouppi, N.P.: i2WAP: improving non-volatile cache lifetime by reducing inter- and intra-set write variations. In: IEEE 19th International Symposium on High Performance Computer Architecture (HPCA), pp. 234–245 (2013)
9. Jokar, M.R., Arjomand, M., Sarbazi-Azad, H.: Sequoia: a high-endurance NVM-based cache architecture. IEEE Trans. Very Large Scale Integr. (VLSI) Syst. **24**(3), 954–967 (2016)
10. Qureshi, M.K., Thompson, D., Patt, Y.N.: The V-Way cache: demand-based associativity via global replacement. In: 32nd International Symposium on Computer Architecture (ISCA 2005), pp. 544–555 (2005)
11. Sanchez, D., Kozyrakis, C.: The ZCache: decoupling ways and associativity. In: 43rd Annual IEEE/ACM International Symposium on Microarchitecture, pp. 187–198 (2010)
12. Das, S., Kapoor, H.K.: Dynamic associativity management in tiled CMPs by runtime adaptation of fellow sets. IEEE Trans. Parallel Distrib. Syst. **28**(8), 2229–2243 (2017)
13. Chen, Y., et al.: On-chip caches built on multilevel spin-transfer torque RAM cells and its optimizations. J. Emerg. Technol. Comput. Syst. **9**(2), 16:1–16:22 (2013). Article 16
14. Wang, S., Duan, G., Li, Y., Dong, Q.: Word- and partition-level write variation reduction for improving non-volatile cache lifetime. ACM Trans. Des. Autom. Electron. Syst. **23**(1), 4:1–4:18 (2017). Article 4
15. Soltani, M., Ebrahimi, M., Navabi, Z.: Prolonging lifetime of non-volatile last level caches with cluster mapping. In: International Great Lakes Symposium on VLSI (GLSVLSI), pp. 329–334 (2016)
16. Mittal, S., Vetter, J.S.: Addressing inter-set write-variation for improving lifetime of non-volatile caches. In: 5th Annual Non-volatile Memories Workshop University of California (2014)
17. Kim, C.H., Kim, J.J., Mukhopadhyay, S., Roy, K.: A forward body-biased-low-leakage SRAM cache: device and architecture considerations. In: Proceedings of the International Symposium on Low Power Electronics and Design, pp. 6–9 (2003)

18. Agarwal, S., Kapoor, H.K.: Targeting inter set write variation to improve the lifetime of non-volatile cache using fellow sets. In: IFIP/IEEE International Conference on Very Large Scale Integration (VLSI-SoC), pp. 1–6 (2017)
19. Wu, X., Li, J., Zhang, L., Speight, E., Xie, Y.: Power and performance of read-write aware Hybrid Caches with non-volatile memories. In: Design, Automation & Test in Europe Conference & Exhibition, pp. 737–742 (2009)
20. Agarwal, S., Kapoor, H.K.: Restricting writes for energy-efficient hybrid cache in multi-core architectures. In: IFIP/IEEE International Conference on Very Large Scale Integration (VLSI-SoC), pp. 1–6 (2016)
21. Park, S.P., Gupta, S., Mojumder, N., Raghunathan, A., Roy, K.: Future cache design using STT MRAMs for improved energy efficiency: devices, circuits and architecture. In: DAC Design Automation Conference, pp. 492–497 (2012)
22. Mishra, A.K., Dong, X., Sun, G., Xie, Y., Vijaykrishnan, N., Das, C.R.: Architecting on-chip interconnects for stacked 3D STT-RAM caches in CMPs. In: International Symposium on Computer Architecture (ISCA), pp. 69–80 (2011)
23. Huai, Y.: Spin-transfer torque MRAM (STT-MRAM): challenges and prospects. AAPPS Bull. 18(6), 33–40 (2008)

A Wearable Neuro-Degenerative Diseases Classification System Using Human Gait Dynamics

Wala Saadeh$^{(\boxtimes)}$ and Muhammad Awais Bin Altaf

Electrical Engineering Department, Lahore University of Management Sciences,
Lahore, Pakistan
{wala.saadeh, awais.altaf}@lums.edu.pk

Abstract. The increasing prevalence of neurodegenerative diseases (NDDs) impose substantial medical and public health burdens on populations throughout the world. NDDs are chronic diseases that affect the human central nervous system causing loss of neurons within the brain and/or spinal cord. This causes deterioration in movement and mental functioning of the patients. The current medications for this group of disorders are limited and aim to treat the symptoms only. A better understanding of the mechanisms underlying neurodegeneration should lead to more effective, disease-modifying treatments in the future. Continuous assessment of NDD patients is a key element of future care and treatment. This contribution proposes a wearable NDD detection system based on patient's gait dynamics using an unobtrusive force resistive sensor embedded in patient's shoe. The NDD classification is based on 3 fundamental gait features: stride time, stride time's fluctuation and the autocorrelation decay factor. It is designed to discriminate between healthy subjects and NDD patients and moreover identify the NDD type: (Huntington's disease (HD), Parkinson Disease (PD), and Amyotrophic Lateral Sclerosis (ALS)). The proposed NDD classification algorithm is implemented on FPGA and verified experimentally using Gait Dynamics dataset from Physionet. It offers a classification accuracy of 93.8%, 89.1%, 94% and 93.3%, for ALS, HD, PD, and healthy person, respectively, from a total set of 64 subjects.

Keywords: Amyotrophic Lateral Sclerosis (ALS) · Huntington's disease · Parkinson Disease · Neurodegenerative disorders · Classifier · Wearable sensor

1 Introduction

Patients with Neurodegenerative diseases (NDDs) suffer from medical conditions that directly affect the neurons within the brain [1]. NDDs cause changes in neuromuscular control causing degradation in muscle movements control, muscle tone, involuntary movements and smoothness of movement. One of the key diagnostic approaches for defining the NDD is the study of patient's gait [2–4]. Parkinson's disease (PD), Huntington's disease (HD) and Amyotrophic Lateral Sclerosis (ALS) are the main types of NDDs deteriorating the patient's gait [1].

© IFIP International Federation for Information Processing 2019
Published by Springer Nature Switzerland AG 2019
M. Maniatakos et al. (Eds.): VLSI-SoC 2017, IFIP AICT 500, pp. 72–91, 2019.
https://doi.org/10.1007/978-3-030-15663-3_4

1.1 Parkinson's Disease

PD is a chronic and progressive movement disorder causing trembling in the hands, arms, legs, jaw, and face, stiffness the limbs and trunk, slowed movement, and impaired balance and coordination [5]. After Alzheimer, PD is the second most common neurodegenerative disease affecting approximately 1 million Americans (estimates range between 4 and 6.5 million people worldwide) and about 1% of older adults. It usually affects people over the age of 50 [5]. In the US alone, 60,000 new cases are diagnosed with PD each year. There is currently no accurate test for the diagnosis of PD and it is highly uncertain in the early stages of the disease. These symptoms usually begin gradually and worsen with time. The gait of PD patients is characterized by small shuffling steps and a general slowness of movement [3]. The stride length and walking speed during free ambulation are also reduced.

1.2 Huntington's Disease

HD is a genetic NDD that affects muscle coordination and leads to cognitive decline and physical, mental and emotional changes [6]. It is estimated that around 30,000 people in the US only are affected by HD, and more than 150,000 people have $\sim 50\%$ potential risk of developing HD. Patients with HD are not able to think, talk and move properly [6, 7]. This disease is responsible for destroying the cells in the basal ganglia, the part of the brain that controls these capacities. HD usually develops at mid-age and can cause a very wide range of symptoms. The general symptoms in early stages can include a poor memory; difficulty in making decisions; mood changes such as depression, anger or irritability; a growing lack of coordination, twitching or other uncontrolled movements; difficulty in walking, speaking or swallowing [8, 9].

1.3 Amyotrophic Lateral Sclerosis (ALS)

ALS is known as motor neuron disease characterized by progressive weakness, difficulty in speaking, swallowing, breathing, muscle twitching (involuntary muscle contraction and relaxation), and muscle stiffness. The patients suffering from ALS have difficulty in maintaining regular normal locomotion [10]. The earliest signs of ALS include muscles weakness of arms and legs that eventually, prevent the patients from walking and talking and be bedridden. The spreading rate of ALS disease is 1 to 2 per 100,000 each year, most cases of which are sporadic while 5%–10% are inherited. The treatment of ALS is very limited. It becomes necessary to understand the pathological mechanism of this disease.

1.4 The Fall Risk

An important risk factor for NDDs at old age is the increasing fall chances. PD-old patients suffer falls more frequently compared to healthy old people which increase the chances of injuries and may lead to death [9, 11, 12]. Currently, the most common practice to analyze and evaluate the progress of the treatment in NDD patients is mainly based on interviewing the patients. However, depending only on the information provided by patients can produce misleading data. A more practical and successful approach is to assess the physical functional performance of patients', which helps the physicians to create a more effective treatment plan and more technical assessment of the results of the treatment [1]. Therefore, it is desirable to have a non-invasive wearable continuous gait monitoring system that provides quantitative analysis to detect and classify any movement disorders through monitoring the gait dynamics of the NDD patient. For such system, it is more applicable to utilize wearable sensors with a detection algorithm since it can be used anywhere and not limited to certain location and it does not cause discomfort for the patient.

1.5 Goal of This Work

The primary goal of this work is to study and distinguish the gait dynamics of the NDD patients and compare it with healthy individuals. Specifically, we compare how the three different types of NDDs (PD, HD, and ALS) degrade the patient's ability to control the movement of two feet. This contribution proposes a wearable gait dynamics detection system that will be utilized with foot sensors implanted on the shoe of the patient to analyze the gait dynamics and identify the corresponding NDD disease.

The contribution is structured as follows. First, we give an overview of related work that covers approaches for classifying the gait dynamics in each NDD in Sect. 2. Following this, we explain the proposed Wearable NDD Detection System in Sect. 3. In Sect. 4, we describe the NDD classification algorithm and define a number of comparison criteria in order to show the strengths of our approach. Finally, the results of the discussion are presented in Sect. 5 in which we point out the achieved benefits.

2 Previous Work

The analysis of the gait dynamics of NDD patients has been widely applied for studying movement patterns in NDD patients. Multiple recent studies record the gait dynamics in different NDD patients and extract various features to distinguish each NDD [12–20]. Reference [1] utilized a deterministic learning method that divides the classification process into two phases: a training phase followed by a classification phase using neural networks to categorize the gait dynamics. The gait data of the patients suffering from NDDs were recorded using foot switches with Support Vector Machine (SVM) classifier. The classification results that ALS can be more easily distinguished from PD with an accuracy of 85.47%, HD with an accuracy of 86.52% and the healthy subjects with an accuracy of 93.96% [15]. The swing time series from a patient with PD and a control subject under usual walking conditions were studied in [12] and classified based on Coefficient of variability (CV). Detrended Fluctuation Analysis (DFA) was also used to analyze the fluctuation of the gait cycle based on 200 m walk of 17 PD patients and 12 healthy young people tests as reported in [16]. The least-squares support vector machine (LS-SVM) was used to distinguish the stride patterns between the ALS patients and healthy controls with an accuracy of 82.8% using data recordings from Physionet.org [17]. An Associated Discrete Index (ADI) was defined in [18] in order to measure the discrete degree at the same frequency. 93 patients with PD and 72 healthy controls were selected. Foot pressure was analyzed including vertical ground reaction force. Power spectra were obtained to compare gait signals of PD and control subjects. Compared with PD patient, the frequency features of gait in control subject are more random, since the spectral lines are loose as well as different with others. On the other hand, those lines in PD patient are comparatively close to each other. This feature can be indicated by ADI, which shows that PD patients always possess larger ADI than that of control subjects [18]. Reference [19] presented an algorithm to analyze a gait pattern in PD patients using deep brain stimulation (DBS). Features were extracted to classify the PD subjects from healthy control subjects with deep brain stimulation (DBS). A mobile sensor based gait analysis system to measure gait patterns in PD and to distinguish mild and severe impairment of gait was proposed in [20–24]. Gait test was performed using sports shoes equipped with inertial sensors. The signals were recorded for both left and right foot, and the features were extracted and classified using different classification algorithm. The sensitivity and specificity were obtained 88% and 86% respectively.

3 Proposed Wearable NDD Detection System

The proposed wearable NDD detection system is composed of a sensing part simulated using CMOS 180 nm technology and a detection algorithm implemented on Field Programmable Gate Array (FPGA) as shown in Fig. 1 [25]. The sensing part is based on Flexi-force resistor (FSR) that measure the force between two surfaces. FSR is robust against most environmental variations [26]. The FSR single element force sensor acts as a force sensing resistor in an electrical circuit. The resistance can be read by connecting a multimeter to the outer two pins, then applying a force to the sensing area. The FSR force sensor is an ultra-thin, flexible printed circuit where the force sensor is constructed of two layers of substrate (polyester/polyamide) film, which does not hinder the normal routine of the person or cause any discomfort. On each layer, a conductive material (silver) is applied, followed by a layer of pressure-sensitive ink. The active sensing area is defined by the silver circle on top of the pressure-sensitive ink. It is renowned for its versatility, ease of integration, and cost-effectiveness. It can be attached to many surfaces and can be combined with plastic or metal films for increased stiffness or for added protection from abrasion. The sensing area is 9.53 mm (0.375 in.) diameter located at the end of the sensor and placed in the shoe sole. It can measure a force ranging up to (1000 lb.) using the readout circuit shown in Fig. 2. In order to measure forces above 100 lb (up to 1000 lb), a lower drive voltage (−0.5 V, −0.25 V, etc.) should be applied with a feedback resistor (1 kΩ min). The FSR data is acquired and processed using Analog Front End (AFE) and then forwarded to NDD classifier to classify the subject's condition as ALS, HD, PD patient or healthy person. The NDD classifier is implemented on FPGA. The processed information will be then transferred to the doctor's/care-giver mobile through Bluetooth/Cloud network associated with the proposed system.

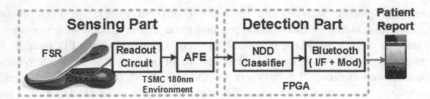

Fig. 1. System level diagram of the proposed wearable system for the NDD detection.

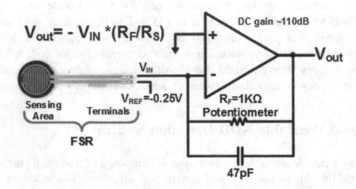

Fig. 2. FSR Readout circuit to measure more than 100 lb. force.

Figure 3 shows the power comparison of FSR based NDD detection system for two different approaches. Transmitting the FSR raw data for off-sensor processing via a low power Bluetooth interface consumes 1.09 mW [27]. However, if the NDD detection is performed on-sensor, the power consumption is reduced by 72% (0.31 mW), which proofs the advantage of on-sensor processing for the wearable systems [27–29].

The block diagram of the proposed on-sensor wearable NDD classifier and AFE is shown in Fig. 4. The proposed processing system is comprised of Instrumentation Amplifier (AMP) to ensure operating of FSR in the desired weight range, followed by a buffer (BUF), an Analog-to-Digital Converter (ADC), a classifier (detection of disorder), and Bluetooth module/interface for communication with the external world. Since the target is a wearable environment, a 12 bits Successive Approximation (SAR) ADC is utilized as an optimum choice with a sampling rate of 300 Samples/s. The digitized data is then collected and filtered with a median filter to eliminate the noise; followed by an NDD classifier. Based on the captured gait features, the NDD classifier categorize the person into (1) ALS, (2) PD, (3) HD or (4) Normal Person (NP). In addition, the proposed classifier also identifies the severity of the disease.

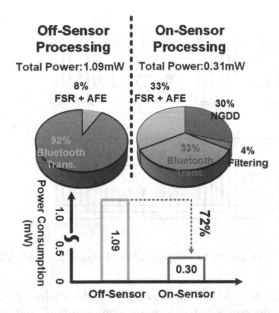

Fig. 3. Power breakdown for two possible on-sensor processing scenarios.

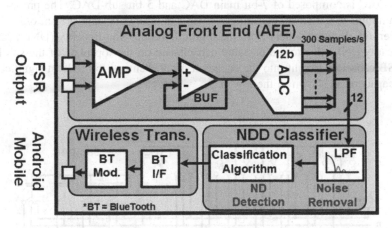

Fig. 4. Block diagram of NDD AFE and the detection processor.

A successive approximation register (SAR) ADC architecture is the natural choice for the wearable/portable biomedical systems [30]. SAR ADC is suited for low speed, moderate resolution, and ultra-low power applications. The designed ADC has a fixed resolution of 12 bits and has a sampling rate of 2.4 kHz. To enhance the common-mode rejection ratio (CMRR) and to eliminate the second order harmonics, a full differential architecture is adopted with the minimal overhead of doubling the digital to analog converter (DAC) power [31]. Figure 5 depicts the architecture of the fully differential ADC which includes differential capacitive DAC, digital comparator, SAR Logic, and switches. The 12b SAR ADC is implemented and simulated using CMOS 180 nm process.

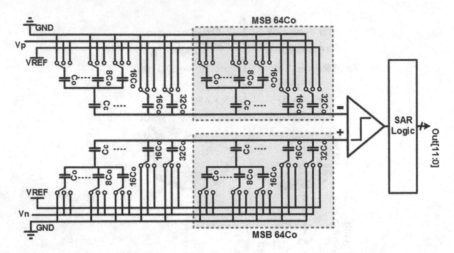

Fig. 5. The architecture diagram of the designed 12b SAR ADC.

The designed 12b SAR ADC utilizes a binary weighted fully differential capacitive DAC. To minimize the power and area consumption sub-DAC and split-capacitor for the most significant bit (MSB) is utilized [32].

The DAC is composed of 7-bit main DAC and 5 bit sub-DAC. The proposed 7/5 division minimize the power consumption while utilizing the same area as 6/6 division. Moreover, 6/6 division suffers from the high differential non-linearity (DNL)/ integral non-linearity (INL) due to the parasitic capacitance on the top plate of the sub-DAC. The MSB capacitor is split into the capacitor array identical to the least significant bit (LSB) capacitor as shown in the Fig. 6.

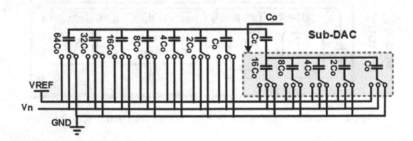

Fig. 6. Binary weighted DAC with 7-bit main-DAC and 5-bit sub-DAC.

The SAR ADC area is mainly dominated by the area of the capacitive DAC. In a binary weighted DAC of N bit resolution, the ratio of MSB to LSB is equal to 2^{N-1}, which is equal to 2048 for 12 bit SAR ADC. To reduce the area of the capacitor array, the capacitive DAC is divided into an M-bit main-DAC and an L-bit sub-DAC that is connected to the main-DAC through a coupling capacitor [33], where the SAR ADC resolution N is equal to M+L. Figure 6 shows the single-sided capacitive DAC split in

M bit main-DAC and L bit sub-DAC where M and L are equal to 7 and 5, respectively, in the implemented design. The coupling capacitor has a value of $2^L Co/2^{L-1}$ which is the $32Co/31$. Therefore, the overall effective capacitance of the sub-DAC and coupling capacitor is equal to Co. Figure 7 shows the utilization of superposition principle to depict the effect of voltage V_{TOP} based on each capacitor in the main-DAC and sub-DAC. The effective capacitive divider individually connects the bottom plate of each capacitor in the main-DAC V_{REF}. First, if the bottom plate of the MSB capacitor (64 Co) is connected to V_{REF} and the bottom plate plates of the rest of the capacitors are connected to the GND. A capacitive divider with two capacitors each is equal to 64-Co occurs and voltage V_{TOP} is equal to half the V_{REF} value. If the capacitor 32Co is the one connected to V_{REF} instead the voltage is equal to quarter V_{REF} and so on.

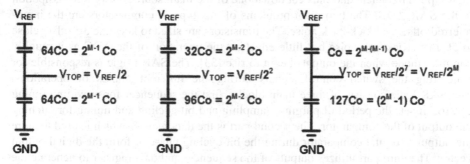

Fig. 7. Explanation of the DAC effective capacitive divider while individually connecting the bottom plate of each capacitor in the main-DAC to V_{REF} and the rest of capacitors to GND.

Thevenin equivalent is utilized to apply same procedure for the sub-DAC evaluation. Figure 8 shows the effective capacitive divider while connecting the bottom plate of the MSB capacitor of the sub-DAC to V_{REF} and the rest of capacitors to the GND. The voltage V_{TOP} is equal to $V_{REF}/2$ divided by 2M which is the half the value yielded by the LSB of main-DAC. The same analysis can be applied to the rest of the capacitors of the sub-DAC. It should be noted the Thevenin equivalent capacitance shown in Fig. 8 is the same while switching any of sub-DAC capacitors.

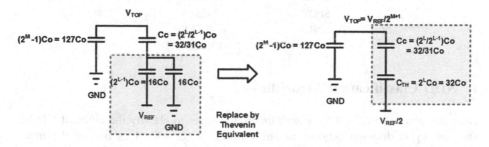

Fig. 8. Thevenin equivalent circuit for analyzing passive sub-DAC.

The only problem with sub-DAC interpolation is its sensitivity to the parasitic capacitance at the top plate of sub-DAC capacitors. This leads to INL/DNL errors due to the compression of transition steps by the sub-DAC. However, this problem can be compensated by an increase in the size of the coupling capacitor by RTP [33] as given in the following equation where C_P is the extracted parasitic capacitance from the top plate of subDAC to GND and $C_{sub\ DAC}$ is the total capacitance of the sub-DAC which is equal to $2^L Co$ (32 Co in this case).

$$R_{RP} = 1 + \frac{C_P}{C_{subDAC}} \tag{1}$$

To reduce the power consumption, dynamic comparators are utilized which are highly power efficient and thus cut down one of the main sources of power dissipation in the SAR ADC. The two main problems of this type of comparators are the input-referred offset and kick-back noise. The transistors are sized to keep the 3σ offset close to 50 mV. Kickback noise has little effect on the operation of the ADC as it roughly common mode when the outputs begin to rise [33]. The SAR Logic is responsible for generating the switch control signals during the different phases of operations. The SAR logic consists of three main blocks, first the sequencer for providing timing control. It sets the period of purging, sampling and bit-cycling and timing for latching the output of the comparator. The second part is the data register which is used to store the output of digital comparator during the bit-cycling phase to form the digital output vector. The third part utilizes outputs of the sequencer and data register to generate the switches control signals of the main-DAC and sub-DAC.

The performance summary of implemented SAR ADC is shown in Table 1. The SAR ADC achieves an effective number of bits (ENOB) of 11.4, signal-to-noise-distortion ratio (SNDR) of 60 dB, spurious free dynamic range (SFDR) of 72 dBFS which provides information about the difference between maximum amplitude tone in frequency spectrum and the fundamental input tone, DNL and INL of 0.275 LSB and 0.3 LSB, respectively, which gives deviation of actual conversion from the ideal one.

Table 1. 12b SAR ADC performance summary.

Power consumption	57 nW
ENOB	11.4
SNDR	60 dB
SFDR	72 dB
DNL	0.275 LSB
INL	0.3 LSB

4   NDD Classification Algorithm

The main goal is to extract the discriminating features to classify the different NDDs. The gait cycle duration (known as stride-time), is considered as one of the main features to identify person's gait dynamics [1]. The heel strike is defined as the heel first touches the ground and ends until the whole foot touches the ground. As shown in the Fig. 9, the early flatfoot strike occurs, when the whole foot is on the ground. The late flatfoot stages end when the heel lifts off the ground. The rise begins when the heel starts to leave the ground. The toe-off phase occurs when the toe leaves the ground. 60% of the walking consists of stance phase. The Stance phase occurs when the whole foot is on the ground. Swing phase is basically defined as the one foot is on the ground and the other is in the air. Figure 10 shows the digitized FSR output from the ADC for an ALS patient for a duration of 100 s along with right and left stride intervals in red and blue, respectively. Close analysis of the graph shows that stride interval of both left and right foot gives same information about the human behavior. Moreover, the left stride time seems to be more sensitive and gives more details in comparison to the right. These results are consistent among all the patients (ALS, HD, PD) and therefore in this work only left stride is utilized in the processing to save power and area utilization.

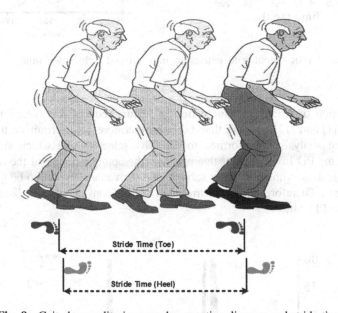

Fig. 9. Gait abnormality in neurodegenerative diseases and stride time.

Figure 11 shows the average left stride time interval for different NDD i.e. ALS, PD, HD and NP. Subjects with ALS, have longer average stride time interval compared with that of the HD, PD and the healthy subjects. Therefore, the average stride time interval is an effective feature for the NDD detection that is used in our proposed NDD classifier. It is also observed that the stride-time interval is a key feature to distinguish between ALS and other NDDs based on Fig. 11. Another important feature for NDD detection is the stride-time fluctuation w.r.t corresponding mean which is more dominant in the HD relative to other NDDs [23] except ALS as shown in the Fig. 12.

But the ALS can be detected based on stride time, therefore stride time fluctuations can be treated as a feature for the HD detection. Stride time fluctuation is calculated by taking the derivative of the stride time and the Fig. 12 shows the relative maximum and continuous fluctuation in the stride time compared to the NP, ALS, and PD.

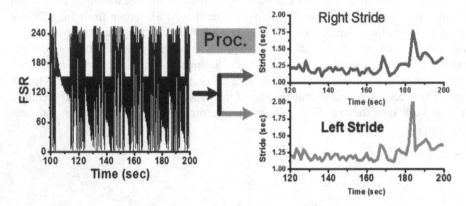

Fig. 10. Digitized FSR output with extraction into left and right stride time. (Color figure online)

The selection of stride time fluctuation as feature reduces the overall feature set compared to [1] and [12] by more than 60%. Furthermore, to discriminate the PD and NP, a detailed analysis is performed to carefully select feature which significantly distinguishes the PD from NP. For this purpose, the autocorrelation of the decay time for the NDD is done with the healthy subject, and the value came out to be greatest for the PD patients. Therefore, the autocorrelation is also considered as a discriminatory feature for the PD patients.

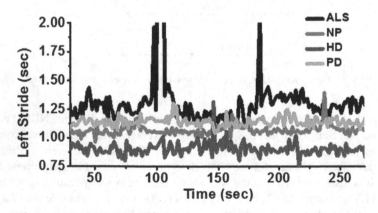

Fig. 11. Average stride time comparison of different NDD (ALS, PD, HD) and NP.

Figure 13 shows the computed auto-correlation factor value of different NDD's used in this work. The values show ALS achieves maximum value but since stride time alone is enough to determine the ALS, therefore, stride time along with auto-correlation factor discriminate PD from all other NDD's and NP with good classification accuracy, since PD has the second maximum value of auto-correlation factor among NP and HD.

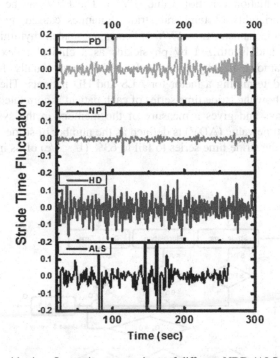

Fig. 12. Average stride time fluctuation comparison of different NDD (ALS, PD, HD) and NP.

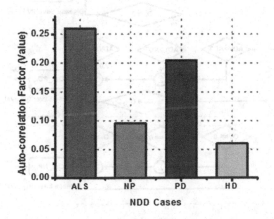

Fig. 13. Average auto-correlation factor comparison of different NDD (ALS, PD, HD) and NP.

Figures 14 and 15 shows the state flow diagram and the algorithm for the proposed NDD classification method based on 3 features: (1) stride-time, (2) fluctuation in the stride time and (3) autocorrelation decay factor. The stride time value is the duration of gait cycle which is the time interval between two consecutive heel strikes of the same foot in milliseconds. Fluctuation in the stride time is an indication of the inconsistent limb movements. Therefore, the mean and standard deviation of stride time are utilized to estimate the fluctuation variation value (FVV). The FVV can be considered as a measure of the variability of temporal stride dynamics caused by the imbalanced rhythmic walking mechanism. Low FVV indicates automated rhythmic characteristics of gait dynamics and is utilized by physicians as a clinical index for stable gait dynamics. FVV among healthy individuals is low and usually below 3% [34]. Explicitly can be determining a factor for ALS and HD patients. The autocorrelation function indicates how the stride time series of each patient is correlated with itself over different time delays and gives a measure of the memory in the system. The auto-correlation decay-time value (ADV) is defined as the number of strides required for the autocorrelation of the stride time series to fall to 63% $(1 - 1/e)$ of its initial value [35].

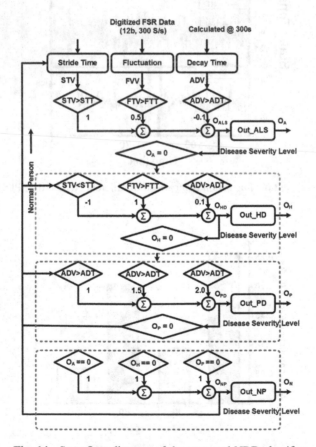

Fig. 14. State flow diagram of the proposed NDD classifier.

The O_A, O_H, O_P, and O_N are outputs of corresponding NDD and their values are calculated based on the STV (Stride time value), FVV, and ADV (Autocorrelation decay-time value) in relation to the STT (Stride time threshold), FVT (Fluctuation variation threshold), and ADT (Autocorrelation decay-time threshold). The detection time for one cycle of evaluation is 5 min (300 s) and will continue repeating if NDD goes undetected.

Algorithm Proposed NDD Classification Algorithm

1: **Input:** STV, STT, FVV, FVT, ADV, and ADT
2: **Output:** O_A, O_H, O_P, O_N
3: **for** the kth iteration **do**
4:   Load the original 300 sec data
5:   $O_{ALS} \leftarrow (STV > STT) + 0.5 * (FVV > FVT) - 0.1 * (ADV > ADT)$
6:   **if** $O_{ALS} \leq 0.5$ **then**
7:     $O_A \leftarrow 0$
8:   **else if** $O_{ALS} > 0.5$ and $O_{ALS} < 1.0$ **then**
9:     $O_A \leftarrow 1$
10:   **else if** $O_{ALS} > 1$ and $O_{ALS} < 1.4$ **then**
11:     $O_A \leftarrow 2$
12:   **else**
13:     $O_A \leftarrow 3$
14:   **end if**
15:   **if** ($O_A = 0$ or $O_A = 3$) **then**
16:     Load the original 300 sec data
17:     $O_{HD} \leftarrow (FVV > FVT) - 1 * (STV < STT) + 0.1 * (ADV > ADT)$
18:     **if** ($O_{HD} > -0.2$ and $O_{HD} < 0.2$) **then**
19:       $O_H \leftarrow 0$
20:     **else if** $O_{HD} > 0.9$ **then**
21:       $O_H \leftarrow 2$
22:     **else**
23:       $O_H \leftarrow 3$
24:     **end if**
25:   **end if**
26:   **if** ($O_H = 0$ or $O_H = 3$) **then**
27:     Load the original 300 sec data
28:     $O_{PD} \leftarrow (ADV > ADT) + (ADV > 1.5 * ADT) + (ADV > 2 * ADT)$
29:     **if** $O_{PD} = 0$ **then**
30:       $O_P \leftarrow 0$
31:     **else if** $O_{PD} = 1.0$ **then**
32:       $O_H \leftarrow 1$
33:     **else if** ($O_{PD} > 1.0$ and $O_{PD} < 2.6$) **then**
34:       $O_P \leftarrow 2$
35:     **else**
36:       $O_P \leftarrow 3$
37:     **end if**
38:   **end if**
39: **end for**
40: **if** ($O_A = 0$ and $O_H = 0$ and $O_P = 0$) **then**
41:   $O_N \leftarrow 1$
42: **else**
43:   $O_N \leftarrow 0$
44: **end if**

Fig. 15. Proposed NDD classification algorithm.

Additionally, based on threshold level and the proposed NDD algorithm, the two bits output of the classifier also describe the severity of the corresponding disorder. If none of the diseases is detected, the patient will be claimed as a normal scenario. Since it's also important to detail severity level of ND and action item, therefore the relation of NDD output, the severity of the disorder and corresponding action are detailed in Table 2. This information will be presented to the concerned person himself, caregiver and physician via cloud/Bluetooth link. The NDD classifier output is 2 (two)-bit with binary encoding utilized for each corresponding NDD, for example, the 2'b11 means a high score of specific NDD, meaning the person has the severe symptom of that NDD and needs to take precautionary measures on urgent basis.

Table 2. NDD output with score description and action item.

NDD Output	Score Description	Action Item
2'b00	Low Score of NDD	Need to monitor Situation
2'b01	Medium Score of NDD	Need to visit Doctor
2'b11	High Score of NDD	Emergency Situation
2'b10	Not enough data	Need further analysis

To form a mathematical model for the detection based on the above discrimination, the fall detection algorithm is as follows. The decision weights are carefully selected based on the rigorous simulation for the Neuro-Degenerative Disease Data Base [35].

5   Results and Discussion

The system is verified with the Gait Dynamics in Neuro-Degenerative Disease Data Base 35, which contains 64 subjects having ALS, HD, PD and Healthy Subjects of 13, 20, 15 and 16, respectively. To measure the real-time performance and working, the complete implementation is also done on FPGA. The average overall classification accuracy was computed using the Xilinx Virtex 5 LX-110T FPGA board and Logic analyzers were used to display and verify the NDD classification. The sensitivity and specificity are defined by (2) and (3), respectively, along with the definition of True Positive, True Negative, False Positive, and False Negative in (4)–(7).

$$\text{Sensitivity} = \frac{\text{True Positive}}{\text{True Positive} + \text{False Negative}} \tag{2}$$

$$\text{Specificity} = \frac{\text{True Negative}}{\text{False Positive} + \text{True Negative}} \tag{3}$$

$$\text{True Positive} = \frac{\# \text{ of pattern classified Normal}}{\text{Total } \# \text{ of Normal Patterns}} \tag{4}$$

$$\text{True Negative} = \frac{\# \text{ of pattern classified Abnormal}}{\text{Total } \# \text{ of Abnormal Pattern}} \tag{5}$$

$$\text{False Negative} = \frac{\# \text{ of pattern classified Abnormal}}{\text{Total } \# \text{ of Normal Pattern}} \tag{6}$$

$$\text{False Positive} = \frac{\# \text{ of pattern classified Normal}}{\text{Total } \# \text{ of Abnormal Pattern}} \tag{7}$$

The evaluation shows the proposed system achieves an averaged sensitivity and specificity of 90.8% and 94.5%, respectively for total 64 subjects. The verification results of the proposed system are shown in Fig. 16. It also achieves a classification accuracy of 93.8%, 89.1%, 94% and 93.3%, for ALS, HD, PD, and normal person, respectively.

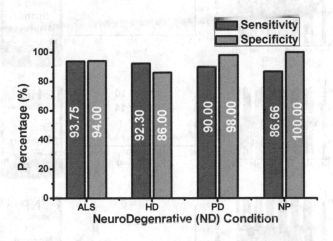

Fig. 16. Measured sensitivity and specificity of NDD.

Figure 17 shows the performance of the proposed system, the digitized FSR data is processed to evaluate the stride time and based on the stride time, fluctuation in the stride and autocorrelation decay time; the specific NDD is determined and the final information is transferred to the doctor/caretaker mobile via Bluetooth. Different scenarios are shown in the Fig. 17 for the working of the proposed NDD classification system along with the computed values (STV, ADV, and FVV) and their corresponding threshold values (STT, ADT, and FVT). The message showing the severity level of the disease along with proposed action item is displayed on caregiver or physician smartphone through a low-energy Bluetooth link. Table 3 compares the performance of the proposed NDD processor with the state-of-the-art works. All other works focus on software implementation only whereas this work target a wearable device with on-sensor processing. It also utilizes only 3 features to distinguish between the different NDDs and healthy persons. The system achieves an overall sensitivity, specificity and classification accuracy of 90.8%, 94.5%, and 92.9%, respectively. Since the proposed system is targeting a wearable environment, therefore an area and power efficient 12b-SAR ADC are implemented using 65 nm CMOS technology consuming <60 nW.

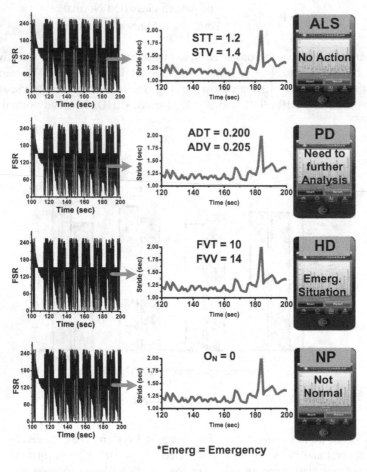

Fig. 17. The measured result showing the system working.

Table 3. Comparison with state-of-the-art works.

Parameter	Zeng [1]	Ren [2]	Wu [17]	Barth [20]	Aziz [21]	This work
Sensor type	FSR	FSR	FSR	Inertial sensors	FSR	FSR
Sensor location	Foot	Foot	Foot	Foot	Foot	Foot
On sensor detection	X	X	X	X	X	O
No. of features	12	10	1	12	1	3
Avg. sensitivity	91.7%	93.7%	76.9%	88%	89.3%	90.8%
Avg. specificity	100%	78.3%	87.5% [20–24]	86%	78.3%	94.5%
Target application	NDD	NDD	ALS	PD	NDD	Wearable: NDD

6 Conclusion

This contribution proposes a wearable novel NDD detection system for the detection and classification of ALS, HD, and PD. The proposed system is based on the minimum feature set of 3 features which will ensure lower power and area implementation without affecting the overall detection performance. The proposed system aims to provide a solution for the next generation of miniaturized wearable devices to detect the NDD at an early stage and may help in reducing the severity of NDD. The proposed system is tested on patient's recordings from Physionet Gait Dynamics dataset and achieves a classification accuracy of 93.8%, 89.1%, 94% and 93.3%, for ALS, HD, PD, and healthy person, respectively, from a total set of 64 subjects

Acknowledgement. This work was funded by the Lahore University of Management Sciences (LUMS), Lahore, Pakistan startup grant number STG-EED-1216. The authors thank Dr. Muhammad Shoaib Bin Altaf for algorithm support and technical advice and Saad Adnan Butt for his help. The authors also thank Cadence for its CAD support, and Euro-practice for the PDK support.

References

1. Zeng, W., Wang, C.: Classification of neurodegenerative diseases using gait dynamics via deterministic learning. J. Inf. Sci. **317**(1), 246–258 (2015)
2. Ren, P., Zhao, W., Zhao, Z., Bringas-Vega, M.L., Valdes-Sosa, P.A., Kendrick, K.M.: Analysis of gait rhythm fluctuations for neurodegenerative diseases by phase synchronization and conditional entropy view document. IEEE Trans. Neural Syst. Rehabil. Eng. **24**(2), 291–299 (2016)
3. Scafetta, N., Marchi, D., West, B.J.: Understanding the complexity of human gait dynamics. Chaos **19**(2), 026108–026110 (2009)
4. Banaie, M., Pooyan, M., Mikaili, M.: Introduction and application of an automatic gait recognition method to diagnose movement disorders that arose of similar causes. Expert Syst. Appl. **38**(6), 7359–7363 (2011)

5. Parkinson's disease Foundation: Statistics. http://parkinson.org/Understanding-Parkinsons/Causes-and-Statistics/Statistics
6. Huntington Disease: Health Conditions, June 2013. https://ghr.nlm.nih.gov/condition/huntington-disease#statistics
7. National Institute of Neurological Disorders and Stroke: Huntington's disease information page. https://www.ninds.nih.gov/Disorders/All-Disorders/huntingtons-Disease-Information-Page
8. Hausdorff, J.M., et al.: Altered fractal dynamics of gait: reduced stride-interval correlations with aging and Huntington's disease. J. Appl. Physiol. 82(1), 262–269 (1997)
9. Grimbergen, Y.A., Knol, M.J., Bloem, B.R., Kremer, B.P., Roos, R.A., Munneke, M.: Falls and gait disturbances in Huntington's disease. Mov. Disord. 23(7), 970–976 (2008)
10. US San Diego, School of Medicine: Center for ALS Research and Therapy. http://als.ucsd.edu/about-als/Pages/incidence.aspx
11. Saadeh, W., Altaf, M.A.B., Altaf, M.S.B.: A high accuracy and low latency patient-specific wearable fall detection system. In: Proceedings of the IEEE International Conference on Biomedical Health Informatics, BHI, pp. 441–444, February 2017
12. Balash, Y., Peretz, C., Leibovich, G., Herman, T., Hausdorff, J.M., Giladi, N.: Falls in outpatients with Parkinson's disease: frequency, impact, and identifying factors. J. Neurol. 252(11), 1310–1315 (2005)
13. Hausdorff, J.M.: Gait dynamics, fractals and falls: finding meaning in the stride-to-stride fluctuations of human walking. J. Hum. Mov. Sci. 26(4), 555–589 (2007)
14. Saadeh, W., Habte, T., Perrott, M.: A > 89% efficient LED driver with 0.5 V supply voltage for applications requiring low average current. In: Proceedings of the IEEE Asian Solid-State Circuits Conference, A-SSCC, pp. 273–276, November 2013
15. Yang, M., Zheng, H., Wang, H., McClean, S.: Feature selection and construction for the discrimination of neurodegenerative diseases based on gait analysis. In: Proceedings of the International Conference on Pervasive Computing Technologies for Healthcare, pp. 1–7 (2009)
16. Ota, L., Uchitomi, H., Suzuki, K., Hove, M.J., Orimo, S., Miyake, Y.: Relationship between fractal property of gait cycle and severity of Parkinson's disease. In: Proceedings of the IEEE/SICE International Symposium on System Integration, SII, pp. 236–239, December 2011
17. Wu, Y., Ng, S.C.: A PDF-based classification of gait cadence patterns in patients with amyotrophic lateral sclerosis. In: Proceedings of the IEEE Engineering in Medicine and Biology Conference, EMBC, pp. 1304–1307, August 2010
18. Han, Y., Ma, Z., Zhou, P.: A study of gaits in Parkinson's patients using Autoregressive model. In: IEEE Proceedings, pp. 104–107 (2009)
19. Fatmehsari, Y.R., Bahrami, F.: Assessment of Parkinson's disease: classification and complexity analysis. In: Proceedings of the Iranian Conference of Biomedical Engineering, pp. 1–4 (2010)
20. Barth, J., et al.: Biometric and mobile gait analysis for early diagnosis and therapy monitoring in Parkinson's disease. In: Proceedings of IEEE Engineering in Medicine and Biology Society, EMBS, pp. 868–871, September 2011
21. Aziz, W., Arif, M.: Complexity analysis of stride interval time series by threshold dependent symbolic entropy. Eur. J. Appl. Physiol. 98(1), 30–40 (2006)
22. Daliri, M.R.: Chi-square distance kernel of the gaits for the diagnosis of Parkinson's disease. Biomed. Signal Process. Control 8(1), 66–70 (2013)
23. Dillmann, U., et al.: Principal component analysis of gait in Parkinson's disease: relevance of gait velocity. Gait Posture 39(3), 882–887 (2014)

24. Huang, A., Mallet, L.: Medication-Related Falls in Older People: Causative Factors and Management. Springer, Heidelberg (2016). https://doi.org/10.1007/978-3-319-32304-6
25. Saadeh, W., Altaf, M.A.B., Butt, S.: A wearable neuro-degenerative diseases classifier system based on gait dynamics. In: IFIP/IEEE International Conference on Very Large Scale Integration, VLSI-SoC, pp. 1–6, October 2017
26. Flex Sensor. https://www.tekscan.com/products-solutions/force-sensors/a201
27. Saadeh, W., Alsuradi, H., Altaf, M., Yoo, J.: A 1.1 mW ground effect-resilient body coupled communication transceiver with pseudo OFDM for head and body area network. IEEE J. Solid-State Circuits (JSSC) 52(10), 2690–2702 (2017)
28. Saadeh, W., Kifle, Y., Yoo, J.: A hybrid OFDM body coupled communication transceiver for binaural hearing aids in 65 nm CMOS. In: Proceedings of the IEEE International Symposium on Circuits and Systems, ISCAS, pp. 2620–2623, May 2015
29. Saadeh, W., Alsuradi, H., Altaf, M.A.B., Yoo, J.: A 1.1 mW hybrid OFDM ground effect-resilient body coupled communication transceiver for head and body area network. In: Proceedings of the IEEE Asian Solid-State Circuits Conference, ASSCC, pp. 201–204, November 2016
30. Altaf, M.A.B., Zhang, C., Yoo, J.: A 16-channel patient-specific seizure onset and termination detection SoC with impedance-adaptive transcranial electrical stimulator. IEEE J. Solid-State Circuits (JSSC) 50(11), 2728–2740 (2015)
31. El-Damak, D.R.: Design of ultra low power analog-to-digital converter for ambulatory EEG recording. M.S. thesis, Massachusetts Institute of Technology, Cambridge (2012)
32. Yazicioglu, R.F., Merken, P., Puers, R., Hoof, C.V.: A 200 pw eight-channel acquisition ASIC for ambulatory EEG systems. In: IEEE International Solid-State Circuits Conference on Digest of Technical Papers, pp. 164–165, February 2008
33. Verma, N.: An ultra-low power ADC for wireless micro-sensor applications. M.S. thesis, Massachusetts Institute of Technology, Cambridge, MA, June 2005
34. Beauchet, O., et al.: Walking speed-related changes in stride time variability: effects of decreased speed. J. NeuroEng. Rehabil. 6, 32 (2009)
35. Hausdorff, J.M., et al.: Dynamic markers of altered gait rhythm in amyotrophic lateral sclerosis. J. Appl. Physiol. 88(6), 2045–2053 (2000)

Self-timed Power-on Reset Circuit for Pseudo Dual/Two Port SRAM Used in Low-Voltage IoT Applications

Vivek Nautiyal$^{(\boxtimes)}$, Lalit Gupta, Gaurav Singla, Jitendra Dasani,
Sagar Dwivedi, and Martin Kinkade

ARM Inc., San Jose, CA, USA
vivek.nautyial@arm.com

Abstract. The purpose of the Power-on Reset (POR) circuit is to reset the latches and flip-flops in an SOC to a known state when the supply is ramping up. During power-up, supply is not stable, and the ramp-up time can vary depending on the applications. A common approach is to generate a POR signal by comparing the supply voltage with a reference voltage. Pseudo dual/two port memories are used in graphic applications where parallel computing is prime factor instead of performance. IoT applications comprise significant image and video processing for which these memories are used. Conventional SRAM does not need a POR circuit but pseudo dual/two port memory face functionality issues without a POR circuit. Low-power applications, like Internet of Things (IoT) devices, comprise of SRAM arrays, sensors, and logic operating at sub-threshold or extremely low voltages. Conventional POR circuits also use a resistor divider circuit along with band gap reference. At these low operating voltages, generating a stable reference voltage is difficult because of band gap reference limitations and process variations. In this paper, we present multiple POR circuits that operates without using a reference voltage, making it robust against different sources of variation. First proposed circuit is self-timed, meaning the reset signal pulse-width varies according to the time needed to reset the latch. The designed circuit has been fabricated in 16 nm FinFET technology. Silicon validation shows that the proposed POR circuit works at a minimum supply voltage of 400 mv. Simulation verifies that the POR circuit is operational in sub-threshold region but is limited to 400 mV on silicon due to the operational voltage of additional testchip logic. Also, the POR circuit does not consume any dynamic power during normal operation of the SOC and has minimal area overhead of 21.3 μm^2. Second proposed circuit is latch based self-feedback circuit which resolves limitations of the initial proposed circuit.

Keywords: Power-on Reset (POR) · Sub-threshold · 16 nm · FinFET · Self timed, Internet of Things (IoT)

© IFIP International Federation for Information Processing 2019
Published by Springer Nature Switzerland AG 2019
M. Maniatakos et al. (Eds.): VLSI-SoC 2017, IFIP AICT 500, pp. 92–111, 2019.
https://doi.org/10.1007/978-3-030-15663-3_5

1 Introduction

At the time of power-up, the POR signal generator senses a minimum threshold voltage, and generates a POR signal as shown in Fig. 1. This POR signal is used to pre-set/reset the flip-flops, latches, and registers to a known state. The supply voltage for the POR circuit is the same as the SOC supply voltage. This presents a challenge because the POR circuit needs to operate while the supply is ramping up. Conventionally, higher-voltage applications use a band-gap reference voltage to compare with supply voltage to generate the reset signal. As low-power devices continue to use supply voltages below the band-gap voltage, conventional POR circuit design becomes difficult. More specifically, the challenges occur as the supply voltage of low-power applications like IoT devices approaches the threshold voltage. Multiple factors increase the complexity of the POR circuit. Slow ramping supply voltage may not generate a POR signal with sufficient voltage level and pulse width to reset the logic circuit. Sharp supply rise times can extend the pulse width of the POR signal, even when supply has fully ramped up because of the longer reaction time of the circuit and the coupling capacitance with supply voltage. The circuit presented in this paper uses a self-timed circuit, to ensure that the reset signal pulse-width varies according to the time needed to reset the latch. The proposed circuit is designed to operate without any reference voltage, thus eliminating these limitations.

The supply voltage requirement of the SOC is based on the maximum supply requirement of all the components. The amount of on-chip decoupling capacitance is also designed based on regular circuit activity. However, at the time of power-up, unpredictable activity of the components causes the supply ramp-up rate to be non-linear. With technology scaling, process variation increases as device dimensions, threshold voltages, and supply voltages have decreased. Device simulation models fit to silicon behavior in limited voltage range, for example nominal voltage, with some tolerance. It is possible that a fully functional POR pulse generator operating in a simulation fails in silicon. To avoid such a situation, the POR signal generator must be simple, and must be thoroughly analyzed. To verify our design, we performed exhaustive simulations involving Monte Carlo tests on different PVT corners with a post-layout netlist. After that, we performed digital testing on silicon.

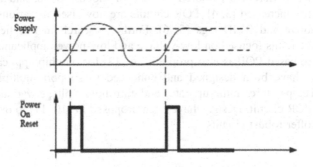

Fig. 1. General POR circuit waveform

This work is an extension of the POR circuit presented in [1]. We propose 2 circuits to set/reset latch at power up correctly.

1. Self-Timed POR circuit [1].
2. Latch based self-feedback POR circuit [2].

First the self-timed circuit is explained. Although it resolves the issue, it comprises of some limitations in terms of its implementation in all scenarios. The latch based self-feedback circuit resolves these issues based self-feedback circuit.

In summary, the major contributions of the proposed circuit are as follows:

- Removing the requirement for a reference voltage. This is useful for low-voltage applications.
- Implementation of a self-timed circuit, to ensure that the reset signal pulse-width varies according to the time needed to reset the latch.
- Use of NAND latch in POR Circuit: - NAND gate resets with 0 voltage level which is the case for all the nodes at power up, making it easier to ensure reset at lower voltage level. Reset of the NAND latch is further used to reset all other latches in the design.
- Latch based self-feedback circuit: To resolve limitations of self-timed circuit.

The paper is organized as follows. Related Work is presented Sect. 2. Requirement of POR circuit in SRAM memories in explained in Sect. 3.1. Overview of the first proposed self-timed circuit is mentioned in Sect. 3.2. Detailed working of the self-timed circuit is provided in Sect. 4. Verification of the proposed circuits is presented in Sect. 5. Section 6 comprises of limitations of self-timed circuit and working of the self-feedback latch-based circuit to avoid these issues. Finally test-chip results and silicon validation are provided in Sect. 7, followed by conclusion in Sect. 8.

2 Related Work

Researchers have been studying and developing POR circuits for a long-time because of their need in analog and digital integrated circuits (ICs). It began with traditional RC circuits, and then researchers explored the use of diodes, BJTs, and MOSFETs as circuit complexity increased [3, 4]. POR circuits are now used in various applications such as automotive and RFID tags [5, 6]. Further research in this field led to the development of circuits focused on low-voltage and low-power applications [7, 9, 13]. A current-source-based POR is also proposed in [12] for on-chip applications.

The circuits have been designed and enhanced to support multiple I/O power supplies [8]. Temperature, ramp-up rate, and threshold voltage variation affect the reliability of a POR circuit. Designs have been proposed in [10, 11] to overcome these variations and offer robust circuits.

Discrete ICs for POR functionality is available. However, designing on-chip POR offers an area reduction advantage. In this study, we propose an on-chip, self-timed, low-voltage POR circuit that is functional at a minimum of 400 mV on 16 nm FinFET technology. The technique uses multiple delay stages and uses a combination of coupling capacitances and resistor divider circuits to generate a reset signal. The area overhead of the POR circuit is minimal, the circuit uses no dynamic power during normal SOC operation, and the pulse width of the reset signal is self-timed.

3 Overview of Self-timed POR Circuit

3.1 Problem Statement

Conventional SRAM architectures have latches to latch data, address and other input signals. These latches are provided CLK input such that it resets the latch as desired for expected functionality. Hence POR circuit is not usually needed in such designs. In latch-based pseudo dual port SRAM memories [14], latches are used for portA but using latch for portB creates the need of POR circuit as will be explained in this section. To resolve this issue flip-flops can be used but at the cost of significant impact on area. Thus, latches were used instead of flip-flop for portB inputs to save area. Figure 2 shows NOR based SR latch that was used in dual/two port memories, to optimize the portB hold time and area. For dual port memories, CLK signal generates 2 internal clocks known as global timing pulse (gtp). Initially data for portA is passed through the mux by selecting the mux_sel signal accordingly. Until then data for portB is latched. At power-up, it is essential that signal qi, which further generates clk_latb and iclk for the latch operation is set to the desired state.

Figure 3 shows both cases where signal qi can be set to different values. When set to low level, data for portB is latched as expected because clk_latb is low. When qi is set to high level, data for portB is not latched correctly. This will result in write failure for the first cycle. Since NOR latch needs a high pulse to reset it, conventional method of resetting it through delaying the supply at the input of NOR latch was showing failures in Monte Carlo simulations.

To resolve this issue, well-known solutions can be implemented but such conventional POR circuit has its own limitations and penalties. To have a high pulse which is enough to latch correctly, amount of required RC is huge. Hence RC and stage delay-based POR circuit costs a lot of area. Stage delay suffers from variability and need big area to provide a reasonable big delay at slow supply ramp. Voltage divider-based POR circuit suffers from significant DC current requirement and are analog in nature. These kind of Power-On-Reset circuits needs silicon validation and are not needed for memory circuits which are supposed to be simple in nature. Based on the mentioned analysis, we propose the following self-timed POR circuit which resolves the SR NOR latch problem and its use is not limited to this scenario.

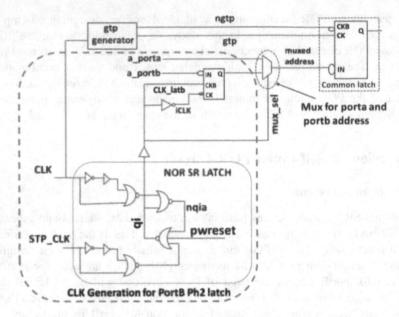

Fig. 2. POR requirement in latch-based pseudo dual port SRAM

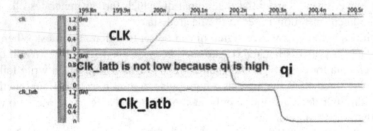

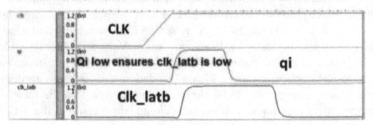

Fig. 3. Signal generation sequence for data latching

3.2   Self-timed POR Circuit

Figure 4 shows the block diagram of the proposed self-timed POR circuit. Initially the supply to POR circuit is delayed by circuit explained in section 4A. When the supply is ramping up, PCTRL and NCTRL signals explained in section 4B and 4C respectively are low. The generation of PCTRL and NCTRL causes the RESET signal explained in section 3D to pulse HIGH which resets the SR latch. After this the feedback circuit switches the PCTRL and NCTRL signals high, such that POR signal remains low until next supply ramp up.

Figure 5 shows the detailed transistor-level diagram of the POR circuit. PCTRL is delayed as compared to the ramping supply. The feedback circuit also generates NCTRL, which prevents any DC current through the POR circuit. This enables the POR circuit to be used in low-power applications. When the supply is ramping up, capacitors C0, C1 and C2 couples with VDD and turns PCTRL and NCTRL signals low causing the latch to reset. After reset output NQ follows the supply, while Q stops following the supply voltage. NQ generates a feedback signal when the reset is complete. The feedback output switches PCTRL and NCTRL signals such that it makes NOR output independent of NQ. The circuit is self-timed, which means that the reset signal turns off depending on the delay of the circuit and the ramp-up time of the power supply. This will help in providing sufficient pulse width for the reset signal.

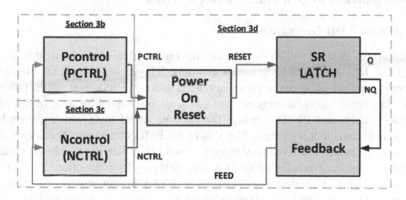

Fig. 4. Block diagram of self-timed POR circuit components

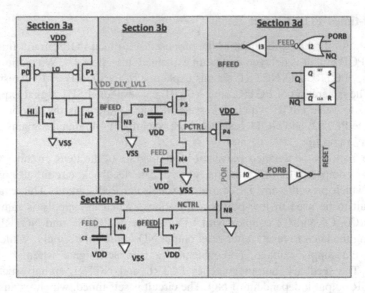

Fig. 5. Overview of self-timed POR circuit components

4   Components of Self-timed POR Circuit

4.1   Delayed VDD Generation

Generation of delayed VDD is shown in Fig. 6. The output of this circuit, VDD_DLY_LVL1, is used to generate a supply-delayed PCTRL signal. Before the power-up operation, all nodes in the circuit are at ground (VSS) level. When power-up begins, the supply starts ramping up, the LO node is coupled because of the Miller capacitance of P0 and P1. This delays the ramping of HI node which in turn helps LOW node to remain at high state. The Vds of the PMOS transistor P0 causes a slight delay in the HI node. The HI node voltage is much lower than the threshold voltage of the NMOS transistor when the ramp-up is slow delaying P1 conduction. The LO node falls with a delay, thus delaying VDD_DLY_LVL1 output supply. N2 acts as a clamping node in case the LO node is coupled higher than Vt as this would turn off the PMOS transistor.

4.2   PCTRL Generation

Figure 7 shows that the VDD_DLY_LVL1 from Fig. 6 and feedback circuit output FEED/BFEED from Fig. 9 generate the PCTRL signal. This signal is also delayed with respect to the VDD supply. Initially at ramp up BFEED = '0', and FEED is ramping up. PCTRL is a delayed VDD signal because of coupling of capacitors C0 and C1 with VDD. When BFEED = '1', PCTRL follows VDD. PCTRL is delayed VDD because of three mechanisms. First, VDD_DLY_LVL1 is used as a source bias for the PMOS transistor P3, whose drain generates the PCTRL signal. The gate of the transistor P3 is connected to coupling capacitance C0. The other node of the coupling capacitor C0 is connected to the supply. As the supply rises, the coupling capacitor makes the gate of the PMOS rise, thereby turning it off. The FEED node at the gate of the NMOS N4 of the PCTRL generator is coupled HIGH through the coupling cap C1. This causes some charge of the PCTRL to leak through the NMOS transistor.

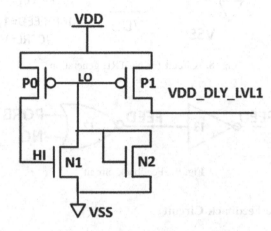

Fig. 6. Circuit for delayed VDD generation

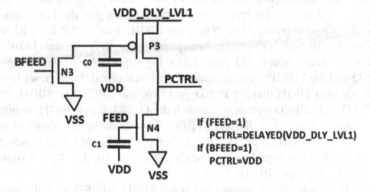

Fig. 7. Circuit for PCTRL generation

4.3 NCTRL Generation

Figure 8 shows the circuit diagram for NCTRL signal generation. At power up, the BFEED signal is LOW while the FEED is coupled HIGH. FEED is coupled HIGH due to C2 as well as it being driven by feedback circuit in Fig. 9. This ensures that at the start of supply ramp-up NCTRL signal remains at VSS. When the RESET operation is complete, the BFEED signal goes HIGH, making NCTRL go HIGH (VDD-VT) because of the NMOS N7.

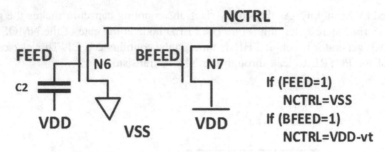

Fig. 8. Circuit for NCTRL generation

Fig. 9. Feedback circuit

4.4   POR and the Feedback Circuit

The POR circuit is shown in Fig. 10 which corresponds to section 3d in Fig. 5. PCTRL and NCTRL are the inputs to this circuit and the output is a reset signal for the SR latch. PORB and NQ signals are inputs to the feedback circuit shown in Fig. 9. Since PCTRL is delayed with respect to the ramping supply, the POR signal which follows VDD is also delayed. After POR goes HIGH, then the SR latch RESET goes HIGH. When the SR latch is reset, the corresponding output Q becomes LOW and after the latching operation, output NQ starts following supply. As shown in Fig. 9, logic NOR of NQ and the PORB signal generate a feedback signal. When reset is executed, the NQ signal goes HIGH making FEED go LOW and BFEED go HIGH.

The FEED and BFEED signals will switch the PCTRL signal HIGH, turning off the PMOS transistor P3 in Fig. 7. Similarly, BFEED turns on the N7 transistor in Fig. 8, making NCTRL go HIGH. Now, PCTRL, which is HIGH, and NCTRL, which is also HIGH, turn off the reset signal as per the circuit in Fig. 10. The PORB signal in the feedback circuit also turns HIGH.

When PORB turns HIGH, the state of reset, FEED, BFEED, and all other signals stay the same and becomes independent of NQ, making normal operation of SR latch independent of RESET signal. Based on process variation, the forward path, or feedback path, of the SR latch will make one of the nodes go HIGH and other go LOW. This state of the SR latch is probabilistic. If the state of the SR latch is as desired, an initial RESET pulse will be generated, which will do nothing to latch as it is already in the desired state. After some time, when NQ disables the RESET pulse operation, the SR latch will become independent of the POR circuit. If the state of the SR latch is not as desired, the initial HIGH pulse on the SR latch will make sure that the latch flips to the desired state, and afterwards the RESET pulse will be disabled. Since this is a simple feedback mechanism it doesn't need any reference voltage generation; hence it operates very well at low voltages. In proposed circuit, a feedback circuit is used. In case there are multiple flip-flops and latches that need to be reset, it is not possible to take feedback from all the latches. The circuit can be used in such cases as well. Instead of taking feedback from all the latch outputs, feedback will be still taken from a single latch. However, the output NQ of that latch will act as RESET signal for all the other latches. the feedback with a single latch will not be enough for timing if a reset signal is propagated through a buffer tree. This is resolved by considering worst RC distance for the POR latch. Additionally, the latch is skewed to account for variation and a buffer is inserted in the feedback path.

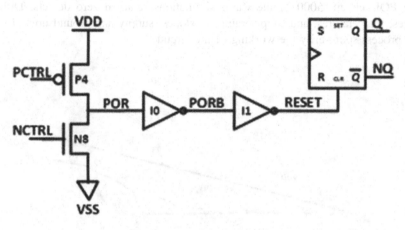

Fig. 10. Self-timed POR circuit

5 SPICE Verification for Self-timed POR Circuit

Figure 11 shows timing waveform from self-timed POR circuit simulation. All the internal signals along with the reset signal can be seen in the figure. The VDD signal is ramping up which generates the reset signal and turns PORB high. As mentioned earlier, factors such as temperature and process variation, device models, supply ramp-up rate, and supply noise increase complexity of the POR circuit. To make sure, that our proposed POR circuit functions correctly, we exhaustively verified it. For global variation, we took different global process corners and for local variation, we ran 5000 Monte Carlo simulations for each of the global corner with the criteria shown in Table 1.

Table 1. Simulation criteria

Simulation type	Post layout full chip extraction
Supply ramp up time	100 ns, 1 µs, 1 ms, 10 ms
Temperature	−40 C, 85 C, 125 C
Supply voltage	0.4 V, 0.51 V, 1.2 V
Parasitic Extraction- RC extraction for metals	−40 C and 125 C for worst R and worst C
VSS noise	50 mV sinusoidal wave
Supply noise	Sinusoidal wave of 10% of instant supply value
Process corners	SS, TT, SF, FF, FS
Monte Carlo simulations	5000

On-chip or on-board supply and ground are not always ideal. They are susceptible to different kinds of variations and noises. For simulating noise at power up, we superimposed 50 mV sinusoidal noise on VSS and 10% of instant supply sinusoidal noise on the supply for the POR block. As shown in Fig. 12, when RESET or BFEED signals are at VSS level, 50 mV noise is present. Also, the supply ramping up shows 10% instant supply value as noise in the VDD. As shown in Fig. 11, when the BFEED signal switches from HIGH to LOW, after some delay. The reset signal also switches from HIGH to LOW. Before that, the RESET signal has been following supply because of the POR circuit. 5000 Monte Carlo simulations returned zero defects. Different voltages, temperatures, and supply ramp-up slopes, supply and ground noise for different process split verify the working of the circuit.

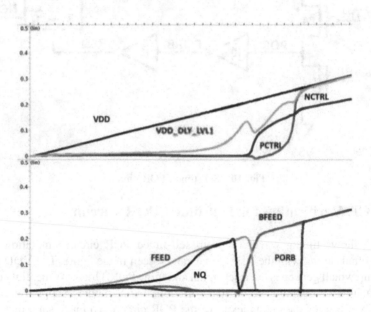

Fig. 11. Simulated waveform for self-timed POR circuit

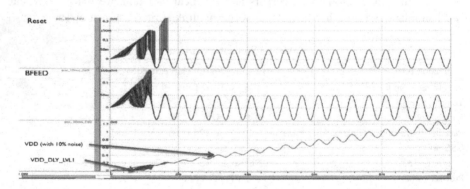

Fig. 12. MC simulations of POR with 10 ms supply slope

6 Latch Based Self-feedback POR Circuit

To address dual/two port latch wrong initialization issue, if we use flip-flop for portB, we don't need power on reset circuit. That will not be area efficient for dual port ultra-high-density design where area is most important.

Although the self-timed circuit resolves the latch issue discussed in Sect. 3.1, it comes with some limitations. The proposed self-timed circuit is completely based on capacitive coupling. Since it was implemented on 16 nm technology where advanced technology helped with the coupling, older technology nodes comparatively have lesser coupling capacitance. In some cases, at lower voltages, coupling might not be as desired for functional operation of the circuit. These issues can lead to limitation of the circuit to be used for older nodes. Here latch based self-feedback circuit is proposed which overcomes these limitations of the self-timed circuit.

Figure 13 shows the block diagram of self-feedback circuit. The idea is to receive feedback from the NOR SR latch, and provide a reset signal to the NOR latch using the NAND SR latch. As shown in the figure, the NAND SR latch uses delayed VDD. Figure 14 shows the detailed diagram for self-feedback POR circuit. Vdd is delayed using RC circuit and logic gates. A NAND SR latch is used after delayed supply Vdd. Since i/p of NAND latch, 'Vdd_delay' starts with 0 V, o/p 'pwreset' will follow Vdd, assuming when latch is in wrong state, nqia=low, feed will follow Vdd. NAND latch will fast latch the pwreset signal. Latched pwreset from NAND latch makes latching of NOR latch independent of logic delay in vdd_delay.

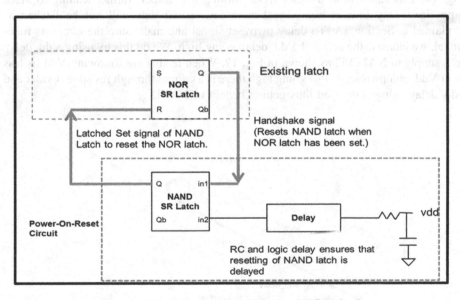

Fig. 13. Block diagram for self-feedback POR circuit

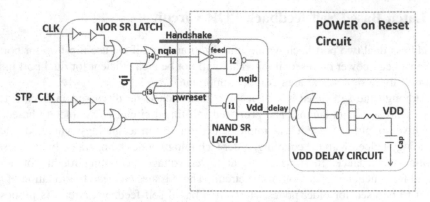

Fig. 14. Detailed diagram for self-feedback POR Circuit

Figure 15 shows the simulated waveform for self-feedback circuit shown in Fig. 14. As shown in the figure, initially nqia is low, once it goes high, feed signal turns low making nqib high. Once nqib turns high, the NAND gate i1 turns pwrreset low. Pwrreset signal stays low thus making nqia stay high. Our assumption is when latch is in wrong state, nqia=low, feed will follow Vdd but this assumption is not always correct. Nqia can initially follow Vdd before finally setting to wrong low state, and so feed is not following Vdd. In this case we do not get benefit of NAND latch.

Figure 16 shows a case where Vdd_delay is not enough with circuit shown in Fig. 14. This can lead to pwrreset signal turning low earlier, further leading to make nqia signal stay low. If nqia signal stays low, portB data will not be latched as explained in Section 3A. To delay pwrreset signal and make sure the circuit is functional, we increase the delay of Vdd_delay going high. We do this by using Vdd_delay as a supply to NAND i2 as shown in Fig. 17. When feed is not following Vdd (is less than Vdd) and pwreset is also going high there is a current through resistive divider and vdd_delay rising is delayed thus getting benefit of NAND.

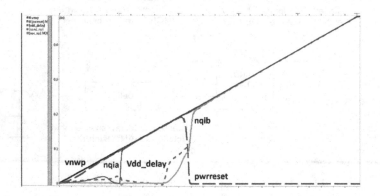

Fig. 15. Simulated waveform for self-feedback POR circuit

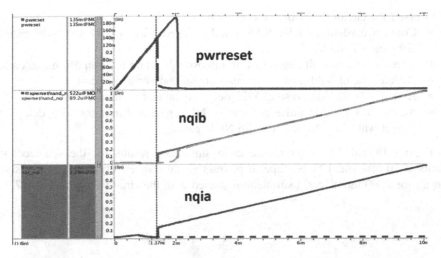

Fig. 16. Simulated waveform for pass and failure depending on nqia voltage level

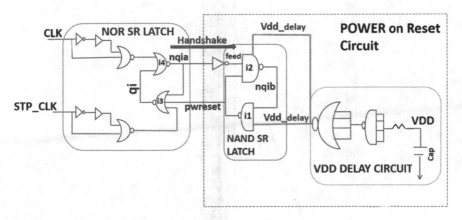

Fig. 17. Modified self-feedback POR circuit

The self-feedback circuit was tested and validated under stress conditions like self-timed POR circuit. The stress conditions are listed below:-

– Validation:
  • Vddpe ramp-up slews (10 ns, 100 ns, 1 ms).
  • SS/FS/SF/FF with −40 C/125 C at low voltage and high voltage margin corners.
  • 5000 Monte Carlo Simulations with not a single failure.

– Stressed the circuit under below conditions:
  • Connected vddpe to 4 I/p NAND and changed 4 I/p NAND and NOR gate to different VT mode.
  • Skewed manually all gates 25% in opposite direction and ran 5k monte carlo.
  • Added 10% of Vdd noise at pwreset signal and verified circuit.
  • Added 10% of Vdd noise at Vdd_delay signal and verified circuit.
  • Added 20% of Vdd noise at input of NOR gate and monitor Vdd_delay and pwrset with 4 I/p NOR and 3 I/p NOR gates.

Figures 18 and 19 shows monte carlo simulation results for the self-feedback results at 10 mns and 100 ns slope of pwreset signal respectively. Both figures show that all the 5000 monte carlo simulations passed with the circuit show in Fig. 17.

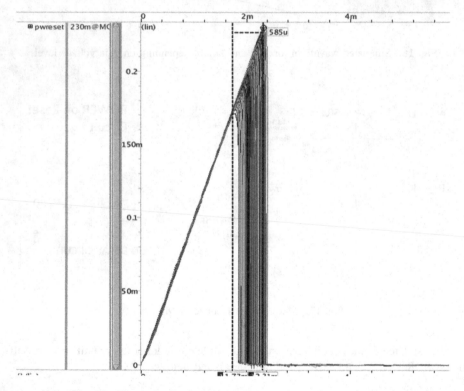

Fig. 18. Monte Carlo simulation at 10 ms slope of pwreset signal

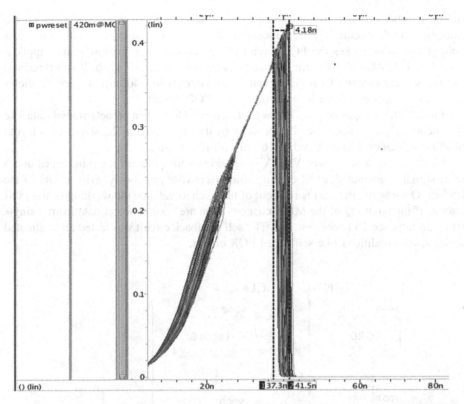

Fig. 19. Monte Carlo simulation at 10 ms slope of pwreset signal

7 Test Chip and Silicon Test Results

To do silicon validation of designed POR circuit and to get statistical yield data we designed and fabricated a POR validation IP. This IP consists of 16 samples of POR; it has two different latch structures which need to be reset. Figure 20 is the block diagram of POR validation IP. 16 latches, each associated with one POR circuit can be written parallel with the help of D and CLK pin. This is used to initialize the latch with a value opposite to the reset value. Output of 16 latches can be read serially through output Q of a 16:1 mux. The POR validation IP has two supplies: VDDD for digital latches and isolated supply VDDA for POR block. For testing purpose, it is important to initialize the latches. Since supply is ramping up for the POR circuit, we need to have 2 supplies, one of which VDDD is used to initialize, while VDDA is used to generate POR pulse.

We tested multiple samples per process split. For each process split we had 20 packaged chips, each packaged chip contains 16 POR circuits. In total, we tested 320 samples per process split. The process split included "SS, TT, FF, SF, and FS". Based on the number of silicon samples tested on different process splits, we observed the self-timed POR circuit is fully functional at a minimum voltage of 400 mv. Low voltage operation makes the POR circuit an attractive choice for low power applications like IoT. Also, the 400 mv limitation is because of the SR latch. If sub-threshold flip-flops/latches are used, the circuit can be used even below 400 mv. Figure 21 shows the timing diagram followed for testing of the POR circuit.

First, VDD is supplied and DIN and CLK is used to write a predetermined data into the latches. Then the data is read out serially by the Q pin. Figure 22, shows chip layout of POR validation IP fabricated in 16 nm FinFET process.

Once that is done, power VDDA is provided with different ramp-up times and a reset signal is generated. POR circuit should overwrite previously written data in the latches. Once again, the data is read out of the latch to validate the working of the POR circuit. If the output Q of the MUX changes from are used to select data from a single latch amongst the 16 latches present. The self-feedback circuit was tested and validated under stress conditions like self-timed POR circuit.

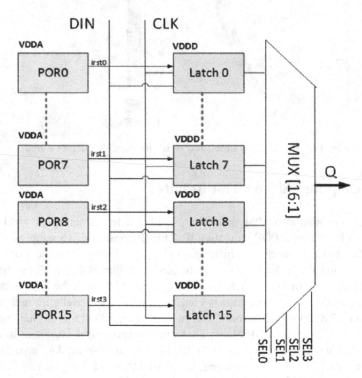

Fig. 20. POR validation IP block diagram

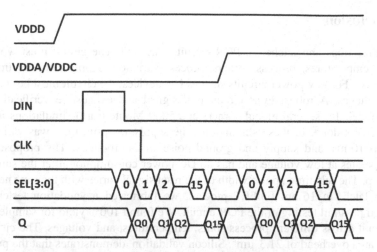

Fig. 21. Timing waveform for POR testing

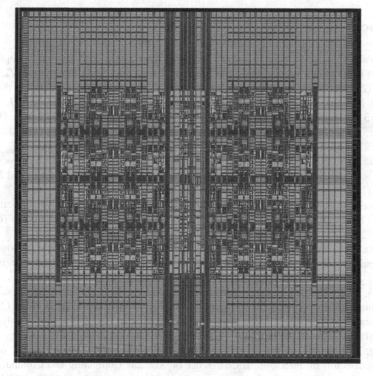

Fig. 22. 16 nm chip layout

8 Conclusion

To initialize flops and latches, a POR circuit is needed. The circuit must work with different temperatures, process corners, process variation, supply ramp-up time, and supply noise. For low-power circuits such as IoT devices, the circuit must be functional at low voltages. A robust POR circuit is designed and exhaustive verification with SPICE models for several global corners and 5000 Monte Carlo simulations for local variations was done. In these simulations, the supply ramp-up time was varied from 100 ns to 10 ms, and supply and ground noise was introduced. The proposed POR circuit operates at low voltage and has no DC power consumption after the supply has ramped up. The self-timed pulse width of the reset signal varies with the time needed to reset the latch. In 16 nm FinFET process, we fabricated a validation testchip and performed pass/fail testing of the POR circuit. We found 100% yield for samples of the POR circuit across different process splits, temperatures, and voltages. The circuit has minimal area overhead of 21.3 μm^2. Silicon validation, demonstrates that the proposed POR circuit works at a minimum supply voltage of 400 mV.

References

1. Nautiyal, V., et al.: Robust, self-timed power-on reset circuit for low-voltage applications. In: 2017 IFIP/IEEE International Conference on Very Large Scale Integration (VLSI-SoC). IEEE (2017)
2. Gupta, L., et al.: Power-on-reset circuit. U.S. Patent Application No. 15/143,197
3. Shen, S.N.: Power-on reset pulse generator. U.S. Patent No. 4,591,745, 27 May 1986
4. Hanke, C.C., Obregon, C.D., Sutton, T.W.: CMOS power-on reset circuit. U.S. Patent No. 4,970,408, 13 November 1990
5. Guo, J., et al.: Power-on-reset circuit with power-off auto-discharging path for passive RFID tag ICs. In: 2010 53rd IEEE International Midwest Symposium on Circuits and Systems. IEEE (2010)
6. Giuffredi, L., et al.: A programmable power-on-reset circuit for automotive applications. In: 2015 11th Conference on Ph. D. Research in Microelectronics and Electronics (PRIME). IEEE (2015)
7. Yasuda, T.R., Yamamoto, M., Nishi, T.: A power-on reset pulse generator for low voltage applications. In: The 2001 IEEE International Symposium on Circuits and Systems 2001, ISCAS 2001, vol. 4. IEEE (2001)
8. Burdia, D., et al.: Power-on reset circuit for SoC with multiple I/O power supplies. In: 2011 10th International Symposium on Signals, Circuits and Systems (ISSCS). IEEE (2011)
9. Chhabra, A., Vaderiya, Y.D.: Low-energy power-on-reset circuit for dual supply SRAM. IEEE Trans. Very Large Scale Integr. (VLSI) Syst. **24**(5), 2003–2007 (2016)
10. Zhang, J., Jiang, L., Zeng, Z.: Design of a novel power-on-reset circuit based on power supply detector. In: International Conference on Scalable Computing and Communications; Eighth International Conference on Embedded Computing 2009, SCALCOM-EMBEDDEDCOM 2009. IEEE (2009)
11. Yen, W.-C., Chen, H.-W., Lin, Y.-T.: A precision CMOS power-on-reset circuit with power noise immunity for low-voltage technology. IEICE Trans. Electron. **87**(5), 778–784 (2004)

12. Katyal, A., Bansal, N.: A self-biased current source-based power-on reset circuit for on-chip applications. In: 2006 International Symposium on VLSI Design, Automation and Test. IEEE (2006)
13. Prakash, R.: Zero quiescent current delay adjustable power-on-reset circuit. In: Circuits and Systems Conference (DCAS) 2014. IEEE, Dallas (2014)
14. Nautiyal, V., et al.: An ultra-high-density pseudo dual-port SRAM in 16 nm FINFET process for graphics processors. In: 2017 30th International Symposium on System-on-Chip Conference (SOCC). IEEE (2017)

Pulsed Decimal Encoding for IoT Single-Channel Dynamic Signaling

Shahzad Muzaffar$^{(\boxtimes)}$ and Ibrahim (Abe) M. Elfadel

Khalifa University of Science and Technology,
Masdar City, 54224 Abu Dhabi, UAE
{shahzad.muzaffar,ibrahim.elfadel}@ku.ac.ae

Abstract. Pulsed-Index Communication (PIC) is a recent technique for single-channel communication that is based on the principle of transmitting the indices of only the ON bits as a series of pulse streams. In this paper, a modified version of PIC, called Pulsed Decimal Communication (PDC), is presented that uses the same underlying principle but with key improvements in data rate and reliability. Like PIC, PDC is a protocol for single-channel, high-data rate, low-power dynamic signaling that does not require any clock and data recovery. It consists of a three-step algorithm, comprising a segmentation, an encoding, and a sub-segmentation step to achieve higher data rates. The segmentation step splits the data word into smaller segments and therefore smaller decimal numbers to represent them. The encoding step reduces the number of ON bits in the data and relocates them to lower indices. The sub-segmentation step further splits the segments into smaller sub-segments. The complete process significantly reduces the total number of pulses required for transmitting binary data, thus improving the data rate by about 78%. A theoretical model of the PDC protocol is exploited to estimate its data rate and derive the optimum segmentation. Furthermore, PDC is shown to be more reliable than PIC as it eliminates the variations in the number of symbols to be transmitted. The FPGA and ASIC (65 nm technology) implementations of PDC show that the low-power operation and small footprint of PIC are preserved. PDC consumes around 25 μW of power at a clock frequency of 25 MHz with a gate count of approximately 2150 gates.

Keywords: Dynamic signaling · Single-channel ·
Low-power communication · Clock and data recovery ·
Internet of Things · Automatic protocol configuration ·
Pulsed-decimal communication · Pulsed-index communication

1   Introduction

The basic structure of an Internet of Things (IoT) application is that of a two-tier architecture in which the first tier acts as a gateway to the Internet of People

© IFIP International Federation for Information Processing 2019
Published by Springer Nature Switzerland AG 2019
M. Maniatakos et al. (Eds.): VLSI-SoC 2017, IFIP AICT 500, pp. 112–132, 2019.
https://doi.org/10.1007/978-3-030-15663-3_6

(IoP) and has privileged cloud access [8] while the second tier is made of the remaining sensing and instrumented devices that are connected to the gateways using simple, low-power physical links and protocols. An example of such two-tier architecture can be found in smart homes where a range of electronic devices pertaining to lighting, air-conditioning, security, fire protection, as well as several other common electronic household items, need to be controlled remotely by a smartphone or computer. Some of these devices can be selected as gateways while others remain on the edge to communicate with the gateways. Single-channel protocols are very promising to achieve the connectivity between the first and second tiers as they provide easy and scalable networking options. The main requirements of such protocols are low-power for long battery life, high data rates for reliable transmission during bursts of activity and small form factor for lowering silicon implementation costs. Unfortunately, the existing protocols fail to meet these requirements simultaneously. Protocols providing high data rates, such as WiFi, WLAN, TCP/IP, USB, etc. [1,2,4], are power-hungry and involve complex controllers to handle two-way communications. On the other hand, low-power protocols such as 1-Wire [5], UART [3], etc. have low data rates.

To fill up the gap, a new single-channel communication technique, called Pulsed-Index Communication (PIC) has recently been introduced [6,7,10]. Its fundamental novelty lies in the replacement of the transmission of *data bits* with the transmission of *ON bit indices* in the packet stream. PIC achieves very low power consumption as it does not require any clock and data recovery (CDR). It also achieves high data rates due to a novel encoding scheme that guarantees error-free decoding even in the presence of clock discrepancies between transmitter and receiver. Additionally, PIC offers a flexible and scalable single-channel networking option for the connectivity of devices in a variety of IoT use cases [8]. Though PIC has shown very competitive figures of merit, it does have few disadvantages. One of them is that PIC is prone to complete packet failure, especially when there is a corruption in either the ON bit index number or in the number of ON bit indices. At the root of this packet failure is the fact that two adjacent data words can have vastly different *numbers* of ON bits or significant differences in the *locations* of the ON bits.

The objective of this paper is therefore to present a modified PIC protocol that significantly improves packet transmission reliability while maintaining its core idea of transmitting information in the form of pulse streams instead of transmitting data bits. The novel protocol, called Pulsed Decimal Communication (PDC), is based on transmitting a number of pulses which is equal in count to the decimal number represented by the data. For long data words, it is intuitive that such transmission will need a large number of pulses. To reduce the represented decimal number, and hence the pulse count, PDC uses a three-level data segmentation and encoding algorithm with the twofold goals of reducing the decimal value of the bit stream *and* controlling the number of pulses per data segment. The three levels of the algorithm are:

1. *First-level segmentation*: This is similar to PIC and is meant to break the data word into smaller data segments to split a number into smaller decimal numbers.
2. *Encoding*: This is applied to each segment and is meant to further reduce the number by *relocating* the ON bits to the least-significant part of the segment.
3. *Second-level segmentation or sub-segmentation*: This step is applied to each of the encoded segments. Each sub-segment is made of 4 bits. This step is meant to equalise the number of pulses in each first-level segment and thus improve transmission reliability.

Like PIC, PDC is dynamic in that it can accommodate several data rates in the range of 4.87–12.9 Mb/s with an average of 7.33 Mb/s using a 25-MHz clock. The main advantage of PDC is that it generates a fixed number of symbols per data word, which results in a simpler and more reliable transmission with respect to packet failures. Other important side advantages of PDC with respect to PIC include a simpler packet header, a more compact decoding, and an improvement of about 78% in data rate. Furthermore, ASIC synthesis of the PDC protocol, using GLOBALFOUNDROES 65 nm process, has shown that it is well within the power and area envelopes of PIC.

This chapter is a significantly expanded version of [11] with the following important additions:

1. We have introduced a new example to better explain the PDC protocol. See Subsect. 3.6
2. We have added a detailed PDC performance analysis and derived the PDC optimum segment size. See Subsect. 4.3.
3. We have added a new treatment of the PDC tolerance to clock jitter and its robustness with respect to clock rate discrepancies between transmitter and receiver. See Subsect. 4.5.
4. We have clarified the power management aspects of PDC and commented on the additional power savings that can be achieved through pulse width control. See Subsect. 4.7.
5. We have added a discussion on automatic PDC parameter setting at the power-on phase in a realistic master-slave network context. See Subsect. 4.6.
6. We have expanded Sect. 5 on Experimental Results and added several benchmarking charts and tables.

2   Review of PIC

Pulsed-Index Communication (PIC) [10] is a recent single-channel protocol that does not require any circuitry for clock and data recovery (CDR). The protocol is based on the concept of a pulsed index where instead of transmitting the bits themselves, only the indices of the ON bits in a data word of length B bits are transmitted. These indices are encoded as pulse counts. The core of the protocol is to encode these indices so as to *minimize* the number of ON bits, and *move* them to the Least Significant Bit (LSB) end of the packet. The encoding process includes a segmentation step where the data is broken into N independent segments of size l bits each (i.e., $N = B/l$). To maximize data rate, PIC uses, on each segment, an encoding combination of bit inversion and/or segment reversion/flipping. This combination is meant to reduce the number of ON bits and decrease their index values so as to lower the number of pulses required to transmit the data bits. To facilitate decoding, flag pulses representing the type of encoding performed (i.e., inversion (1 pulse), reversal (2 pulses), both (3 pulses), or none (4 pulses)) are added to each segment. All the pieces of information including flags, number of indices, and the indices themselves are transmitted in the form of pulse streams. The pulse is characterized by its width which is the number of clock cycles during which it remains high. Within a given packet, segment pulse streams are separated by an inter-symbol delay, α, as shown in Fig. 1. The receiver counts the number of pulses for each pulse stream and applies the decoding according to the flags received. The data rate depends on the number of clock cycles required to transmit a packet. Beside the elimination of CDR, the implementation of PIC is very area-efficient, low-power and highly tolerant of clocking differences between transmitter and receiver. As empirically found in [10], PIC is dynamic and provides data rates in the range of 3.1–8.5 Mb/s with an average of 4.1 Mb/s operating at a clock rate of 25 MHz and transmitting data words of 16-bits each. For an ASIC implementation using 65 nm technology, PIC can reduce area by more than 80% and power by more than 70% in comparison with a CDR-based serial bit transfer protocol.

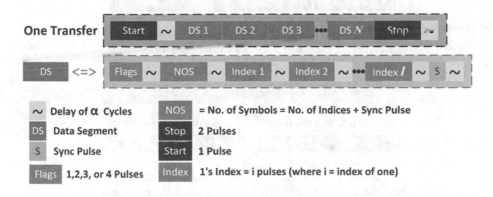

Fig. 1. PIC packet format

3 Pulsed Decimal Communication

Like PIC, the core concept of PDC is to break the data packet into smaller segments, and to transfer these segments as series of pulses. The number of transferred pulses of a given segment is equal in count to the decimal number represented by the segment bits. Hence the name of this technique: Pulsed Decimal Communication (PDC). High-data rates are achieved by a three-step

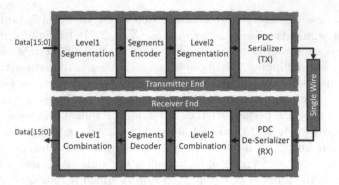

Fig. 2. Conceptual block diagram of PDC

encoding process of the raw bit stream so that the segments have decimal number representations that are as small as possible. The three-step encoding process comprises three operations: first-level (L1) segmentation, encoding (inversion, and/or reversal), and second-level (L2) segmentation. The conceptual block diagram of the encoding and transmission processes is shown in Fig. 2, whose blocks are explained in the following subsections.

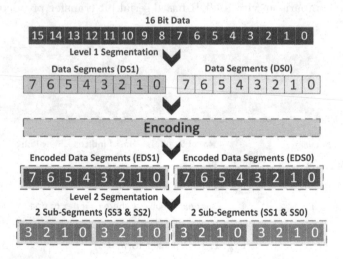

Fig. 3. PDC three-step encoding process

3.1 First Step: L1 Segmentation

The decimal number represented by the data word increases exponentially with the number of bits. The count of pulses to represent a number becomes large and it becomes infeasible to transfer this count in pulses. Therefore, segmentation is required to break a data word into several independent segments with lower number of bits, hence representing smaller numbers. It is mentioned in [10] that a segment size of 8 bits optimizes the number of delays for PIC to increase the data rate. For PDC, 8 bits is not an optimum segment size and the segments need to be cut down further before the pulses can be transferred. On the other hand, increasing the number of segments before encoding would decrease the data rate. This is because each time a segment is encoded, flags are generated to represent the type of encoding applied. The process of encoding will be explained in the following subsection. The encoding flags are also transmitted in the form of a separate pulse stream, and an increase in the number of segments increases the number of flag streams to be transferred, which would of course reduce the data rate. Additionally, there is an increased area and power overhead associated with the encoding of each of the segments. Therefore, it is not feasible to break the data word into a large number of segments before the encoding is applied. To address this, we have introduced two levels of segmentation, pre- *and* post-encoding as shown in Fig. 3. In the first segmentation level, data is broken into segments called *Data Segments (DS)* each of which is 8 bits long. One could think of applying encoding on a 16-bit data word instead of performing the first level of segmentation, but it has been experimentally observed that encoding 8 bits is far better than encoding 16 bits in order to reduce the decimal number represented by the segment bits.

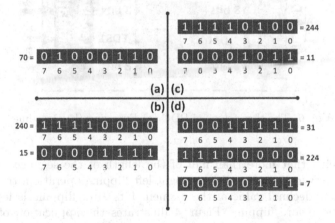

Fig. 4. PDC encoding: (a) No reversal or inversion (b) Reversal (c) Inversion (d) Inversion and reversal

3.2   Second Step: Encoding

The PDC encoding is similar to that of PIC [10]. Reducing the number of ON bits, within each segment, and mapping these bits to the locations with smallest possible indices results in a smaller decimal number represented by each segment. This can be achieved using bit-wise inversion and segment-wise reversal. Bit-wise inversion is a conditional one's complement operation on the segment bits, the

Pulses	Inverted	Reversed
1	NO	YES
2	YES	NO
3	YES	YES
0	NO	NO

Fig. 5. PDC flags

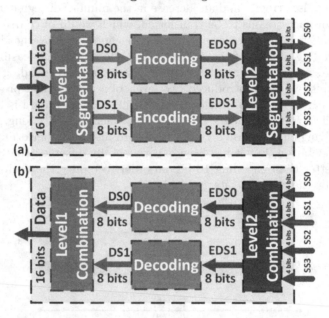

Fig. 6. The three steps of PDC (a) Encoding (b) Decoding

condition being that more than half of the length of the segment is occupied by ON bits. Reversal is a conditional right-left flipping operation, the condition being that the decimal value of the segment bits after flipping is less than its decimal value before flipping. Figure 4 illustrates the application of inversion and reversal on a 8-bit data segment. In particular, it shows that inversion and reversal alone cannot minimize the number of pulses. On the other hand, combining inversion and reversal results in the smallest decimal number, namely 7, for that particular example. One's complement and flipping on short data words are not only very easy to implement in hardware but also very energy-efficient. Each of the four types of encoding is represented by a flag number as shown in Fig. 5.

3.3 Third Step: L2 Segmentation

As mentioned earlier, PDC needs to have a second level of segmentation post-encoding to further reduce the number of pulses per segment. This second level of segmentation, shown in Fig. 3, breaks each data segment (DS) into *Sub-segments (SS)*, each of which is 4 bits long. The 4-bit length is the optimum segment size for PDC as will be explained in Sect. 4. The complete three-step process is shown in Fig. 6(a). EDS0 and EDS1 represent the two 8-bit encoded first-level data segments.

3.4 Serialization

The serializer collects the encoded data from the encoder and transmits it serially according to the format shown in Fig. 7. Unlike PIC, each segment is transmitted independently without any header to indicate the encoding flags. The body of the message includes the pulses of the L2 sub-segments (SS) only. The flag information is transmitted along with the start pulse prior to the transmission of SS's. As mentioned earlier, each flag is a 2-bit code representing one of the 4 encoding cases (Fig. 5) for each DS of the L1 segments. The PDC serializer combines all DS flag codes to generate one flag code that is 4 bits long, called the *CFlags*, as shown in Fig. 7. It must be remembered that in the absence of any encoding PIC used the flag code 4 instead of 0 because it needed at least one pulse to represent the absence of data pulses which is already assigned as another flag code. On the other hand, PDC replaces the flag code of 4 with 0 as the "CFlags" pulses are transmitted along with the start pulse, which helps in recognizing 0 without any additional pulse. "SSn" (SS0 to SS3) represents the number of pulses being transmitted for a particular L2 SS. Each of these parts is sent in the form of a pulse stream (one pulse is equal to 1 clock cycle), and each stream is followed by an inter-symbol delay, α, made of 4 clock cycles. Transmission is initiated with a start pulse followed by all the message pulses. It ends with two stop pulses. There is inter-symbol delay, α, of 4 clock cycles after the "Start+CFlags" and "Stop" pulses. The waveforms for PDC transmission are shown in Fig. 8.

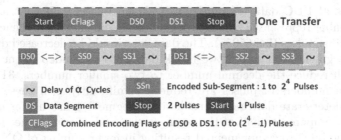

Fig. 7. PDC transmission format

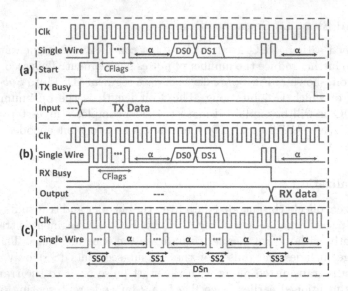

Fig. 8. (a) Transmission (b) Reception (c) L2 segment format

3.5 De-serialization, Decoding and Combination

The receiver counts the pulses of each stream using rising edge detection which eliminates the need for CDR. The count of CFlags pulses is used to infer the segment encoding type which will be used in the segment decoding process. Next, the count of each of the pulse streams is considered as SS. At the reception of last sub-segment SS3, all the sub-segments are combined and decoded to generate data segments, and the decoded segments are combined to assemble the full length of transmitted data. The complete process of three-step decoding is shown in Fig. 6(b), where EDS0 and EDS1 represent the received 8-bit encoded DS. The waveforms for PDC reception are shown in Fig. 8.

3.6 PDC Example

An example of PDC data transmission is shown in Fig. 9. If we transmit the decimal number represented by data without any segmentation and encoding, we need numerous pulses (i.e. 65055). The data rate would be decreased drastically. In the L1 segmentation step, if we break data into two independent segments then we will reduce the decimal number to two smaller numbers, 31 and 254. Though the numbers of pulses are reduced significantly, still these are large enough to deteriorate data rate considerably. Segment 1 has higher number of ON bits as compared to half of the segment size and, therefore, need encoding where all the bits are complemented resulting in fewer number of ON bits. The resulting segment number is increased to 224 instead of decreasing because the ON bits are now located at higher index numbers. This needs the second step of encoding that is to flip the segment bit-wise which results in a smaller number that is 7. The flag for segment 1 is set to $\{1,1\} = 3$ to indicate that both steps of encoding are applied. On the other hand, Segment 2 only need inversion of bits as it results in fewer ON bits which are located at lower index numbers. The resulting number in segment 2 is 1. The flag for Segment 2 is set to $\{1,0\} = 2$ to indicate that bits are inverted only. In L2 segmentation step, if we break data into four independent sub-segments then the number of pulses needed for each sub-segment would reduce further. Both flags are combined to generate one 4-bit CFlags. In serialization or transmission process, we have one start pulse, one CFlags with pulse count of 14, four sub-segments with pulse counts of 8, 1, 2, and 1, and two stop pulses. All of these pulse streams are then transmitted in a packet format as shown in Figs. 7, 8, and 9.

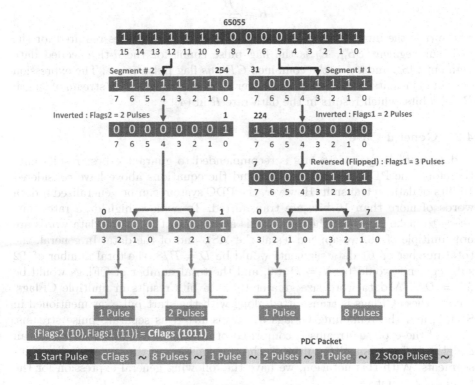

Fig. 9. PDC example

4   PDC Protocol Analysis and Optimization

4.1   Preliminary Equations

Let b_i^n denote the i-th bit in the n-th sub-segment and f_i^d denote the i-th bit of the flags code for d-th encoded data segment. We assume the number of bits per segment and the number of sub-segments in the data stream to be both 4. Then the total number of pulses C is given by

$$C = 3 + 6\alpha + \Phi_C + \sum_{n=0}^{3} P_n \qquad (1)$$

$$P_n = 1 + \sum_{i=0}^{3} 2^i b_i^n \qquad (2)$$

$$\Phi_C = 1 + \sum_{d=0}^{1} 4^d F_d \text{ with } F_d = f_0^d + 2f_1^d \qquad (3)$$

$$R = \frac{B}{TC} \qquad (4)$$

where α is the inter-symbol delay, P_n is the number of pulses required for the n-th sub-segment SS_n, F_d is the flag pulse count for the d-th encoded data segment DS_d, and Φ_C is the combined $CFlags$ flag pulse count. The expression of C in (1) results from a summation over all segments in a data stream of length $B = 16$ bits, which results in the data rate R in (4).

4.2   General Case

A data word length of 16 bits is recommended to guarantee best results and, therefore, the PDC discussion so far and the equations above have considered 16 bits of data to transmit. However, the PDC system can be generalized if data words of more than 16 bits are transmitted. To achieve high data rates, one needs to make sure that the data size is a multiple of 16. If the data words are not multiple of 16, we append 0's at the MSB end of the data. In general, the total number of $L1$ data segments would be $D = B/8$, the total number of $L2$ sub-segments would be $N = D \times 2$, and the total number of CFlags would be $M = D/2$. A data word size greater than 16 bits results in multiple CFlags. One of these CFlags is transmitted along with the start pulse, as mentioned in Sect. 3, and the remaining CFlags are transmitted as separate pulse streams. Each of these pulse streams is comprised of $CFlags + 1$ pulses followed by an α delay, and is transmitted prior to the transmission of the corresponding data segments. With this notation, we have the following general expression for the total pulse count

$$C = 2 + M + (M + N + 1)\alpha + \sum_{m=0}^{M-1} \Phi_{Cm} + \sum_{n=0}^{N-1} P_n \qquad (5)$$

where l is the size of the $L2$ sub-segment, which is 4 in our implementation of PDC. Recall that each of the Φ_{Cm} represents the encoding flags of two adjacent data segments. For example, if $B = 32$ bits, the number of CFlags would be $M = 2$. Φ_{C0} would represent the 16 LSBs (i.e., two data segments, DS0 and DS1). Similarly, Φ_{C1} would represent the 16 MSBs (i.e., the two next data segments, DS2 and DS3). The generalized transmission packet format is shown in Fig. 10.

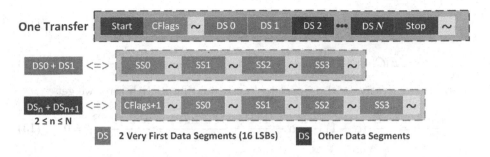

Fig. 10. Generalized PDC transmission format

4.3 Optimum Sub-Segment Size

The L2 sub-segment (SS) size is chosen to maximize data rate. For a short SS, α delays inserted between pulse streams to separate symbols increase linearly and reduce the data rate. Similarly, for longer SS, segments have large decimal number representations and, therefore, require a large number of pulses to transmit. The number of pulses increase exponentially with the size of SS, which in turn reduces the data rate rapidly. It is therefore intuitive that there is a segment size for which the data rate is maximum. For PDC, our experimental results have shown that the data rate is maximized when the number of bits per L2 SS is 4.

To find the optimum L2 sub-segment length, we will minimize the number of clock cycles needed to transmit the PDC packet. We know from the previous section that the number of segments is $N = B/l$. Because there is one CFlags for two consecutive segments, the number of CFlags would then be $M = N/2 = B/2l$. For a length l, the number of pulses P_n of (2) becomes

$$P_n = 1 + \sum_{i=0}^{l-1} 2^i b_i^n \qquad (6)$$

Assuming that bits 0 and 1 are equally likely, the expected value of P_n is

$$E[P_n] = \frac{2^l + 1}{2} \qquad (7)$$

Similarly, using

$$E[F_d] = E[f_0^d] + 2E[f_1^d] = \frac{1}{2} + 2 \times \frac{1}{2} = \frac{3}{2} \qquad (8)$$

the expected value of Φ_{Cm} as expressed in (3) is given by

$$E[\Phi_{Cm}] = 1 + E[F_0] + 4E[F_1] = 1 + \frac{3}{2} + 4 \times \frac{3}{2} = \frac{17}{2} \qquad (9)$$

Using $N = B/l$ and $M = B/2l$, the expected value of the total number of clock cycles C as given in (5) becomes

$$E[C] = 2 + M + (M + N + 1)\alpha + ME[\Phi_{Cm}] + NE[P_n] \qquad (10)$$

$$E[C] = 2 + M(\alpha + 1) + N\alpha + \alpha + \frac{17M}{2} + N\frac{2^l + 1}{2} \tag{11}$$

$$E[C] = 2 + \frac{B}{4l}(\alpha + 1) + \frac{B}{l}\alpha + \alpha + \frac{17B}{8l} + \frac{B(2^l + 1)}{2l} \tag{12}$$

Taking the derivative with respect to l and equating it with zero, we get

$$\frac{\partial E[C]}{\partial l} = -\frac{B}{4l^2}(\alpha + 1) - \frac{B}{l^2}\alpha - \frac{17B}{8l^2} + \frac{B\,2^l\ln(2)}{2l} - \frac{B\,2^l}{2\,l^2} - \frac{B}{2l^2} = 0 \tag{13}$$

$$-2(\alpha + 1) - 8\alpha - 17 + 4l\,2^l\,\ln(2) - 4\,2^l - 4 = 0 \tag{14}$$

$$2^l(l\,\ln(2) - 1) = \frac{1}{4}(23 + 10\alpha) \tag{15}$$

which gives the following expression of α as function of l

$$\alpha = \frac{2}{5}\left[2^l(l\,\ln(2) - 1) - \frac{23}{4}\right] \tag{16}$$

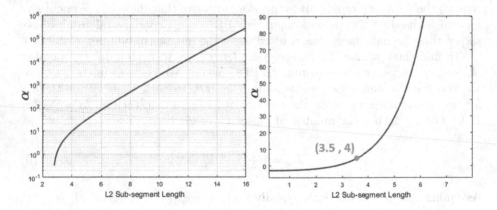

Fig. 11. α vs. L2 Sub-segment length

This function is plotted in Fig. 11 and can be used to obtain the optimum sub-segment size for any value of α. For instance, when $\alpha = 4$, we get $l_{opt} = 3.5 \approx 4$. An alternative graphical method to find l_{opt} for a given α is to plot the left- and right-hand sides of

$$l\,\ln(2) - 1 = \frac{1}{4}(23 + 10\alpha)2^{-l} \tag{17}$$

as function of l. The optimal segment size l is at the intersection of these two curves. Such plot is shown in Fig. 12 for $\alpha = 4$, which corresponds to

$$l\,\ln(2) - 1 = \frac{63}{4}2^{-l} \tag{18}$$

Again, the optimum value of the L2 sub-segment length is found to be

$$l_{opt} = 3.5 \approx 4 \tag{19}$$

If the sub-segment length is increased or decreased from this optimum value, the data rate declines rapidly. To achieve maximum data rate at a given cock frequency, one must therefore operate the PDC signaling with an L2 sub-segment length of 4 bits.

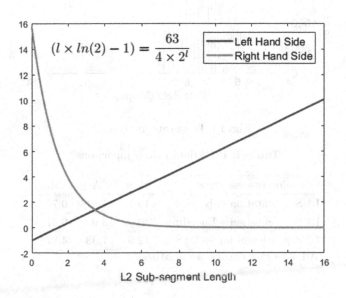

Fig. 12. Optimal segment length for $\alpha = 4$

4.4 Data Rate

PDC is dynamic in that the actual data rate of the protocol is dictated by the pulse C count which is very much data dependent as is clear from (1) and (5). We have analyzed the statistical distribution of PDC data rates using exhaustive sampling of 16-bit data words ($2^{16} - 1$ PRBS), each segmented into four 4-bit sub-segments. For data rate calculations, we use a 25 MHz clock. The analysis has shown that the three-step encoding process (L1 Segmentation + Encoding + L2 Segmentation) is generally needed not only to maximize the (average) data rate but also to tighten the distribution of dynamic rates around the average data rate. The effect is shown in Table 1. Note that after full three-step encoding, there is a significant improvement in the average data rate and a tightening of the data rate distributions around the average. The histogram of data rate is shown in Fig. 13.

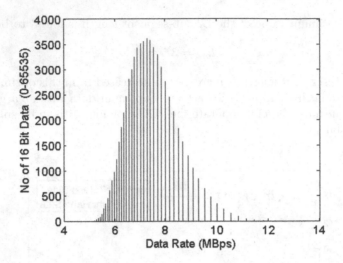

Fig. 13. Data rate analysis

Table 1. PDC data rate comparisons

Encoding process steps	*Max.	*Avg.	*Min.
L1 Segmentation only	19	1.81	0.75
L1 Segmentation + Encoding	19	3.92	0.97
L1 Seg. + Encoding + L2 Seg.	12.9	7.33	4.87

*All data rate entries are in Mb/s.

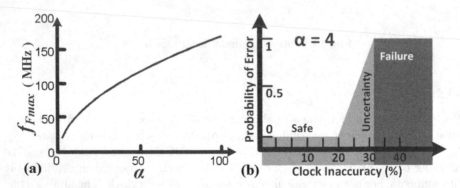

Fig. 14. (a) α vs Inaccuracy limit (b) Regions of operation ($f_S = 25$ MHz) [7]

4.5   Tolerance with Respect to Clock Variations

Even if similar clock generators are used at the transmitter and receiver end, there would be a slight difference between their clock frequencies due to the various sources of variability. Considering the slow speed end as a reference and keeping the inter-symbol delay α the same for both ends, the rate of the fast clock should not exceed a limit above which decoding errors start to occur [7]. In Fig. 14(a), we plot the maximum limit on the clock speed of the fast clock, f_{Fmax}, for a range of α while the slow clock, f_S, is at 25 MHz. Figure 6(b) identifies different regions of operation. Beyond the safe region of operation, there is a region of uncertainty in which errors start occurring randomly. At a certain level of clock discrepancy, total failure occurs due to the failure in detecting even a single inter-symbol delay. The recommended region of operation is of course the one delimited by f_{Fmax}.

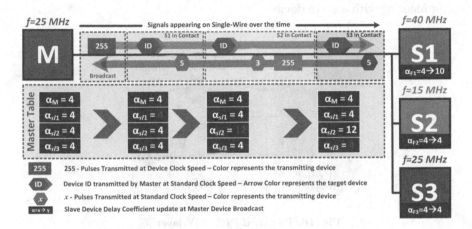

Fig. 15. An example of automatic parameter detection [9]

4.6   Automatic Protocol Configuration

While PDC is tolerant towards clock discrepancies, its per-device parameters have to be adapted in order to support high level of clocking differences. The device parameter setting may be done manually or at the factory in a way similar to existing low-power, single wire solutions. Not only does manual or factory setting method limits the scalability of IoT network to an arbitrary number of devices, but also it prevent the devices from communicating at the highest data rate allowed by the protocol. To overcome this limitation an algorithm for automatically detecting and setting the PDC protocol parameters at the power-on phase can be used that to help remove the restriction on the IoT devices in the PIC network to communicate at a pre-specified baud rate and allows the devices with different capabilities to communicate reliably. At power-on, based on clock-rate differences the master device configures all the slave devices connected to a single-channel network prior to the start of any device-to-device communication. Pulse count differences between the pulse trains at the transmitter and receiver are used in closed-form formulas to find a suitable inter-symbol delay coefficient so as to eliminate the need to know the exact clock rates at both ends of the link. An example flow of the configuration process is shown in Fig. 15 where

128   S. Muzaffar and I. (Abe) M. Elfadel

the master device broadcasts a clock pulse stream and then contacts the slave
devices one-by-one to receive their responses. Each of the slave devices receives
the incoming clock stream and compares with its local clock speed. At master
device request, if the device is at higher clock speed as compared to master, five
pulses are transmitted back and the slave device updates it's α accordingly. If
the device is at lower clock speed as compared to master, three pulses followed by
255 pulses are transmitted back at local clock rate. Depending on the response
format, the master updates a table of α entries for the slave devices. Later, the
master device picks up the corresponding α from the look-up table and starts
communicating with a slave device.

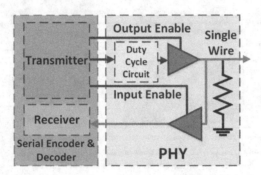

Fig. 16. Proposed PIC PHY layer [6]

4.7 Power Management

Although PDC [10] itself is power-efficient, the PDC physical layer can be the
source of significant power consumption. A PDC power management policy can
be used to improve further its ultra-low power characteristics without impacting
data rates. This policy shows that an additional 22% power saving at the PIC
PHY layer can be achieved using the duty cycle of the pulse as a power control
parameter, as shown in Fig. 16. A mathematical model helps in selecting the
physical design parameters related to PDC PHY power management. For an
input duty cycle of 20 ns, the implementation of this policy in 45 nm CMOS
technology shows that the smallest duty cycle of 0.39% can be generated to
achieve 22% of extra power saving.

4.8 Reliability

In this subsection, we analyze PDC in terms of its robustness and reliability
in comparison with PIC. We use packet failure rates as a comparison metric.
Considering the PIC transmission format for 16 bits of data, there exist several
locations in the packet which, if corrupted, may be the source of complete packet
failure. For instance, there are 8 to 16 locations of α delays, and each can be
a source of packet failure if it gets corrupted. This corruption makes it difficult

for the receiver to detect α and sample the subsequent pulse streams at the expected instants of transmission. Similarly, if the information on the number of indices (NOI, one for each packet) is not received successfully, there is no way for the receiver to know about the number of incoming index pulse streams. Additionally, the corruption of two sync pulses can also misalign the pulse streams during PIC decoding. The number of locations, PE_{PIC}, whose corruption in a PIC stream of 16 bits results in a complete packet failure during transmission has been found in the range

$$8 + 2NOI_{min} + 2 \leq PE_{PIC} \leq 8 + 2NOI_{max} + 2 \tag{20}$$

$$10 \leq PE_{PIC} \leq 18 \tag{21}$$

when $0 \leq NOI \leq 4$. Analyzing the PDC transmission stream, we know there would always be a fixed number of pulse streams that directly eliminates the threat of packet failure due to the NOI and sync pulses, as these are not included in the packet at all. In terms of α delays, there are only 6 locations ($PE_{PDC} = 6$) for all the possible 16 bit data words. This makes PDC simpler and more reliable even when compared with the best PIC case, $PE_{PIC} = 10$ in (21).

5   Experimental Results

A full experimental setup, similar to that of PIC [10], is implemented in Verilog on the Xilinx Virtex-7 FPGA platform. The prototype platform is used to verify PDC functionality and performance. Extensive simulations and real time hardware verification are performed in order to verify the results. To make a fair comparison with PIC, we have used 16-bit data words and a clock rate of 25 MHz as in the PIC testing system [10]. The same experimental flow is adopted in which the PDC transmitter sends the 16-bit data starting at 0 with an increment of 1 at each transmission. The receiver resends the same data back. The returned and original data words are compared to verify the complete round-trip chain.

To get the most realistic comparison with PIC in terms of power and area, we have synthesized the PDC system using GLOBALFOUNDRIES 65 nm technology and found that PDC consumes around 25 μW with a gate count of around 2150, while offering dynamic data rates in the range of 4.87–12.9 Mb/s (7.33 Mb/s average) with a 25-MHz clock. As compared to PIC, the PDC increases average data rate by 78%, makes the transmission more reliable with respect to packet failure rates, and still remains well within the power and area budget of PIC. Table 2 shows a comparison between PIC and PDC. In Fig. 17, an overall comparison of PIC and PDC is presented. Along with the increased data rate, the gate count, power consumption and energy per bit in PDC are also reduced as compared to PIC. The reliability in terms of vulnerable locations is also reduced by 40% as compared to the best reliability case in PIC transmission.

Table 3 presents a comparison of PDC with CDR based simple serial transfer technique. The ASIC synthesis results show that PDC can reduce power consumption by more than 72% and area by more than 89% as compared to the best cases of CDR based serial transfer techniques available to-date.

Table 2. Synthesis results

	Data rate (Mb/s)	Power (μW)	Avg. E_b (pJ/bit)	Area (gate count)
PDC	4.87–12.9 (7.33 Avg.)	≈25	3.41	≈2150
PIC	3.1–8.5 (4.1 Avg.)	≈26.6	6.49	≈2356

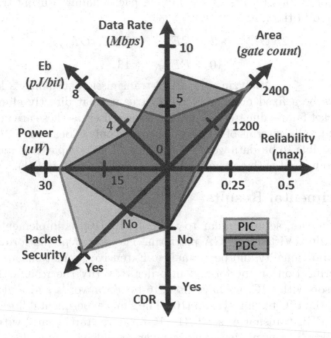

Fig. 17. PDC vs. PIC

Table 3. PDC comparison with simple-serial

	Power (μW)			Area (gate count)			
	SRL[a]	CDR	Total[d] (PI)[e]	SRL	CDR[c]	Total[d] (PI)[e]	
PDC	25	N/A	25	2150	N/A	2150	65 nm
NST[b]	32.1	70	102.1 (75.5%)	1327	15600	16927 (87.3%)	90 nm [12]
		62.5	94.6 (73.6%)		60000	61327 (96.5%)	90 nm [14]
		90	122.1 (79.5%)		N/A	N/A	90 nm [15]
		57.5	89.6 (72.1%)		19800	21127 (89.8%)	65 nm [16]
		60.6	92.7 (73%)		N/A	N/A	28 nm [13]

[a]Serializer
[b]Normal Serial Transfer
[c]Estimated calculation
[d]SRL+CDR
[e]%Increase as compared to PDC

6   Conclusions

Pulsed Decimal Communication (PDC) is an improved version of Pulsed Index Communication (PIC). It is a novel, simple yet robust method of signaling over single-channels that fulfils the requirements for high-data rate, ultra-low power protocols for IoT sensors. The concept of transmitting the indices of ON bits is replaced with the transmission of reduced decimal numbers. The PDC segmentation and encoding process reduces the overall number of transmission pulses by reducing decimal numbers, hence improving the data rate by 78% with respect to PIC. The average data rate is 7.33 Mb/s with a 25-MHz clock consuming a power of $25uW$ with a gate count of 2150 in 65 nm technology. Unlike PIC, there are fewer inter-symbol delays α in the PDC packet. Moreover, a fixed number of pulse streams is used for transmission, thus providing a simpler and more reliable communication technique that results in a significant decrease in packet failures, especially for low-end devices and sensors. The elimination of variations in the number of pulse streams makes the use of error detection and correction schemes easier. Like PIC, the PDC reduces silicon area and power consumption significantly by eliminating the need for a CDR. It is also robust with respect to skews, jitters, and clock variations as its decoding is based on counting the rising edges of the transmitted pulses. Additionally, all the presented PIC-related work for robustness analysis [7], auto detection of communication parameters [9], and power management [6] are valid for PDC without any change.

Acknowledgments. This work has been supported by the Semiconductor Research Corporation (SRC) under the Abu Dhabi-SRC Center of Excellence on Energy-Efficient Electronic Systems (ACE4S), Contract 2013 HJ2440, with customized funding from the Mubadala Investment Company, Abu Dhabi, UAE.

References

1. Byun, J., Kim, S.H., Kim, D.: Lilliput: ontology-based platform for IoT social networks. In: IEEE International Conference on Services Computing, Anchorage, AK, USA, June–July 2014, pp. 139–146 (2014)
2. Dayu, S., Huaiyu, X., Ruidan, S., Zhiqiang, Y.: A GEO-related IoT applications platform based on Google map. In: 7th IEEE International Conference on e-Business Engineering (ICEBE), Shanghai, China, pp. 380–384, November 2010
3. dos Reis Filho, C.A., da Silva, E.P., Azevedo, E.D.L., Seminario, J.A.P., Dibb, L.: Monolithic data circuit-terminating unit (DCU) for a one-wire vehicle network. In: Proceedings of the 24th European Solid-State Circuits Conference (ESSCIRC 1998), Hague, Netherlands, pp. 228–231, September 1998
4. Hou, J.M., Chen, C.Y.: A sensor information gateway based on thing interaction in IoT-IMS communication platform. In: Tenth International Conference on Intelligent Information Hiding and Multimedia Signal Processing (IIH-MSP), Kitakyushu, Japan, pp. 835–838, August 2014
5. MAXIM. OneWireViewer User's Guide, Version 1.4. AN3358 (2009)
6. Muzaffar, S., Elfadel, I.A.M.: Power management of pulsed-index communication protocols. In: 33rd IEEE International Conference on Computer Design (ICCD), New York, NY, USA, pp. 375–378, October 2015

7. Muzaffar, S., Elfadel, I.A.M.: Timing and robustness analysis of pulsed-index protocols for single-channel IoT communications. In: 23rd IFIP/IEEE International Conference on Very Large Scale Integration (VLSI-SoC 2015), Daejeon, South Korea, pp. 225–230, October 2015

8. Muzaffar, S., Elfadel, I.A.M.: A versatile hardware platform for the development and characterization of IoT sensor networks. In: 59th IEEE International Midwest Symposium on Circuits and Systems (MWSCAS 2016), Abu Dhabi, UAE, pp. 1–4, October 2016

9. Muzaffar, S., Saeed, N., Elfadel, I.A.M.: Automatic protocol configuration in single-channel low-power dynamic signaling for IoT devices. In: 24th IFIP/IEEE International Conference on Very Large Scale Integration (VLSI-SoC 2016), Tallinn, Estonia, pp. 1–6, September 2016

10. Muzaffar, S., Yoo, J., Shabra, A., Elfadel, I.A.M.: A pulsed-index technique for single-channel, low-power, dynamic signaling. In: Design, Automation and Test In Europe (DATE 2015), Grenoble, France, pp. 1485–1490, March 2015

11. Muzaffar, S., Elfadel, I.A.M.: A pulsed decimal technique for single-channel, dynamic signaling for IoT applications. In: 25th IFIP/IEEE International Conference on Very Large Scale Integration (VLSI-SoC), Abu Dhabi, UAE, pp. 1–6, October 2017

12. Loh, M., Emami-Neyestanak, A.: All-digital CDR for high-density, high-speed I/O. In: 12th IEEE Symposium on VLSI Circuits (VLSIC 2010), Honolulu, HI, USA, pp. 147–148, June 2010

13. Soh, L.-K., Wong, W.-T.: A 2.5–12.5 Gbps interpolator-based clock and data recovery circuit for FPGA. In: 4th Asia Symposium on Quality Electronic Design (ASQED), Penang, Malaysia, pp. 373–379, July 2012

14. Loh, M., Emami-Neyestanak, A.: A 3x9 Gb/s shared, all-digital CDR for high-speed, high-density I/O. IEEE J. Solid-State Circ. (JSSC) **47**(3), 641–651 (2012)

15. Du, Q., Zhuang, J., Kwasniewski, T.: A 2.5 Gb/s, low power clock and data recovery circuit. In: 20th Canadian Conference on Electrical and Computer Engineering (CCECE), Vancouver, BC, Canada, pp. 526–529, April 2007

16. Urano, Y., Yun, W.-J., Kuroda, T., Ishikuro, H.: A 1.26 mW/Gbps 8 locking cycles versatile all-digital CDR with TDC combined DLL. In: 45th IEEE International Symposium on Circuits and Systems (ISCAS 2013), Beijing, China, pp. 1576–1579, May 2013

Electromigration Analysis of VLSI Circuits Using the Finite Element Method

Matthias Thiele$^{(\boxtimes)}$, Steve Bigalke, and Jens Lienig

Institute of Electromechanical and Electronic Design (IFTE),
Dresden University of Technology, Dresden, Germany
{matthias.thiele,steve.bigalke,jens.lienig}@tu-dresden.de
https://www.ifte.de

Abstract. Addressing electromigration (EM) during physical design has become crucial to ensure reliable integrated circuits. Simulation methods, such as the finite element method (FEM), are increasingly overwhelmed by the complexity of the task. With further technology scaling, it is predicted that FEM will not be usable anymore for a full-chip EM analysis due to complexity reasons. To address this bottleneck, we present a new methodology enabling an FEM-based full-chip EM analysis for future technologies down to 10 nm feature sizes. Our solution reduces analysis costs significantly by establishing pre-validated layout patterns without losing accuracy of the verification results. We thoroughly evaluate the necessary pattern geometries, pattern library size and the calculation time savings. We show that a number of 10 to 20 different patterns is sufficient for generation and analysis of layouts provided that the same pitch is used for each metal layer. Our full-chip meta-model EM analysis allows speedups of at least 10X compared to current FEM-based verification methods.

Keywords: FEM · Electromigration · Interconnect · Reliability · Physical verification · Routing

1 Introduction

Excessive current density within interconnects is a major concern for integrated circuit (IC) designers because it causes electromigration (EM). Due to smaller feature sizes, this is a growing reliability issue in modern ICs [1]. While analog designers have been aware of this issue for some time, digital designs are now being affected as well [2–4].

EM is a migration process mostly driven by momentum transfer between electrons and metal ions of the wire. It causes damage through formation of voids and hillocks. While directly depending on current density, damage takes place mostly in locations of inhomogeneous electric currents, such as vias or non-linear wiring shapes.

© IFIP International Federation for Information Processing 2019
Published by Springer Nature Switzerland AG 2019
M. Maniatakos et al. (Eds.): VLSI-SoC 2017, IFIP AICT 500, pp. 133–152, 2019.
https://doi.org/10.1007/978-3-030-15663-3_7

EM analysis by simulation helps to find excessive current densities in the layout. Hence, current-density verification has emerged as an important verification step in VLSI physical design. The most common method of analysis is the finite element method (FEM). While it has been widely accepted in analog layout verification, using FEM in significantly more complex digital circuits faces numerous challenges.

FEM uses meshes for discretization of arbitrary shapes of continuous matter (Fig. 1). Each node and element of the mesh has its degrees of freedom to contribute to a linear system of differential equations. Therefore, the size of this system of equations and the calculation time depends on the number of nodes in the mesh.

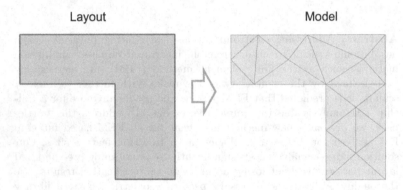

Layout   Model

Fig. 1. Example for meshing of a model for FEM simulation.

Digital integrated circuits usually contain a large number of transistors and nets. Additionally, current densities are growing with decreasing feature sizes [1]. To make matters worse, current density limits are also shrinking due to smaller structure sizes (Fig. 2 and Sect. 2).

As stated by [1], all minimum-sized wires in integrated circuits have been EM-affected since 2018. Subsequently, all wiring elements (segments, vias) of these circuits must be subjected to EM verification and analysis; totaling billions of elements for some circuits.

As FEM is commonly used for detailed analyses, the complexity of future circuits will demand excessive calculation cost. For full-chip analysis, other simulation methods are more time-efficient, but with the drawback of less detailed results and information loss in terms of potential void locations, for example. To the authors' knowledge, only FEM and similar methods, such as the finite-difference method (FDM), possess the capability of spatially resolved analysis to visualize excessive current densities.

The FDM is numerically very simple and therefore well suited for theoretical analysis or very fast calculations. Due to its simplicity, its results are not as accurate as with FEM. As its name suggests, the system of equations is based on the differences in the degrees of freedom.

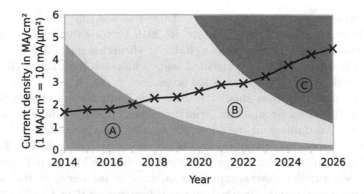

Fig. 2. Evolution of the required current density for driving four inverter gates for leading edge technologies according to ITRS roadmap [1]. As also shown, the maximum tolerable current density limits are shrinking due to smaller structure sizes. Region A/green: local EM issues, region B/yellow: all wires EM-affected, region C/red: no EM-solutions known yet. (Color figure online)

A similar methodology exists in the finite volume method (FVM). It uses polyhedrons to divide the given geometry, while solving the equations only at the center of each polyhedron. The FVM is best suited for conservational equations, such as mass flow calculations for fluid and gas transport. It can be applied to migration when modeling atomic flux similar to gas diffusion.

FDM and FVM are less favorable for EM simulations then FEM due to their reduced accuracy and the missing availability of simulation tools. FEM based verification will only be usable in the future if we achieve a significant reduction in simulation time. To meet this demand, we proposed in [5] a new methodology that reduces simulation time at least tenfold by using FEM for pre-layout pattern analysis without accuracy loss.

This chapter extends our previous work [5] significantly by describing in detail the implementation of the pattern generation process (Sect. 6). We also performed a more elaborate quantification of the benefits of our approach. Furthermore, the basic simulation methods are discussed in detail.

The remainder of this chapter is structured as follows. We first discuss the EM challenges of future VLSI design (Sect. 2), introduce the FEM as a method for EM analysis (Sect. 3) and formulate its limitations (Sect. 4). A solution for the complexity problem is presented in Sect. 5, accompanied by an implementation of the pattern generation method in Sect. 6 and a verification of its benefits in Sect. 7. Section 8 summarizes our results.

2   The Need for EM Analysis

Size reduction of semiconductor structures is mainly driven by the need for higher circuit performance, efficiency at higher frequencies and smaller footprints. Furthermore, line widths and wire cross-sectional areas decrease over time to meet routing requirements of semiconductors. Table 1 shows that the cross-sectional area of Metal 1 shrinks from 1600 nm^2 in 2016 to roughly 600 nm^2 in 2020. Although currents are decreasing as well due to shrinking gate capacitances and supply voltages (see Table 1), current densities increase because of the significantly larger decrease of cross-sectional areas.

To make matters worse, smaller feature sizes limit the maximum tolerable current densities, because small material defects will cause a dramatic change in resistance or even damage of the wires. As a result, maximum tolerable current densities must decrease to maintain a constant reliability [1,2]. The ITRS [1] indicates that all minimum-sized interconnects have been EM-affected since 2018. Therefore, any further downscaling of wire sizes is increasingly restricted by current density constraints (marked by the yellow region B in Fig. 2).

Taking into account that the total interconnect length per IC will continue to increase, reliability requirements per length unit of the wires need to increase in order to maintain overall IC reliability. However, the future decrease in interconnect reliability due to EM – as noted above – conflicts with these requirements. As the ITRS states that there are no known solutions to meet the EM-related reliability requirements of technologies in the near future (Fig. 2, red region C), there is a strong need for time-efficient, full-chip EM analysis.

3   Finite Element Method for EM Analysis

3.1   General Approach for EM Analysis

The finite element method can help analyzing the EM susceptibility by different approaches. The most obvious application of FEM in EM analysis is the calculation of current densities. As it is impracticable to calculate current densities analytically, the use of finite elements enables to lower the calculation costs. Current densities are calculated by solving the linear field equation for the electric field under voltage or current boundary conditions [6].

Nevertheless, not only current density influences migration. Also temperature and, especially at small feature sizes, mechanical stress must be considered in the simulation. This multi-physics problem is described by the diffusion equation [7] and results in an atomic flux under electromigration, thermomigration and mechanical stress as in

$$J_{\text{total}} = J_{\text{EM}} + J_{\text{TM}} + J_{\text{SM}}, \tag{1}$$

where J_{total} is the whole mass flux, and J_{EM}, J_{TM}, J_{SM} describe the mass flux caused by electromigration, thermomigration and stress migration, respectively.

Diffusion can be determined using quasi-static simulation by calculating the initial atomic flow. Lifetime and robustness will be estimated by extrapolation of this flow.

The applicability of finite element models for simulating migration processes and void growth until failures occur has been shown in [8,9]. However, those simulations are very time-consuming and therefore not applicable to a full-chip EM analysis in VLSI physical design.

Table 1. Technology parameters based on the ITRS, 2013 edition [1]; maximum currents and current densities for copper at 105 °C

Year	2016	2018	2020	2022	2024	2026
Gate Length (nm)	15.34	12.78	10.65	8.88	7.4	6.16
On-chip local clock frequency (GHz)	4.555	4.927	5.329	5.764	6.234	6.743
DC equivalent maximum current (μA)[a]	29.09	23.19	16.52	12.40	10.00	7.90
Metal 1 properties						
Width – halfpitch (nm)	28.35	22.50	17.86	14.17	11.25	8.93
Aspect ratio	2.0	2.0	2.0	2.1	2.1	2.2
Layer thickness (nm)[a]	56.70	45.00	35.72	29.76	23.63	19.65
Cross sectional area (nm^2)[a]	1607.4	1012.5	638.0	421.7	265.8	175.5
DC equivalent current densities (MA/cm^2)						
Maximum current density without EM degradation[b]	3.0	1.8	1.1	0.7	0.4	0.3
Maximum current density (solution unknown)[b]	15.4	9.3	5.6	3.4	2.1	1.2
Required current density for driving four inverter gates	1.81	2.29	2.59	2.94	**3.76**	**4.50**

[a] Calculated values, based on given width W, aspect ratio A/R, and current density J in [1], as follows: layer thickness $T = A/R \times W$, cross-sectional area $A = W \times T$ and current $I = J \times A$.
[b] Approximated values from the ITRS Figure INTC9 [1].
All remaining values are from the ITRS 2013 edition [1].

3.2   Benefits of FEM

As already indicated, FEM has great benefits compared to faster techniques. In contrast to lumped element simulations, FEM offers simulation results with spatial resolution. This information is especially important when dealing with problems like EM, which cause failures by local damage. At the same time, FEM is more flexible and less time-consuming than analytic or continuous methods, when dealing with complex geometries. By scaling of the elements' size, calculation effort can be optimized depending on accuracy requirements.

3.3   Application in Physical Design

Current physical design tools such as [10–12] have built-in functionality for current density and, thus, EM analysis. Most analysis tools are based on the finite element method for calculating current density and temperatures. Still, those practical CAD applications only implement a small portion of the capability FEM tools used in other disciplines possess. Mostly, they use single-physics elements due to limitation of computing time. These tools cannot consider all effects connected with EM, such as mechanical stress and temperature gradients.

Analog designers make extensive use of the offered analysis tools. In digital designs, the available tools are increasingly limited to power and ground nets due to the excessive number of signal nets. Some authors, e.g. in [13], propose filter functions to address this complexity problem. Those filters rely on the availability of current information for all nets. This, and the fact that all nets become potentially critical in future digital designs, limit the use of the mentioned filters. As a result of this increase in verification complexity, FEM will no longer be usable for full-chip current density calculation.

4   Problem Formulation: Limitations of FEM

4.1   Model Size Restriction

More and more nets are becoming EM-affected in digital designs [1], while at the same time design complexity increases due to down-scaling. It is practically impossible to use FEM for digital full-chip analysis. Based on the ITRS roadmap, Fig. 3 shows a prediction of the analysis problem complexity for current and future digital circuits.

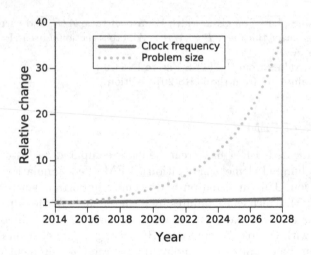

Fig. 3. Complexity of finite element simulations of all signal nets in current and future technologies, as predicted by the ITRS relative to 2014. The respective clock frequency of CPUs is also depicted for comparison. Calculated from ITRS [1].

FEM works with meshed geometric models, where physical properties are assigned to discrete nodes and elements. Generally, precision and calculation time of FEM problems depend on model size, i.e. on the number of nodes and elements of the mesh. To gain a result in a given time, model size has to be limited. Precision demands a certain number of nodes per volume, therefore, the simulated volume per FE model has to be restricted.

FEM is limited to small portions of a layout. Hence, critical layout areas have to be identified and filtered. However, filters, like those proposed in [13], will no longer mitigate the complexity problem. Hence, FEM will not be usable anymore, as simulation cost would grow enormously.

Due to the large scale of whole chip models, the number of sub-models used in FEM will increase with technology progress. To limit this increase, we suggest the use of re-usable sub-models. That means, *standardized* sub-units of the interconnect structure have to be established and re-used. This leads to a layout composed of a large number of few, pre-determined basic building blocks in terms of interconnect structures that would facilitate the FEM analysis. The gained efficiency for EM verification from our approach increases with growing layout complexity.

4.2 Atomic Scale Restriction

Further downscaling imposes limitations due to influences of the atomic scale. At feature sizes in the range of 4 to 5 nm, single atoms affect the failure probability, i.e., if there is a failure or not. Hence, the wire cannot be regarded as a continuum. The violation of this fundamental demand for FEM disallows further use of this method in those size ranges. When going near this point, strong inhomogeneities may occur. These can be dealt with by using non-linear models for EM calculation as it has been applied to different other inhomogeneities on a micro scale. Hence, our approach is restricted to all technologies with a metal pitch not smaller than 10 nm.

5 Our Approach: Pattern Verification

Our approach uses the advantages of FEM without the necessity of large models or a great number of smaller FE models consuming a lot of computing power. The basic principle is to simulate patterns of wire structures that are used for routing afterwards. Layout patterns with a high repetition rate in layout, i.e., that are common, have to be determined and pre-simulated. Hence, simulation costs of the final layout verification can be significantly reduced (see Sect. 7.3).

5.1 Basic Principle

We propose a pre-layout simulation of metalization patterns and the restriction of routing to those simulated patterns. Our method is based on the following (Fig. 4):

- Technology restrictions will be taken into account for FE simulation.
- All common patterns needed for interconnection analysis are generated and simulated by FEM.
- These pre-defined layout patterns comprise typical wiring elements, such as via connections, long and short wires, and in-layer junctions (T-shaped or crossing).

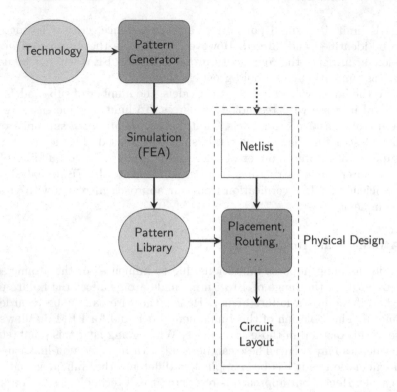

Fig. 4. Layout synthesis using our proposed pattern verification method.

- The EM robustness of the patterns for individual current constraints is verified by simulation.
- Routing is performed using wiring patterns suitable for particular currents of the nets.

While these measures alone cannot guarantee a reliable design, they are the foundation to enable a full-chip verification to ensure circuit reliability (see subsequent sections).

5.2   Pattern Choice

The requirements for deducing a full-chip verification from the verification of all its elements are as follows:

- currents should be equally distributed at model boundaries,
- temperature influences and mechanical stress from the neighborhood should be negligible, and
- diffusion at the boundaries should be known or zero.

The last point is easily satisfiable if model boundaries with current flow are always at the boundary between different materials, e.g. at tungsten plugs connecting to silicon or metal-via interfaces containing diffusion barriers. However, the first requirement is not fulfilled in this case, as the interfaces are always near current crowding regions due to turns of the current direction from horizontal to vertical or vice versa. By adding geometric appendices to the model at such boundaries, the correct current distribution at the boundary can be achieved while the results inside the appendix are ignored.

Mechanical and thermal influences are harder to neglect, as they do not only influence a pattern or segment from two sides but they take effect from all around the simulation model. Both temperature and mechanical stress are transmitted through the surrounding dielectric material.

5.3 From Pattern Verification to Full Chip Verification

We will show how FE simulations can be performed without knowing the surrounding of a wiring pattern, as this is always the case when running a simulation prior to routing. A successful verification using a limited number of FE simulation is based on one of the following constraint assumptions:

1. A worst case analysis (all patterns are verified for the largest current in the circuit) is performed, where only the constraints have to be verified for the full-chip verification. This leads to robust, but over-sized designs.
2. An average estimation of constraints (FE simulations for typical loads) is performed. This can lead to partially unreliable systems.
3. The exact constraints are calculated. This is not feasible in pre-layout analysis.
4. New estimation metrics for constraints based on known current values are used. This approach works with meta-models of the design patterns that can be used in a full-chip analysis using concentrated elements.
5. Different variants of the same pattern type are simulated, where a certain pattern can be selected from the library depending on actual constraints.

The approach (4) using meta-models is the most promising. It demands some additional simulation time during or after routing, but this time is limited due to the use of simple models. The proposed meta-models are mathematical relations between FE model constraints and result quantities, e.g. maximum current density. Additional constraints to be implemented are current values (from circuit simulation) and hydrostatic stress. As a first implementation, both are only propagated at the electrically conducting boundaries between neighboring interconnect patterns. Therefore, a limited amount of additional simulation data is created.

When proceeding to smaller scale, it might also become necessary to propagate hydrostatic stress between wiring elements that are not electrically connected. Here lies the limitation of this approach, because the full-chip model complexity will then increase comparably to interconnect simulation models incorporating capacitive crosstalk.

Given the before mentioned circumstances, the pattern analysis allows a reliability prediction of the entire wiring structure.

6   Pattern Generation

6.1   Number of Needed Patterns

A large variety of patterns might be necessary to model the whole wiring of an integrated circuit. The number of needed patterns depends strongly on the metallization layer system and the technology/routing constraints of each interconnect layer. However, a small number of patterns is required if all considered metal layers have the same routing pitch and only single vias are used. This simplified case will be analyzed in the following section. Redundant vias and a variance in wire widths or interconnect pitches will increase the pattern number, while restrictions in routing direction or via pitch will decrease this number.

6.2   Generation of Sample Patterns

Using the above mentioned restrictions (i.e., only one wiring pitch for all layers, only single vias, and minimum wire widths), the number of possible patterns can be calculated. If we do not restrict the routing to certain directions on each layer, there are four ways (in a rectilinear or Manhattan routing fashion) to approach a via on a metal layer. We label these directions north (n), west (w), south (s), and east (e) as they can be represented by the directions of a compass. Every combination of directions, e.g. n, nw or we, can be allowed on a single layer, as the via of interest can be a Steiner or branching point in the net. We add the letter c to mark the center of our pattern, hence, we obtain cn, cnw or cwe as the names of our single-layer patterns. These combinations in one layer can be connected to each of these combinations on a second wiring layer, e.g. cn_c_cnw or cnw_c_cwe, where the c between the two underscores stands for a single via in the center, and the letters following the second underscore represent the directions on the second layer. This nomenclature also allows for redundant vias at either of the compass directions, e.g. cn_cn_cnw, which we do not consider in the remainder of this chapter. Figure 5 illustrates the nomenclature for some application-relevant patterns.

Theoretically, there are $2^8 = 256$ different patterns for a via structure if we assume that each wire direction can either be present or absent. The number of patterns can be dramatically reduced by looking for equal patterns, that can be transformed into each other only by rotation around the z-axis or mirroring at the xz or yz-plane. Obviously, up to eight different transformations are possible, while some of the transformation results end up in identical patterns. We developed a brute-force algorithm to calculate the number of distinct patterns (Algorithm 1).

Please note, that mirroring at the xy-plane leads to a different pattern, as the layer structure is not necessarily symmetric, e.g., there are usually diffusion barriers at the lower end of a via. This is especially the case when considering interconnects that are made by the dual-damascene technology.

The further naming convention for our distinct patterns is the following: We start on the lower metal layer in the north and continue counter-clockwise on the

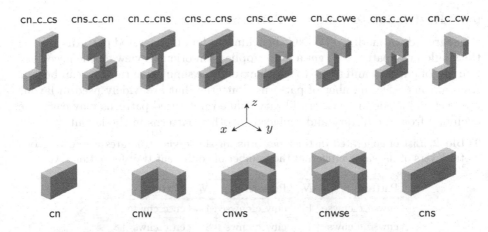

Fig. 5. Example patterns with their names; top: typical two-layer via patterns; bottom: all distinct single-layer patterns in rectilinear routing.

Algorithm 1. Generate a list of distinct patterns for single-via structures

---

1: **for** $i=0$ to 255 **do**
2:      $pattern \leftarrow$ binary code of i
3:      $variant[0..3] \leftarrow$ rotate($pattern$)
4:      $variant[4..7] \leftarrow$ rotate(mirror($pattern$))
5:      **if** $pattern$ **not** in $variants\_list$ **then**
6:          add $pattern$ to $pattern\_list$
7:          add $variants$ to $variants\_list$

---

lower layer and finish on the second metal layer. That is, cnw is preferred over cne and cns_c_cw over cns_c_ce. The 55 patterns, generated by Algorithm 1, are listed in Table 2. There are different numbers of equivalent patterns, that can be transformed into one distinct pattern. This number is 1, 2, 4 or 8, depending on the symmetry properties of each pattern.

In addition to the via patterns in Table 2, there are five single-layer patterns (see Fig. 5, lower line), of which only three (cnw, $cnws$ and $cnwse$) are useful for FEM analysis. The electrical contacts of the pattern can either be at the ends of the wire segments that continue to certain compass directions or on the top or bottom surface of the centered via. The latter is obvious in the case of via pillars running across more than just two metal layers. Hence, more than the 55 patterns might be needed if we also consider branching of nets into some of the middle layers of a via pillar.

6.3   Restriction to Relevant Patterns

We searched our modified MCNC[1] benchmarks for all generated patterns and for the single-layer patterns to get a more application-oriented view on the necessary number of patterns and to see to which extend the simulation runtime can benefit from an increasing number of patterns. Patterns that are widely used in layout are best to include in a pattern library, while rarely used patterns may easily be excluded from the library and replaced by other patterns in the layout.

Table 2. List of generated distinct patterns for single via structures connecting two metal layers of the same pitch and the number of equivalent transformations N_{tr}.

Pattern	N_{tr}	Pattern	N_{tr}	Pattern	N_{tr}
cnwse_c_cnwse	1	cnw_c_cnwse	4	cn_c_cnwse	4
cnwse_c_cnws	4	cnw_c_cnws	8	cn_c_cnws	8
cnwse_c_cnw	4	cnw_c_cnw	4	cn_c_cnwe	4
cnwse_c_cns	2	cnw_c_cnse	8	cn_c_cnw	8
cnwse_c_cn	4	cnw_c_cns	8	cn_c_cns	4
cnwse_c_c	1	cnw_c_cne	8	cn_c_cn	4
cnws_c_cnwse	4	cnw_c_cn	8	cn_c_cwse	4
cnws_c_cnws	4	cnw_c_cse	4	cn_c_cws	8
cnws_c_cnwe	8	cnw_c_cs	8	cn_c_cwe	4
cnws_c_cnw	8	cnw_c_c	4	cn_c_cw	8
cnws_c_cnse	4	cns_c_cnwse	2	cn_c_cs	4
cnws_c_cns	4	cns_c_cnws	4	cn_c_c	4
cnws_c_cne	8	cns_c_cnwe	4	c_c_cnwse	1
cnws_c_cn	8	cns_c_cnw	8	c_c_cnws	4
cnws_c_cwe	4	cns_c_cns	2	c_c_cnw	4
cnws_c_cw	4	cns_c_cn	4	c_c_cns	2
cnws_c_ce	4	cns_c_cwe	2	c_c_cn	4
cnws_c_c	4	cns_c_cw	4	c_c_c	1
		cns_c_c	2		

The results in Tables 3 and 4 show clearly that only a fraction of the generated patterns is found in our benchmark layout. In the analyzed case, not even half of the patterns can be found, while some of them only exist in a small amount.

If we remove the rather *exotic* patterns, e.g., all patterns with a sum (last line of Tables 3 and 4) below 20, we can reduce the number of necessary patterns to 13 in our case. This will enable a compact pattern library. As an increase in library size is inevitable for more complex metalization systems, we should preemptively restrict the library size for our simplified case. A number of 10 to 20 distinct patterns is necessary for the analyzed case.

[1] The MCNC benchmark suite was originally obtained from [14] and adjusted to contain only single vias as outlined in [15].

Table 3. Counts of Patterns in the layouts of the MCNC benchmark suite (part 1/2). The first two columns contain single-layer patterns (cnw and cnws), the remainder shows different via patterns.

Benchmark	Count per pattern									
	cnw	cnws	c_c_c	c_c_cn	c_c_cns	c_c_cnws	c_c_cnw	cn_c_c	cn_c_cw	cn_c_cs
mcc1	552	0	146	1074	76	0	0	306	3988	2
mcc2	2704	1	1151	6601	45	0	0	1215	25175	1
primary1	1606	8	78	943	76	0	0	96	3936	13
primary2	5961	45	271	3475	445	0	0	372	16672	60
s13207	3937	28	205	1204	26	0	1	395	10631	9
s15850	4492	42	303	1544	39	0	0	523	12717	6
s38417	11362	124	599	3429	88	0	1	1002	31145	22
s38584	15649	140	957	4748	145	1	0	1550	41572	18
s5378	1537	9	132	685	15	0	0	243	5019	2
s9234	1480	19	93	486	4	0	0	155	4008	6
struct	3402	19	174	1478	146	0	0	242	5133	29
∑	52682	435	4109	25667	1105	1	2	6099	159996	168

A larger number of patterns might be necessary for different interconnect technologies. This applies especially when different metal wire widths, vias of different sizes, or redundant vias are used. Hence, we conclude, that up to 200 different patterns will be sufficient to tackle interconnect structures with different pitches and redundant vias.

7   Verification

We choose the following method in order to verify our approach: Firstly (A), we show that partitioning FE models of the wiring is possible without losing accuracy of the current density results. Secondly (B), we present an application on full-chip examples to illustrate the scaling effect. Thirdly (C), the reduction in calculation time is estimated based on technology data.

7.1   Example Simulations for Patterns and Their Combination

It is important to verify that partitioning FE models of wiring is possible without losing accuracy of the current density results. This is done by comparing the simulation results of generic sample patterns calculated both separately and in combination. Different manually generated patterns from a generic technology have been analyzed. As an example, a T-shape inside one metal layer and a

Table 4. Counts of Patterns in the layouts of the MCNC benchmark suite (part 2/2). Some patterns are rarely used, e.g. *cnw_c_cn*, and, thus, can be easily removed from the pattern library without significantly changing the layout.

Benchmark	Count per pattern										
	cn_c_cwe	cn_c_cws	cn_c_cnw	cn_c_cnwe	cn_c_cwse	cns_c_c	cns_c_cw	cns_c_cwe	cnw_c_ce	cnw_c_cnw	cnw_c_cn
mcc1	148	0	0	0	0	4	198	3	3	0	0
mcc2	105	0	0	0	0	2	81	0	0	0	0
primary1	163	0	0	0	0	0	227	3	1	0	0
primary2	866	2	0	0	0	2	969	15	5	0	0
s13207	565	17	1	0	1	1	899	16	0	0	1
s15850	699	27	0	0	2	2	1038	19	3	0	0
s38417	1760	50	1	0	3	7	2790	43	2	0	0
s38584	2280	78	0	1	3	10	3941	70	5	2	0
s5378	213	5	0	0	0	1	417	7	0	0	0
s9234	260	8	0	0	2	1	337	5	0	0	0
struct	190	0	0	0	0	1	204	1	0	0	0
$\sum$	7249	187	2	1	11	31	11101	182	19	2	1

via connection are chosen. Figure 6 shows the current density results from two separate (distinct) simulations.

For comparison, the combination of these patterns is used in a second simulation (Fig. 7). The simulation results of the combined configuration are in good agreement with the separately calculated results.

Figure 8 indicates current density distribution at the interface between the two patterns in the common simulation, which is a measure for the error in the separate simulations. The maximum error is 3% in our case; this value has been verified for the other patterns (see Fig. 9) as well.

Hence, under the constraints mentioned in Sect. 5.3, simulation time can be significantly reduced by splitting an FE model into smaller parts while preserving the accuracy of the results.

7.2 Full-Chip Analysis

We chose layouts (Fig. 10) from the MCNC benchmark suite for verification and analyzed it in two ways:

1. FE simulation of the complete circuit *(full-chip, F)* and
2. partitioned simulation re-using repeated patterns *(partitioned, P)*.

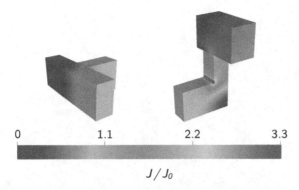

J/J_0

Fig. 6. Results of the separate simulations of single patterns with homogeneous constraints at the cut surfaces.

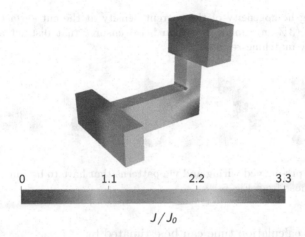

J/J_0

Fig. 7. The results of the common simulation of the two patterns are in good agreement with the results of the separate simulations from Fig. 6.

The first approach produces very large simulation models with $N_F > 10^7$ nodes and excessive simulation times $t_F > 70\,\mathrm{h}$. We can safely assume that FE simulation will be impossible with larger layouts in reasonable time. The second approach uses predefined and verified patterns (compare Figs. 6 and 9). An algorithm to localize the defined patterns has been implemented and applied to the benchmark layouts (Fig. 10). By reusing the patterns, the problem size is reduced to a significantly lower number of nodes N_P enabling a reduced simulation time t_P. Please note that by improving pattern choice, N_P can be reduced further.

Full-chip simulation time t_F is compared directly with simulation time t_P of the partitioned approach (Table 5).

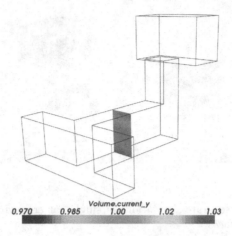

Fig. 8. Verifying homogeneity of the current density at the cut surface between the two sub-models (3 % maximum deviation here) ensures that distinct and combined simulations show matching results.

Fig. 9. Typical, pre-defined wiring and via patterns that have to be simulated by FEM in addition to those from Fig. 6.

The overall calculation time can be estimated by

$$t_F \approx P_C \cdot t_1 \text{ and} \tag{2}$$
$$t_P \approx P_L \cdot t_1 + P_C \cdot t_m, \tag{3}$$

with the number of patterns per circuit P_C, the mean calculation time for FE simulation of a single pattern t_1, the number of patterns in a library P_L, and the mean calculation time for a pattern meta-model t_m.

All critical spots of the full-chip analysis can be detected using only 5 different patterns (see Fig. 9). As shown, simulation time can be reduced by a factor of at least 16 (Table 5). Please note that library buildup time, i.e., FE simulation of individual patterns, is included in our simulation time.

N_P is always 30,000 as similar pattern libraries are used for all benchmarks. Numbers of nodes and calculation times are estimated based on wire length and number of patterns in the layout (see Fig. 10). t_P includes the estimated meta-model evaluation time (see Eq. 3).

A larger pattern library can be worthwhile if a large number of layouts is to be analyzed, reducing the simulation time per layout even further.

7.3   Reduction in Simulation Time

The time needed for simulation using the pattern method comprises (a) the time needed for library buildup (FE simulation of individual patterns) and (b) the full-chip meta-model calculation time. The FE simulation of individual patterns (a) is only necessary once for a variety of similar circuits.

For a number P_L of patterns in a library, the proposed method results in a reduced simulation time compared to full chip analysis if $t_\mathrm{P}(s) < t_\mathrm{F}(s)$ or:

$$P_\mathrm{L} \cdot t_1 + s \cdot P_\mathrm{C} \cdot t_\mathrm{m} < s \cdot P_\mathrm{C} \cdot t_1, \tag{4}$$

with s the number of similar circuits to be analyzed.

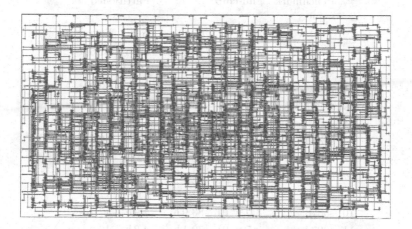

Fig. 10. Layout of the benchmark circuit *s5378*. Red crosses note the location of the example patterns of Fig. 9. (Color figure online)

That means, the approach accelerates the analysis if both the library contains much less patterns than a circuit and FE simulation time is greater than meta-model evaluation time. Due to increasing influences between model partitions with further downscaling of feature sizes, the number of patterns and the calculation time will rise. Figure 11 shows the difference in calculation time for $s = 1$, i.e., the pattern library is only used once (worst-case), illustrating nevertheless a speedup of at least 10 for current and future technologies.

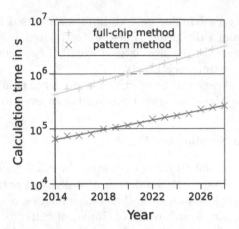

Fig. 11. Comparison of estimated calculation times between full-chip analysis and pattern method for $s = 1$ (one circuit verification per pattern library), calculated from technology parameters from [1].

Table 5. Experimental results of the layouts of the MCNC benchmark suite.

#	Benchmark name	Full-chip		Partitioned	
		N_F	t_F	t_P	Speedup
1	mcc1	3.8×10^7	106.2 h	3.4 h	31.6 ×
2	mcc2	4.0×10^8	1,106.8 h	19.5 h	56.6 ×
3	primary1	5.0×10^7	138.4 h	3.6 h	39.0 ×
4	primary2	2.0×10^8	569.8 h	14.5 h	39.2 ×
5	struct	5.6×10^7	154.6 h	5.5 h	28.2 ×
6	s13207	6.7×10^7	186.3 h	10.7 h	17.4 ×
7	s15850	8.0×10^7	221.9 h	12.7 h	17.5 ×
8	s38417	2.0×10^8	543.2 h	31.4 h	17.3 ×
9	s38584	2.6×10^8	728.1 h	41.8 h	17.4 ×
10	s5378	3.0×10^7	83.9 h	4.9 h	17.1 ×
11	s9234	2.5×10^7	70.1 h	4.2 h	16.7 ×

If the library models can be used multiple times for one circuit or if analyzing several similar circuits, i.e., $s > 1$, the difference between calculation times becomes even more significant. Specifically, when looking at the overall analysis time for large numbers of circuits, a speedup of at least 50 can be achieved, which nearly corresponds to the speedup of a meta-model calculation compared to an FE calculation.

8   Summary

Downscaling of the dimensions in integrated circuits leads to increasing problems with electromigration (EM) which needs to be tackled with greater awareness and more analyses. The finite element method (FEM) is well established in physical design and has proven itself in EM analysis.

Since FEM will struggle with circuit complexity, an alternative strategy is presented. Our approach uses FEM only for calculating generic layout elements (patterns) to build a meta-model library in advance. The layout will be created from a variety of library patterns, enabling a simple meta-model EM analysis. We verified our method using layouts of the MCNC benchmark suite and showed an acceleration of EM analysis by a factor of 16 and more. This acceleration factor will be (at least) the same when using parallel computing for FEM calculations, as our method provides good opportunities for parallelization.

Further work will investigate the practical implications of complex, nano-scale layout synthesis when using the proposed library patterns.

References

1. International Technology Roadmap for Semiconductors (ITRS), 2013 Edition. http://www.itrs2.net/itrs-reports.html
2. Lienig, J.: Electromigration and its impact on physical design in future technologies. In: Proceedings of the ACM International Symposium on Physical Design (ISPD), pp. 33–40 (2013). https://doi.org/10.1145/2451916.2451925
3. Lienig, J.: Interconnect and current density stress - an introduction to electromigration-aware design. In: Markov, I. (ed.) SLIP. ACM, San Francisco (2005). https://doi.org/10.1145/1053355.1053374
4. Lienig, J., Thiele, M.: Fundamentals of Electromigration-Aware Integrated Circuit Design. Springer, Cham (2018). https://doi.org/10.1007/978-3-319-73558-0
5. Thiele, M., Bigalke, S., Lienig, J.: Exploring the use of the finite element method for electromigration analysis in future physical design. In: 2017 IFIP/IEEE International Conference on Very Large Scale Integration (VLSI-SoC), pp. 1–6 (2017). https://doi.org/10.1109/VLSI-SoC.2017.8203466
6. Jerke, G., Lienig, J.: Hierarchical current-density verification in arbitarily shaped metallization patterns of analog circuits. IEEE Trans. Comput.-Aided Des. Integr. Circuits Syst. 23(1), 80–90 (2004). https://doi.org/10.1109/TCAD.2003.819899
7. Scorzoni, A., Neri, B., Caprile, C., Fantini, F.: Electromigration in thin-film interconnection lines: models, methods and results. Mater. Sci. Rep. 7(4–5), 143–220 (1991). https://doi.org/10.1016/0920-2307(91)90005-8
8. Bower, A.F., Shankar, S.: A finite element model of electromigration induced void nucleation, growth and evolution in interconnects. Model. Simul. Mater. Sci. Eng. 15(8), 923–940 (2007). https://doi.org/10.1088/0965-0393/15/8/008
9. Tan, C.M., Hou, Y., Li, W.: Revisit to the finite element modeling of electromigration for narrow interconnects. J. Appl. Phys. 102(3), 033 705-1–033 705-7 (2007). https://doi.org/10.1063/1.2761434
10. Synopsys Inc.: CustomSim Reliability Analysis; IC Compiler. http://www.synopsys.com/
11. Mentor Graphics: Calibre PERC. http://www.mentor.com/

12. Cadence Design Systems Inc.: Virtuoso Power System; Encounter Power System. http://www.cadence.com/
13. Jerke, G., Lienig, J.: Early-stage determination of current-density criticality in interconnects. In: ISQED, pp. 667–774, San Jose, CA (2010). https://doi.org/10.1109/ISQED.2010.5450505
14. Chen, H.Y., Chiang, M.F., Chang, Y.W., Chen, L., Han, B.: Full-chip routing considering double-via insertion. IEEE Trans. Comput. Aided Des. Integr. Circuits Syst. **27**(5), 844–857 (2008). https://doi.org/10.1109/TCAD.2008.917597
15. Bigalke, S., Lienig, J.: Load-aware redundant via insertion for electromigration avoidance. In: Proceedings of the ACM International Symposium on Physical Design (ISPD), pp. 99–106 (2016). https://doi.org/10.1145/2872334.2872355

On the Efficiency of Early Bird Sampling (EBS) an Error Detection-Correction Scheme for Data-Driven Voltage Over-Scaling

Roberto G. Rizzo[1], Valentino Peluso[1], Andrea Calimera[1(✉)], and Jun Zhou[2]

[1] Department of Control and Computer Engineering,
Politecnico di Torino, 10129 Turin, Italy
andrea.calimera@polito.it
[2] University of Electronic Science and Technology of China,
Chengdu, China

Abstract. An efficient implementation of voltage over-scaling policies for ultra-low power ICs passes through the design of on-chip *Error Detection and Correction* (EDC) mechanisms that can provide continuous feedback about the health of the circuit. The key components of a EDC architecture are embedded timing sensors that check the compliance of timing constraints at run-time and drives the computation to safely evolve toward the minimum energy point.

While most of the existing EDC solutions, e.g., *Razor* [1], have proved hardly applicable to circuits other than pipelined processors, our recent work [2] introduced a lightweight EDC alternative for general sequential circuits, what we called *Early Bird Sampling* (EBS). As a key strength, EBS reduces the design overhead by means of a *dynamic short path padding* that alleviates the overhead of timing sensors placement. Moreover, EBS implements an error correction mechanism based on *local logic-masking*, a technique that is well suited for digital IPs w/o an instruction-set. These features make EBS a viable solution to devise Data-Driven Voltage Over-Scaling (DD-VOS) for error-resilient applications.

Aim of this work is to recap the EBS strategy and quantify its figures of merit under different power management scenarios. We thereby provide accurate overhead assessment for different benchmarks and run under different DD-VOS policies. Comparison against a state-of-art EDC scheme, i.e., Razor, demonstrates EBS shows affordable area penalty (3.6% against 71.6% of Razor), still improving the efficiency of DD-VOS. Indeed, EBS leads circuits through lower energy-per-operation (savings w.r.t. Razor range from 36.2% to 40.2%) at negligible performance loss, from 2% to 5% (as much as Razor).

Keywords: Error Detection-Correction · Energy optimization · Error-resilient applications · Data-Driven Voltage-Over-Scaling

© IFIP International Federation for Information Processing 2019
Published by Springer Nature Switzerland AG 2019
M. Maniatakos et al. (Eds.): VLSI-SoC 2017, IFIP AICT 500, pp. 153–177, 2019.
https://doi.org/10.1007/978-3-030-15663-3_8

1   Introduction

1.1   Context

The key to success for the Internet-of-Things (IoT) is the availability of always-on smart objects with embedded Integrated Circuits (ICs) that can process/transmit sensor data ceaseless. Due to the limited budget of energy made available by small batteries [3], such ICs must show ultra-low power consumption thus to guarantee reasonable throughput [4,5]. This poses stringent design constraints that can be hardly achieved with classical low-power techniques, such as Dynamic Voltage Frequency Scaling (DVFS) [6], Clock-Gating [7], Power-Gating [8–10]. Recent trends highlight the rise of adaptive power-management strategies, e.g., Adaptive Voltage Over-scaling (AVOS) [11], which leverage the error resilience of data-driven applications in order to bring computation closer to the point of minimum energy consumption.

The strength of adaptive strategies lies under the ability of tuning low-power knobs at a finer time scale granularity, depending on the actual workload (or context). In standard DVFS both voltage (Vdd) and frequency (fc) are jointly traded over a set of discrete points statically defined at design-time on the base of the worst-case timing path. By contrast, AVOS applies Vdd lowering on the base of the longest *synthesized* timing path, yet keeping the operating frequency untouched. This guarantees larger power savings, zero throughput degradation, and thus, higher energy efficiency. To notice that knobs other than Vdd can still work, e.g., adaptive body-biasing. With no lack of generality this work focuses on AVOS.

As any other adaptive power management strategy, AVOS makes use of *Error Detection and Correction* (EDC) mechanisms that give real-time feedback on the correctness of the circuit; such information is used by the power management unit to identify the most appropriate Vdd scaling. In its more general embodiment a EDC architecture consists of in-situ timing sensors that flag the occurrence of set-up time violations across the flip-flops. The flag count is used as metric to decide whether the circuit is getting too faulty, in which case the Vdd is raised up in order to alleviate the cost of the error correction, or there still enough margin for lowering the Vdd, and thus to save more power. To notice that different Vdd scaling policies may vary depending on the flag threshold(s) that triggers the Vdd scaling, i.e., the *error rate*, the period of observation of the flag count, i.e., the *monitoring period*, the height and number of Vdd steps, i.e., the *Vdd quantization*.

Leaving out the details related to the Vdd scaling policy, the key aspect concerns how timing errors are detected and corrected, namely, the circuit implementation of the EDC architecture. The design of a reliable, low-cost EDC represents the actual bottleneck, indeed.

1.2   Motivation

Among the many EDC solutions appeared in the recent literature, *Razor* [1,12] still represents the main reference. The error detection is implemented by replacing

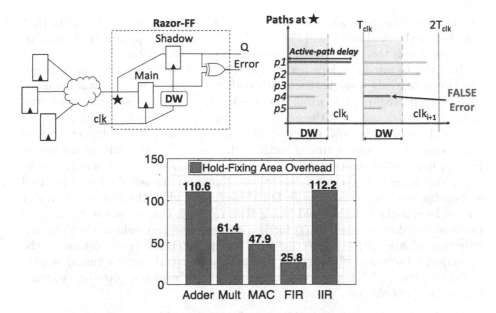

Fig. 1. Razor-FF implementation (left); short path race (right); area overhead due to short-path padding (center down), % w.r.t. baseline circuit [2].

standard flip-flops (FFs) with special FFs, a.k.a. *Razor-FFs* (Fig. 1), that sample logic signals at two different instants of time: first, at the rise edge of the clock, then, after a predefined timing window, the so called *Detection-Window* (DW). The two time-skewed samples are stored by two different FFs, i.e., the *main* flip-flop and the *shadow* flip-flop, and then compared through a XOR gate for parity check. A parity match implies the absence of errors and the availability of some timing slack, whereas a mismatch implies a faulty computation that is then recovered through some correction mechanism. To notice that Razor has been conceived for pipelined processors, hence, error recovery is accomplished through instruction replay.

Although Razor is considered a milestone in the scientific community, it shows intrinsic limitations that prevent its use on sequential circuits other than pipelined processors. The main reasons are two (described below in criticality order).

1. Short path race. While processors show a relative small number of end point FFs (the stage registers of the pipeline) most of which having a regular timing path distributions, generic sequential circuits have many FFs usually driven by logic cones with timing path distributions that seriously complicate the timing closure during logic synthesis. To better understand this critical aspect, one should consider Razor-FFs suffer the so called *short-path race*. As per their internal structure (Fig. 1), Razor-FFs cannot make distinction between the activation of a short-path within the DW and the activation of a long-path beyond the clock edge. This may cause "false" error detections. As depicted in

Fig. 1-center, the value sampled in the main FF at (T_{clk}) may differ from that sampled in the shadow FF at $(T_{clk} + DW)$ due to a short path activation (p4); the error flag is then raised even if there is no timing violation.

In order to avoid overlaps between short- and long-paths, a common design practice is to apply a static short-path padding [1,12]. It is a constrained hold-time fixing procedure (*hold-fixing* hereafter) where buffers are selectively inserted in the logic cones such that the minimum arrival time of any logic path is shifted beyond DW (usually 50% of the clock-period); short paths delaying is done while keeping the longer timing paths untouched. The side effects are many. Firstly, long buffer chains induce huge area penalties. As a preliminary result, Fig. 1 shows the area overhead due to hold-fixing for the set of circuits we used as benchmarks: the worst case is 112%! Secondly, when the timing constraint on the long paths is tight, hold-fixing tries to reach timing closure turning on Boolean transformations that (i) further increase area (ii) reshape the path distribution with negative impact on Vdd scaling efficiency (more details in the experimental section). Finally, long buffer chains exacerbates the timing unpredictability due to PVT variations when the circuit works at ultra-low voltage, e.g., near-threshold [13].

2. Correction through functional redundancy. While pipelined processors offer an easy path to error correction, i.e., instruction reply, implementing the same mechanism on sequential circuits would require a too complex FSM rewind. Hence, alternative circuit strategies are needed [14]. Unfortunately, the design overhead of such correction circuitry might substantially affect the gain brought by adaptive power management.

These two issues make Razor implementation very hard, often impractical, to be adopted in low-power ICs. Also, most of the attempts made to generalize the Razor technique have turned out to be too costly. This work deals with the same design issue by describing a lightweight EDC strategy that orthogonally applies to a wider set of circuits.

1.3   Contribution

Our recent work [2] proposed a simple, yet effective EDC implementation that addresses the key limitations of Razor. We refer it as the *Early Bird Sampling* (EBS). The EBS approach improves over the Razor technique by means of two main components: *dynamic short path padding* and *local logic masking*. The former addresses the short-path race through the insertion of a *Tunable Delay Line* (TDL) shared among *all* the paths that flow onto the same end-point; the result is that of depleting the DW from short-paths thereby avoiding false error detections without any significant overhead[1]. The latter one consists of an error correction mechanism that is applied locally, i.e., on the faulty FFs, cycle-by-cycle, thereby avoiding complex flow re-execution. This solution is inspired by [14].

---

[1] To notice that the availability of tunable delays also enables post-silicon variability compensations (out of the scope of this work).

With this paper we elaborate more on the EBS implementation details and we quantify the figures of merit over different operating scenarios. After a brief overview of related works (Sect. 2), we give a detailed description of the EBS architecture (Sects. 3 and 4). We then demonstrate EBS improves the efficiency of adaptive power management. EBS is validated for *Data-Driven Voltage Over-Scaling* (DD-VOS) (Sect. 5), a VOS scheme where the Vdd lowering follows the actual workload; as shown later in the text, DD-VOS enhanced with EBS well fits the characteristics of error-resilient applications. A customized design framework integrated into a commercial design kit for a 28 nm FDSOI CMOS technology (Sect. 6) is used to validate EBS on a representative class of benchmarks. Those benchmarks are simulated under realistic workloads using different voltage scaling policies: *single-threshold*, *double-threshold* and *saturation-counter*. The collected results (Sect. 7) give a comparative analysis against Razor-based DD-VOS. The main achievements are as follows: (*i*) EBS reduces area overheads: 3.6% (EBS) vs. 71.6% (Razor) on average; (*ii*) EBS improves energy efficiency as it increases the voltage scaling margins DD-VOS can play with: average energy-per-operation savings (w.r.t. baseline) are 38.6% (EBS) vs. 0.7% (Razor); (*iii*) EBS induces a mere performance loss: operations-per-cycles ranges from 0.95 to 0.98 (as much as Razor).

2 Related Works

2.1 Razor-Based Overhead Reduction

In previous works, several solutions for limiting the area overhead of Razor-based monitoring schemes have been investigated. The works [12,15–17] proposed the use of a duty-cycled clock. Nevertheless, this solution was applied on specific designs and it is hard to generalize to random sequential circuit. Moreover, large detection windows may be necessary to cover delay variations over a wide voltage range operation. Authors in [18] presented a novel technique for preventing hold-fixing buffers while maintaining a traditional clock network design. Such method was demonstrated on a loop-accelerator for System-on-Chip designs. The short-path race is avoided through the insertion of negative-phase transparent latches at the middle of each timing path covered by a Razor-FF. In this way, the latches prevents signals propagation through the Razor-FFs during the high-phase of the clock. However, the arrival time to the latches may be affected by process variations, leading to an increase of the error rate. In this work, we opted for a simpler solution, with reduced area overhead and low implementation cost. In [19], the authors proposed an hold-fixing procedure based on a fine-grained load allocation that makes use of spare cells and dummy metals. The integration of this methodology in standard EDA tools might be a concern, whereas our implementation strategy is fully integrated into industrial design tools.

2.2 Existing Voltage Over-Scaling Approaches

Voltage Over-Scaling (VOS) leverages the quadratic relationship of dynamic power with supply voltage. VOS scales the Vdd below the minimum threshold that satisfies the worst-case delay of the circuit. The implementation of this scheme requires error detection and/or correction mechanisms to properly tune the Vdd in case of set-up time violations. The basic idea underlying VOS is the empirical observation that the *sensitization* probability of long (hence, critical critical) paths is usually very low. If this is not the case, some optimization, e.g., those introduced in [20, 21], can be applied in order to meet this requirement. In this way, the overhead of the correction mechanism is minimized.

As reported in [22], different implementations of the VOS strategy have been presented in the literature. The following is a taxonomy of the most representative works in the field.

Error Detection-Correction Schemes. Such techniques take corrective action according the signals coming from error monitors embedded in the logic. Razor [1, 23] represents a milestone for error-detection systems and after more than ten years since its first appearance, is still the state-of-art. The Razor technique has been conceived for pipelined microprocessor architectures. In a Razor Flip-Flop, the signal is double-sampled by a *shadow* flip-flop triggered by a delayed clock (see Sect. 1). In case of detected errors, a recovery strategy is activated by a three-stage mechanism: first, the pipeline is stalled; second, the bits stored in the shadow flip-flops are loaded into the main flip-flops; finally, the last pipe-cycle is repeated. This system enable to remove excessive voltage margin, tuning the Vdd of the circuit according the error rate.

The main issue of Razor is the possible occurrence of metastability. Several works have addressed this problem. Razor II [12], an extension of Razor, proposed to use a transition detector. Another approach is to replace the Razor-FF with time borrowing latches [15, 16].

In order to reduce the performance penalties introduced by error correction, authors in [11] proposed to remove any recovery circuitry. The error detection systems is used tune the Vdd according to the error rate. Such solution is suited for error resilient application, e.g. signal processing, where the degradation of the output marginally impact the quality of the final results.

Another solution is to reduce the number of activations of the recovery mechanisms by just changing the slack distribution. While standard tools optimize the longest timing path, several works [21, 24–27] proposed to speed-up the most frequently exercised paths, thereby forcing timing errors on the most infrequent paths. Therefore, it is possible to further scale the voltage while maintaining the same error rate.

Prediction-Based Schemes. Differently from Razor, they are based on some prediction logic that prevents the occurrence of errors. Authors in [20] introduced a design methodology, called CRISTA, for voltage over-scaled circuits. The basic idea of CRISTA is to reduce the activation probability of the most critical paths through a customized optimization stage carried out during the logic-synthesis; then, at run-time, and provide those paths with an extra clock cycle when they are sensitized. The low activation rate of the long paths allows to minimize performance penalties.

Elastic-clock execution units [28, 29] are another practical example of the CRISTA paradigm. A low overhead prediction logic check whether an input pattern exercise a critical path; then it dynamically allocates an additional clock cycle in order to meet the timing constraints. The remaining input patterns are executed in a single clock cycle.

Algorithmic Noise Tolerance (ANT). The basic principle underlying ANT is to accept errors if the output degradation is below a given threshold. Indeed, ANT [30,31] has been conceived for DSP arithmetic blocks, where the circuit output represents a quantity. Instead of using local timing monitors, the error detection is delegated to a lightweight replica of the main circuit, namely the *estimator*. The output computed by the estimator is checked against the main circuit one and a control unit flags an error if the difference overcomes an user-defined threshold. If this is the case, the estimator's output is forwarded towards the main output of the circuit. The main challenge in ANT-based systems is to limit the area and timing overhead of the estimator for complex arithmetic functions, while guaranteeing the desired output quality.

3   Early Bird Sampling

The objective we intend to pursue by proposing the Early Bird Sampling (EBS) technique is twofold: (*i*) reduce traditional design overhead imposed by Razor system, while (*ii*) maintaining those intrinsic characteristics of the circuit that enable an efficient implementation of VOS.

A schematic representation of the EBS circuit is given in Fig. 2a. Tunable Delay Lines (TDLs) are inserted just before the critical end-points of the circuit. Those end-point are equipped with a variant of the Razor-FF (more details provided later in the text).

The propagation delay of the TDLs can be changed at run-time such that the minimum arrival time (AT_{min}) is greater than the detection window (DW) of the Razor-FFs. Indeed, the delay of a TDL is given by:

$$TDL = DW - AT_{min}; \tag{1}$$

This prevents the activation of short-paths within the detection window, and so, races with long-path in setup time violation, i.e., "false" error detection. For the sake of clarity, we assumed that a TDL is tuned during post-fabrication stage, when also the nominal $Tclk$ can be properly set such that no paths can be delayed beyond the DW in nominal operating conditions. Each critical end-point comes with its dedicated TDL. To be also noticed that the tunable delays enable post-silicon compensation on the short-paths (out of the scope of this work).

The EBS strategy can be seen as a "weak" hold-fixing optimization procedure where the set-up constraints are not taken into account. Indeed, a TDL does not delay short-paths only, actually, it evenly affects all the paths in its fan-in cone. The longest paths may thereby suffer early sampling, which is why we called this technique *Early Bird Sampling*. The relaxation of the timing constraints is the key for a lightweight implementation of the error-detection mechanism.

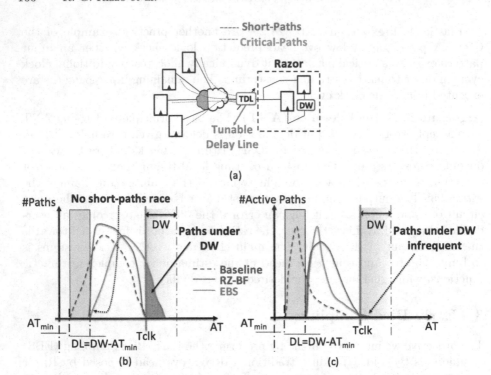

Fig. 2. Early Bird Sampling at a timing critical end-point: circuit implementation (a); static (b) and dynamic (c) timing paths analysis. Plots are illustrative and do not refer to a specific case, rather, they show typical distributions observed on generic circuits. (Color figure online)

To better understand the working principle of EBS, Fig. 2b provides a comparison among the static path distributions at a critical end-point for three different circuits implementations: (i) a generic circuit after synthesis, the *baseline* (dashed line), (ii) the circuit after standard hold-fixing optimization, *RZ-BF* (red-line) (iii) *EBS* (green line). Hold-fixing reshapes the path distributions guaranteeing that all paths are beyond the detection window, namely, outside the gray area in figure, while maintaining the longest path delay unchanged. By contrast, the effect of EBS is to shift the whole timing distribution, hence, some paths move beyond $Tclk$ (purple area).

In principle, this issue may be seen as a potential impediment. However, a more accurate analysis reveals that the problem is less relevant from a practical viewpoint. EBS exploits the fact that for real-life workloads the activation probability of long paths is usually pretty low. This feature, shown by the majority of digital circuits, suggests that latent faults on long paths are rarely excited. Experimental results give evidence of such empirical rule of thumb, which can be inferred by probing the arrival time of timing end-points during workload execution, i.e., through a dynamic timing analysis. Figure 2c plots the dynamic path distribution for a typical workload run on three different implementations of the circuits: baseline, RZ-BF, EBS. As a matter of fact, the number of violating paths is much lower that those estimated using a worst-case static timing analysis (purple area in Fig. 2b).

The most interesting aspect, is that EBS does not alter the shape of the distribution (both static and dynamic); referring to the plots in Fig. 2, the green line is a copy of the dashed line, just shifted on the right. This allows to preserve the intrinsic characteristics of the original circuit, thus enabling a more efficient voltage scaling. The same is not for RZ-BF, where path compression resulting from hold-fixing optimization substantially increases the number of "quasi-critical" paths (i.e., paths close to $Tclk$) as shown in Fig. 2c. As a side effect, even small voltage variations would bring a large number of paths beyond $Tclk$, therefore triggering more timing errors. As a result, power-management techniques, and VOS in particular, would have less margins to operate.

4   Implementation Details

4.1   Tunable Delay Line (TDL)

Different implementations of TDLs have been proposed in literature; as the modeling of a TDL is out of the scope of this work, we opted for the solution presented in [32]. It consists of a pair of inverters with a voltage-controlled variable load between them; the load is a transmission gate whose ON-resistance is controlled by V_{delay}, as shown in Fig. 3. Such solution allows to cover a wide range of delays with a limited area overhead. The main drawback is that an extra power grid is needed for the distribution of V_{delay}. An alternative solution is to use tunable buffers adopted for on-line clock-skew compensation [33].

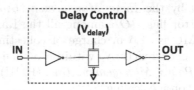

Fig. 3. Tunable Delay Line (TDL) implementation [32].

4.2   Error Detection and Correction

The EBS detection and correction mechanism is implemented using standard Razor-FFs [23] augmented with a logic masking circuitry [14], Fig. 4. Hereafter, we refer to this architecture as *Razor-Logic-Masking* (Razor-LM). A polarity change at the input of the main flip-flop after the rise edge of the clock implies some long-path is violating the timing constraint, i.e., a timing error. This event is flagged through the XOR gate that runs a parity check between the signals at pins D_{FF} and Q_{FF}. The error flag is sampled in a shadow latch triggered on the fall edge of the clock.

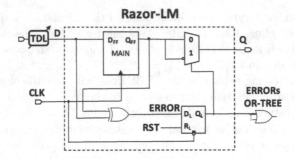

Fig. 4. Error detection and logic masking circuitry in EBS.

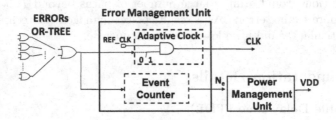

Fig. 5. Error Management Unit in EBS.

This smart solution allows large detection windows (i.e., $DW = 50\%Tclk$) w/o any modification of the clock distribution network. Once detected, the error is locally corrected through logic masking, that is, a MUX switches the output with the complement of the wrong signal stored in the main FF.

In order to let the corrected value propagate toward the fanout logic, the whole circuit has to be stopped for at least one clock cycle. Such an error-driven clock-gating is managed by the *Error Management Unit* (EMU), Fig. 5, that uses a superset of the error flags (OR among all the Razor-LM in the circuit) as clock enable. The EMU is also in charge of collecting the error statistics, i.e., the number of error occurrences N_e within a predefined monitoring period of N clock cycles. The *Power Management Unit* (PMU) uses this feedback to implement the dynamic voltage scaling.

4.3   Design Flow

The EBS design flow encompasses three different stages we integrated into a commercial design platform (the *Synopsys*® Galaxy) using wrappers written in TCL:

1. **Logic Synthesis:** a classical timing-driven, low-power logic synthesis run using 28 nm industrial technology libraries characterized at the nominal Vdd = 1.10 V.

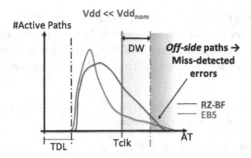

Fig. 6. Miss-detected errors representation.

2. **Identification of critical end-points:** after the clock-tree synthesis, the end-points whose worst-case arrival time at minimum voltage Vdd = 0.60 V (lower bound of the voltage scaling range) miss the clock-period $Tclk$ are labeled as "critical".
3. **Razor-LM re-placement and TDL insertion:** for each critical end-point, the standard FF is replaced with a Razor-LM and the TDL properly inserted; the error OR-tree is also synthesized.

5   Data-Driven Voltage Over-Scaling with EBS

Data-Driven Voltage Over-scaling (DD-VOS) belongs to the class of adaptive voltage scaling [11] techniques. It implements a context-driven voltage lowering, that is, voltage gets regulated by the occurrence of timing errors on the actual *sensitized* critical paths, i.e., those activated by the actual input pattern.

As already discussed, this may lead some of the longest paths beyond the clock period. Those which fall within the detection window (DW) are detected and eventually corrected; that's the basic principle of EBS. However, there might be specific sequences of input patterns that push the supply voltage so down that some of the longest paths could even exceed the *DW*; such *off-side* paths represent the main source of error *miss-prediction*. The latter case is graphically depicted in Fig. 6. Paths in *off-side* run out of control, and their activation is the main source of error propagation. Here's why DD-VOS is particularly suited for error-resilient applications.

It is worth to emphasize that miss-detections mainly raise depending on the voltage scaling policy adopted. We therefore provide a parametric analysis among different DD-VOS parameters and different management policies (the latter being described in the next subsection).

5.1   DD-VOS Policies

The main feedback provided by the error management unit (EMU) is the number of errors N_e within a predefined number of clock-cycles N, the monitoring period (please refer to Sect. 4). The power management unit (PMU) makes use of such error-rate ER in order to implement some voltage scaling policy. More specifically, the ER is compared against a given ER_{th} (or multiple error-thresholds) in order to trigger the voltage scaling. In this work we implemented three different policies as follows.

1. Single-threshold (STh): as shown in Fig. 7a, given ER_{Th} as a user-defined error threshold, the policy works as follow:

- as soon as N_e gets larger than ER_{Th}, the supply voltage is increased w/o waiting for the end of monitoring period.
- if $N_e \leq ER_{Th}$ at the end of the monitoring period, i.e., after N cycles, the supply voltage is reduced for power minimization.

To notice that STh enables the control over the minimum Operation per Clock-cycle (OPC), a measure of performance overhead due to error correction; indeed, ER_{Th} represents the maximum OPC loss.

2. Double-threshold (DTh): conceived to be more conservative, the DTh policy exploits a "neutral" region defined by two thresholds $ER_{Th_{min}}$ and $ER_{Th_{max}}$, Fig. 7b; within this region, the supply voltage is kept untouched. This avoids excessive Vdd ripples thus making the voltage scaling smoother. The policy works as follows:

- as soon as $N_e \geq ER_{Th_{max}}$, Vdd is scaled up w/o waiting for the end of monitoring period;
- if $N_e \leq ER_{Th_{min}}$ at the end of the monitoring period, Vdd is scaled down for power minimization;
- if $ER_{Th_{min}} < N_e < ER_{Th_{max}}$ at the end of the monitoring period, Vdd is kept unchanged in order to avoid excessive Vdd ripple.

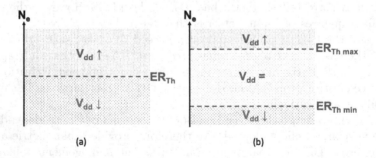

Fig. 7. STh (a) vs. DTh (b) Vdd scaling policies.

3. Threshold-exceeding Saturation Counter (SC): this policy is more elaborated as it takes into account how the supply voltage evolves over time. The working mechanism, depicted in Fig. 8 as a Mealy Finite State Machine (FSM), makes use of a 4-bit saturation counter to decide whether the voltage has to be scaled up/down. It works as follows:

- the policy starts reducing Vdd (*Safe* state);
- if N_e exceeds the ER_{Th} a warning signal is raised ($E=1$) at the end of the monitoring period and the FSM state evolves to *Saturation Count*. Vdd is not increased;
- the Vdd is scaled up if the number of consecutive warning signal c is equal to c_{max} ($2^5 - 1$). In this case, the FSM moves to the *Unsafe* state;
- If the current state is *Unsafe* and no warning signal is raised ($E=0$), the FSM evolves in *Safe* state and Vdd is scaled down;
- anytime FSM reaches the *Saturation Count* state, the warning count c is set to zero.

To notice that the SC policy has been thought to be more aggressive than STh; indeed it allows to increase the time spent at lower Vdd, even when the N_e exceeds ER_{Th}. This enables larger energy savings at the cost of some performance and quality-of-results loss.

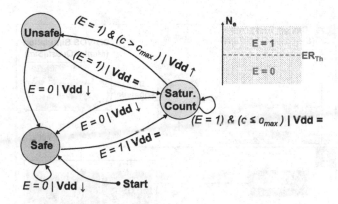

Fig. 8. Saturation counter Vdd scaling policy.

6 Experimental Framework

6.1 Benchmarks and Testbenches

The proposed EBS technique has been tested on a set of open source benchmarks over which we applied a DD-VOS scheme. The five circuits under analysis are:

- *Adder:* 32 × 32-bit + Carry-In Adder; $f_{clk} = 750$ MHz.
- *Multiplier:* 32 × 32-bit Multiplier; $f_{clk} = 500$ MHz.
- *MAC:* 16 × 16-bit Multiply Accum. Unit; $f_{clk} = 650$ MHz.
- *FIR Filter:* Pipelined 16th-order low-pass FIR filter in direct form (12-bit in, 24-bit out); $f_{clk} = 650$ MHz.

– *IIR Filter:* Pipelined 8th-order low-pass IIR filter in direct form I, modeled after a Bessel analog filter (16-bit in, 32-bit out); $f_{clk} = 650$ MHz.

For each benchmark we designed both the EBS and the RZ-BF versions. The difference between them is the method adopted to solve the short-path races, i.e., TDLs for EBS and standard post-synthesis hold-fixing for RZ-BF; in both cases the number of monitored end points is the same. The hold-fixing procedure implemented for the RZ-BF circuits uses multi-V_{th} clock buffers that minimize the area overheads.

The DD-VOS is emulated using a in-house tool (Fig. 9) which runs functional simulations (*Mentor QuestaSim*) with back-annotated sdf delay information. Propagation delays are extracted using a Static Timing Analysis engine (*Synopsys PrimeTime*) loaded with technology libraries characterized at different supply voltages; for those supply voltages not available in the library set we used derating factors embedded into the STA. The power dissipation is calculated using probabilistic models (*Synopsys PrimePower*) with back-annotated signal statistics from saif format files. The energy consumption is estimated considering the supply voltage profiles collected from simulations.

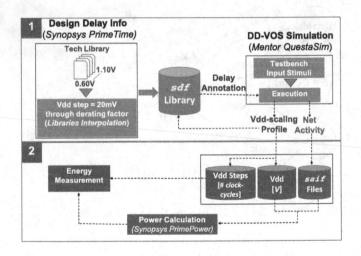

Fig. 9. In-house DD-VOS emulation tool flow diagram.

The emulated workload consists of realistic input stimuli made up of 5×10^6 patterns customized for each benchmark. For arithmetic circuits (*Adder, Multiplier* and *MAC*) we organized the patterns as sequence of Gaussian distributions each of them having a variable mean; for *Adder* and *Multiplier:* $\mu_1 = 2^8$, $\mu_2 = 2^{16}$ $\mu_3 = 2^{28}$ with standard deviation $\sigma = 2^8$; for *MAC:* $\mu_1 = 2^4$, $\mu_2 = 2^8$ $\mu_3 = 2^{12}$ with standard deviation $\sigma = 2^4$. For *FIR* and *IIR filters*, stimulus consists of a set of baseband audio samples.

6.2   Quality Metrics

1. *Average Vdd*: average of the Vdd measured over the testbench trace.
2. *Energy per Operation* (EPO): ratio between energy consumed and number of operations.
3. *Operation per Clock Cycle* (OPC): ratio between the number of operation run and total number of clock cycles.
4. *Miss-detected Errors* (MDE): the count of logic errors due to miss-detected timing faults occurred during simulation, measured in *ppm* (parts per million).
5. *Normalized Root Mean Squared Error* (NRMSE):

$$NRMSE = \sqrt{\frac{\sum_{i=0}^{n}(y[i] - y_o[i])^2}{n}} \cdot \frac{1}{y_{max} - y_{min}} \qquad (2)$$

with y the value sampled at the output of the circuit, y_o the right output value, n is the total number of operations; y_{max} and y_{min} are the max and the min value of y_o, they define output dynamic. $NRMSE$ quantifies the QoR.

To be noticed that our simulations do not consider process variations as they do not affect the functionality of the proposed technique.

7   Results

7.1   Area Overhead

Table 1 collects the statistics of the five benchmarks; column **#FFs** reports the total number of flip-flops (FFs), while column **#Critical-FFs** the percentage of FFs replaced with timing monitors, the Razor-LM.

Table 1. Benchmarks designed for EBS.

Benchmark	Area [μm^2]	#FFs	#Critical-FFs	DW [ps]	TDL [ps]
Adder	339.45	98	22.4%	665	616
Mult	2954.01	128	42.2%	1000	898
MAC	1241.12	72	45.8%	750	656
FIR	1946.32	228	8.3%	750	634
IIR	3296.80	296	78.4%	750	692

The DW is set to 50%·*Tclk*, while *TDL* is sized according to Eq. 1. The analysis reported in [32] ensures that the circuit adopted to implement the delay lines (Sect. 4.1) allows to achieve the values reported in the Table 1.

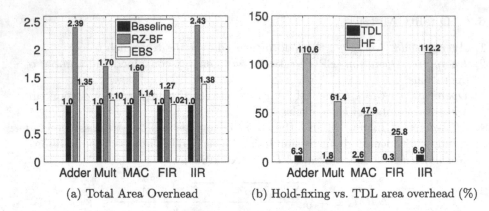

Fig. 10. Area overhead comparison.

The bar-charts in Fig. 10a and b provide a more detailed area comparison between EBS and RZ-BF; both the implementations show the same number of timing monitors (Table 1). Figure 10a shows the overall area overhead normalized w.r.t. the baseline circuit (i.e., w/o any EDC scheme). EBS is by far a more compact architecture; average area overhead is 19.8% against 87.8% of RZ-BF. That's due to the efficiency of the proposed dynamic short path padding. As shown in Fig. 10b, TDLs requires much less area (3.6% on average) than buffers insertion using hold-fixing procedures (71.6% on average). For instance, the *IIR*, which shows a large number of short-paths in the feedback network, area penalty of RZ-BF is 112.2%, while it drastically reduces to 6.9% with EBS.

7.2   DD-VOS Improvement with EBS

In order to quantify the improvements brought by EBS, Tables 2 and 3 summarize the results achieved during DD-VOS emulation on the five benchmarks under analysis. The two tables report a collection of the quality metrics presented in Sect. 6.2. Collected results refer to the *single-threshold* policy (STh) described in Sect. 5 assuming (*i*) a monitoring period $N = 10^3$ clock cycles, (*ii*) a Vdd step 20 mV, (*iii*) two different values for the error-rate ER_{Th}: 2%, i.e., 20 errors in 10^3 cycles - Table 2), and 5%, i.e., 50 errors in 10^3 cycles - Table 3.

A large ER_{Th} accelerates the voltage scaling, hence, it may induce some performance penalty (due to more errors to be corrected) and some QoR degradation (due to a possible increase of miss-detected errors).

Except for the *Mult* benchmark, which we discuss later as a special testcase, the results clearly show EBS outperforms RZ-BF. The savings achieved with EBS are quantified by (*i*) the average Vdd recorded during testbench simulations (column Vdd_{avg}), and (*ii*) the energy-per-operation savings w.r.t. the baseline circuit (column $EPO_{savings}$). The EBS implementation reaches lower Vdd_{avg} (and also minimum Vdd - column Vdd_{min}) for both the ER_{Th} thresholds. This translates into larger *EPO* savings w.r.t. RZ-BF. Best cases have been measured

Table 2. Results summary for DD-VOS set as $N = 10^3$ (clock cycles) and $ER_{Th} = 2\%$. Notes: *EPO* savings w.r.t. Baseline.

Benchmarks	EBS					
	Vdd$_{min}$ [V]	Vdd$_{avg}$ [V]	EPO savings [%]	OPC	MDE [ppm]	NRMSE [%]
MAC	0.74	0.87	43.6	0.98	0	0
Adder	0.60	0.83	41.9	0.98	6	0.001
IIR	0.92	0.95	30.6	0.98	0	0
FIR	0.84	0.96	28.2	0.98	0	0
Mult	1.10	1.10	−5.5	0.98	0	0
Benchmarks	RZ-BF					
	Vdd$_{min}$ [V]	Vdd$_{avg}$ [V]	EPO savings [%]	OPC	MDE [ppm]	NRMSE [%]
MAC	0.94	1.00	9.0	0.98	0	0.0
Adder	0.66	0.87	18.6	0.99	35	0.001
IIR	1.00	1.02	−47.7	0.97	0	0
FIR	0.86	0.98	12.8	0.98	0	0
Mult	1.00	1.04	−23.7	0.98	0	0

Table 3. Results summary for DD-VOS set as $N = 10^3$ (clock cycles) and $ER_{Th} = 5\%$. Notes: *EPO* savings w.r.t. Baseline.

Benchmarks	EBS					
	Vdd$_{min}$ [V]	Vdd$_{avg}$ [V]	EPO savings [%]	OPC	MDE [ppm]	NRMSE [%]
MAC	0.72	0.83	48.6	0.95	6	0.128
Adder	0.60	0.81	44.4	0.97	15	0.001
IIR	0.88	0.90	37.6	0.95	0	0
FIR	0.80	0.93	34.0	0.95	0	0
Mult	1.10	1.10	−8.5	0.95	0	0
Benchmarks	RZ-BF					
	Vdd$_{min}$ [V]	Vdd$_{avg}$ [V]	EPO savings [%]	OPC	MDE [ppm]	NRMSE [%]
MAC	0.94	0.99	9.6	0.95	0	0
Adder	0.66	0.86	20.7	0.97	91	0.002
IIR	0.98	1.01	−45.6	0.96	0	0
FIR	0.86	0.96	21.5	0.96	0	0
Mult	1.00	1.02	−19.5	0.96	0	0

for *MAC* (48.6% for EBS vs. 9.6% for RZ-BF at $ER_{Th} = 5\%$) and *Adder* (44.4% for EBS vs 20.7% for RZ-BF at $ER_{Th} = 5\%$). It is worth to emphasize that in the worst-case (*FIR*), *EPO* savings achieved with EBS are 2.2× larger than those obtained by RZ-BF: 28.2% vs. 12.8% for $ER_{Th} = 2\%$; 34.0% vs. 21.5% for $ER_{Th} = 5\%$.

The *IIR filter* is a kind of circuit for which RZ-BF results quite inefficient; the *EPO* increases w.r.t. the baseline circuit leading to negative savings: −47.7%

at $ER_{Th} = 2\%$ and -45.6% at $ER_{Th} = 5\%$. Such huge design overhead is due to the fact that hold-fixing overwhelms the power savings of voltage scaling. By contrast, EBS still gets remarkable EPO savings: 30.6% at $ER_{Th} = 2\%$ and 37.6% at $ER_{Th} = 5\%$.

For what concerns performance degradations due to errors correction, Tables 2 and 3 clearly shows EBS guarantees a OPC close to that of the RZ-BF strategy: $OPC \geq \{0.98, 0.95\}$ for both the thresholds $ER_{Th} = \{2\%, 5\%\}$. This confirms once again TDLs insertion has marginal effect on the error-rate.

Remarkable results have been also observed in terms of reliability. Although EBS pushes Vdd to values below those achieved with RZ-BF, the number of miss-detections MDE is zero for all the benchmarks. The two exceptions are *Adder* ($MDE = 6\,\text{ppm}$ and $MDE = 15\,\text{ppm}$, with ER_{Th} equals to 2% and 5% respectively) and *MAC* ($MDE = 6\,\text{ppm}$ at $ER_{Th} = 5\%$). Nonetheless only marginal QoR degradation has been observed: $NRMSE$ is a mere 0.128% at worst case. Such a low QoR degradation is achieved thanks to the internal logic topology of the circuits which, in turn, reflects into a low activation of the most critical paths.

As a counterexample, the *Mult* benchmark belongs to that class of circuits whose internal characteristics are not particularly suited for aggressive voltage over-scaling. Both EBS and RZ-BF fail, suggesting DD-VOS might not be a valuable low-power option. To better understand the reasons behind such behavior, we resort to a comparison between two benchmarks, the *Mult* (for which DD-VOS does not work) and the *MAC* (for which DD-VOS gets substantial savings). Figure 11 recalls the qualitative analysis discussed in Sect. 3. More specifically, it shows the dynamic path distribution of three different implementations: baseline, EBS and RZ-BF. The bars represent the cumulative number of timing path activations vs. their arrival time.

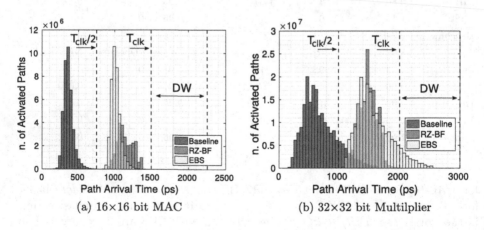

(a) 16×16 bit MAC

(b) 32×32 bit Multilplier

Fig. 11. Dynamic path distribution analysis.

Some key comments are as follows. First. For both EBS and RZ-BF the path distribution is skewed such that none of the short-paths falls behind $T_{clk}/2$ (the width of the detection window DW). This avoids short-path races thus ensuring the right functionality of the error detection mechanism. Second. EBS keeps the path distribution unchanged (just a right shift of the baseline distribution) avoiding the growth of those "quasi-critical" paths that, just standing behind T_{clk}, may prevent voltage lowering. Usually, RZ-BF works on the opposite direction instead, as the number of "quasi-critical" increases due to timing-constrained buffer insertion. This behavior is quite evident for MAC (Fig. 11a), for which the red bars (RZ-BF implementation) stand over the white ones (EBS implementation). Since a larger number of activated "quasi-critical" paths reduces the chance of Vdd lowering, EBS results to be more efficient. That's what makes EBS outperforming RZ-BF. However, there might be particular circuits for which this feature does not hold. Such circuits are those for which the basic principle under which EBS is built, namely, *the longer the path, the lower its activation*, gets weaker. That's the *Mult*. As reported in Fig. 11b, the original dynamic path distribution (baseline implementation) is pretty large, with very active paths that take the whole clock-period. This negatively affects EBS, where the TDLs push many paths into the DW; as a result, the supply voltage is stuck at high values and the EPO gets larger than the original circuit due to error corrections: 1.06× and 1.09× for $ER_{Th} = 2\%$ and $ER_{Th} = 5\%$ respectively. Also RZ-BF suffers from the same problem, as the number of active paths across T_{clk} is huge; EPO increases w.r.t. the baseline circuit: 1.24× and 1.20× for $ER_{Th} = 2\%$ and $ER_{Th} = 5\%$ respectively. However, the overhead of RZ-BF gets larger than that of EBS.

As a final comment, one should consider that circuits on which DD-VOS does not work properly, may radically change their behavior when integrated into more complex architectures. That's the case of *Mult* integrated into MAC.

7.3 EBS Characterization Under Different DD-VOS Implementations

The main goal of this section is to quantify the figures of merit of EBS under different DD-VOS settings, and thus, to demonstrate EBS performs well under several power management scenarios. We therefore characterize the quality metrics according to: *(i)* the Vdd step, namely, the ΔVdd used for voltage scaling; *(ii)* the monitoring period, that is, the clock cycles N used to measure the error-rate; *(iii)* the Vdd scaling policies presented in Sect. 5. For the sake of space, we just report the analysis for MAC. Similar results hold for the other benchmarks.

Vdd Step. The collected results refer to three different values of ΔVdd: 20 mV, 50 mV, 100 mV, 250 mV. In order to make the analysis more realistic, we also take into consideration different voltage steps may require different clock-cycles to be properly delivered; we therefore assume a latency of {1, 2, 5, 12} clock cycles for {20 mV, 50 mV, 100 mV, 250 mV} respectively.

Simulations are conducted on EBS and RZ-BF using the *Single Threshold* Vdd scaling policy (STh) under two different values of error-threshold, $ER_{Th} = 2\%$ and 5%.

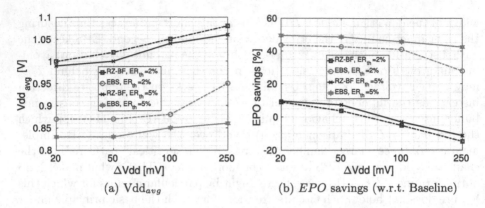

(a) Vdd$_{avg}$ (b) *EPO* savings (w.r.t. Baseline)

Fig. 12. Energy efficiency vs. Vdd step width (ΔVdd).

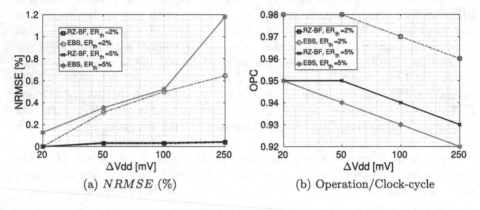

(a) *NRMSE* (%)   (b) Operation/Clock-cycle

Fig. 13. QoR and performance vs. Vdd step width (ΔVdd).

EBS outperforms RZ-BF for any of the vdd-steps values under analysis. As shown in Fig. 12b, EBS brings the circuit to a lower average Vdd; along the whole ΔVdd range, the average improvement w.r.t. RZ-BF reaches 140 mV at $ER_{th} = 2\%$ and 180 mV at $ER_{th} = 5\%$. The same results hold for energy efficiency; average EPO savings are: 46.6% and 38.8% at $ER_{th} = 5\%$ and $ER_{th} = 2\%$ for EBS vs. a mere 0.6% and 0.01% for RZ-BF. More in details, Fig. 12 shows how savings drift with ΔVdd. Vdd$_{avg}$ reaches lower values using a finer voltage resolution. For instance, considering the EBS at $ER_{Th} = 2\%$, it reduces from 0.95 V at ΔVdd = 250 mV to 0.87 mV at ΔVdd = 20 mV. As a result, the energy savings reported in Fig. 12b show substantial improvements, from 27.8% at ΔVdd = 250 mV to 43.6% at ΔVdd = 20 mV.

The voltage resolution does also impact the QoR. As shown in Fig. 13a, the lower the Vdd step, the better the QoR. Indeed, a larger ΔVdd makes harder to control the occurrence of miss-detected errors. For $ER_{Th} = 5\%$, the *NRMSE* measured for EBS reduces from 1.2% at ΔVdd = 250 mV to 0.1% at ΔVdd = 20 mV. By contrast, the *NRMSE* of the RZ-BF implementation is less

sensible (variation in the range [0.0%–0.1%]); that's mainly due to the fact that
the Vdd scaling is slower than in EBS, therefore, less miss-detections do occur.

Concerning the performance, the STh Vdd-scaling policy is conceived as a
mechanism to control the minimum OPC value; ideally, as introduced in Sect. 5,
ER_{Th} represents the max. OPC loss, thus the minimum OPC equals $1 - ER_{Th}$.
However, since larger Vdd steps come with larger latencies, the performance
achieved by EBS and RZ-BF are substantially affected and OPC may drop
below that ideal minimum boundary if OPC loss $>ER_{Th}$. Figure 13b shows this
drawback through OPC vs. ΔVdd plot; both EBS and RZ-BF OPC losses are
still kept lower than ER_{Th} only for ΔVdd $= 20$ mV (both the ER_{Th}s). In the
worst case, i.e., $ER_{Th} = 5\%$, OPC loss raises from 5% (i.e., the ideal max. loss
value) to 8% for EBS and from 5% to 7% for RZ-BF in the interval ΔVdd $=$
[20 mV $-$ 250 mV].

Monitoring Period. The plots reported in Fig. 14 show Vdd_{avg} and EPO
using different monitoring period N. Simulations are conducted on EBS and
RZ-BF using the Single Threshold Vdd (STh) scaling policy ΔVdd $= 20$ mV and
two different values of error-threshold, $ER_{Th} = 2\%$ and 5%.

EBS performs more efficiently than RZ-BF for all the operating conditions.
Considering the case $ER_{Th} = 5\%$ (the best case), EBS reaches lower Vdd_{avg},
0.91 V vs 1.02 V of RZ-BF, and larger EPO savings, 36.4% vs. 5.4% of RZ-BF
(average values on N interval).

As a general rule, the larger the N the slower the Vdd scaling. While this
trend is less evident in RZ-BF (Vdd_{avg} increases by just 40 mV), EBS amplifies
the effect showing an overall spread of 180 mV (from 0.83 mV to 1.01 mV). The
same consideration can be inferred for EPO, where savings gets smaller with N,
from 48.6% ($N = 10^3$) to 19.3% ($N = 5 \cdot 10^5$).

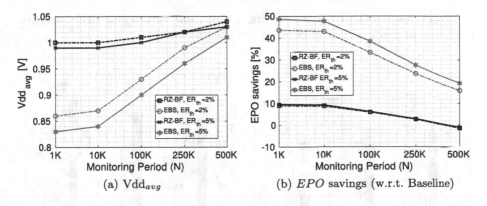

(a) Vdd_{avg} (b) EPO savings (w.r.t. Baseline)

Fig. 14. Energy efficiency vs. monitoring period (N).

Finally, the analysis reported in Fig. 15 shows that a more aggressive voltage
scaling strategy, i.e., smaller N, affects output quality and performance due to

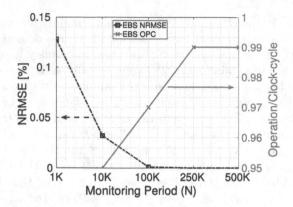

Fig. 15. EBS with $ER_{th} = 5\%$: QoR and performance vs. monitoring period (N).

an increasing number of error corrections. Results for RZ-BF are omitted as the $NRMSE$ gets always zero whatever the value of N. The $NRMSE$ of EBS increases, yet, only marginally: from zero to 0.128%. Also the OPC drops: from 0.99 to 0.95 when N reduces from $= 5 \cdot 10^5$ to 10^3 for both EBS and RZ-BF. That's the cost to be payed for a more energy efficient DD-VOS.

Vdd Scaling Policies. Simulations of the three Vdd scaling policies described in Sect. 5 have been run fixing the DD-VOS parameters as follows:

- Vdd step, ΔVdd $= 20$ mV;
- monitoring period, $N = 10^3$.
- error-threshold: $ER_{Th} = \{2\%, 5\%\}$ for STh and SC, $ER_{Th_{max}} = ER_{Th} = \{2\%, 5\%\}$ and $ER_{Th_{min}} = 0.2 \cdot ER_{Th_{max}}$ for DTh.

Figure 16 plots the collected results, which show once again EBS improves the figures of merit of DD-VOS, whatever the adopted policy.

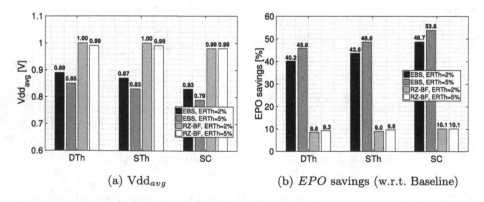

(a) Vdd$_{avg}$ (b) EPO savings (w.r.t. Baseline)

Fig. 16. DD-VOS policies energy efficiency comparison.

Table 4. Results summary for DD-VOS policies OPC and $NRMSE$.

Benchmarks	RZ-BF				EBS			
	OPC		NRMSE		OPC		NRMSE [%]	
	ER_{Th}= 2%	ER_{Th}= 5%	ER_{Th}= 2%	ER_{Th}= 5%	ER_{Th}= 2%	ER_{Th}= 5%	ER_{Th}= 2%	ER_{Th}= 5%
Double Th	0.99	0.97	0.000	0.000	0.99	0.97	0.000	0.000
Single Th	0.98	0.95	0.000	0.000	0.98	0.95	0.000	0.128
Saturation Counter	0.87	0.86	0.000	0.000	0.95	0.90	0.158	0.185

The DTh is more conservative. In this case EBS reaches a lower Vdd_{avg} than that of RZ-BF: at $ER_{Th} = 5\%$ (best case), 0.85 V vs. 0.99 V. With a lower Vdd, also EPO savings improve: 45.8% vs 9.3%. At the opposite corner, the SC approach pushes a more aggressive Vdd scaling. EBS reaches the lowest Vdd_{avg}, hence, the largest EPO savings: 0.79 V with 53.8% energy savings, against 0.98 V and 10.1% of RZ-BF. This comes at the cost of some miss-detection. As shown in Table 4, the adoption of the SC policy induces a $NRMSE$ degradation, mainly due to miss-detected errors: 0.185% in the worst case ($ER_{Th} = 5\%$). By contrast DTh ensures zero miss-detected errors, both for EBS and RZ-BF.

For what concerns performance, DTh affects OPC only marginally: 3% loss for both EBS and RZ-BF in the worst case ($ER_{Th} = 5\%$); DTh reduces Vdd ripples thus bringing to a lower number of error corrections. On the contrary, SC heavily impacts performance with OPC loss in the order of 10% for EBS and 14% for RZ-BF (at $ER_{Th} = 5\%$).

8   Conclusions

Early Bird Sampling (EBS) is a Razor variant strategy that applies to generic low-power sequential designs. The EBS allows to solve the problem of short-path races bypassing tedious hold-time fixing design stages, and enables aggressive Data-Driven Voltage Over-Scaling (DD-VOS), suited for ultra-low power error-resilient applications. Simulation runs on a representative set of circuits under realistic workloads using different voltage scaling policies provide a fair comparison with a standard Razor strategy. Collected results show EBS reduces area overheads (3.6% against 71.6% for Razor) and improves the voltage scaling thereby achieving higher energy efficiency (savings w.r.t. Razor range from 36.2% to 40.2%).

References

1. Ernst, D., Kim, N., et al.: Razor: a low-power pipeline based on circuit-level timing speculation. In: 36th Annual IEEE/ACM International Symposium on Microarchitecture, MICRO-36, Proceedings, pp. 7–18. IEEE (2003)
2. Rizzo, R.G., Peluso, V., Calimera, A., Zhou, J., Liu, X.: Early bird sampling: a short-paths free error detection-correction strategy for data-driven VOS. In: 2017 IEEE 25th International Conference on Very Large Scale Integration (VLSI-SoC). IEEE (2017)
3. Benini, L., Castelli, G., Macii, A., Macii, B., Scarai, R.: Battery-driven dynamic power management of portable systems. In: Proceedings 13th International Symposium on System Synthesis, pp. 25–30 (2000)
4. Alioto, M.: Ultra low power design approaches for IoT. Singapore-Hotchips (2014)
5. Bortolotti, D., Rossi, D., Bartolini, A., Benini, L.: A variation tolerant architecture for ultra low power multi-processor cluster. In: 2013 23rd International Workshop on Power and Timing Modeling, Optimization and Simulation (PATMOS), pp. 32–38. IEEE (2013)
6. Peluso, V., Rizzo, R.G., Calimera, A., Macii, E., Alioto, M.: Beyond ideal DVFS through ultra-fine grain vdd-hopping. In: Hollstein, T., Raik, J., Kostin, S., Tšertov, A., O'Connor, I., Reis, R. (eds.) VLSI-SoC 2016. IAICT, vol. 508, pp. 152–172. Springer, Cham (2017). https://doi.org/10.1007/978-3-319-67104-8_8
7. Benini, L., De Micheli, G., Macii, E., Poncino, M., Scarsi, R.: Symbolic synthesis of clock-gating logic for power optimization of control-oriented synchronous networks. In: Proceedings of the 1997 European Conference on Design and Test, EDTC 1997, p. 514. IEEE Computer Society, Washington, DC (1997)
8. Babighian, P., Benini, L., Macii, A., Macii, E.: Post-layout leakage power minimization based on distributed sleep transistor insertion. In: Proceedings of the 2004 International Symposium on Low Power Electronics and Design, ISLPED 2004, pp. 138–143. ACM (2004)
9. Calimera, A., Bahar, R.I., Macii, E., Poncino, M.: Temperature-insensitive dual-Vth synthesis for nanometer CMOS technologies under inverse temperature dependence. IEEE Trans. Very Large Scale Integr. (VLSI) Syst. 18(11), 1608–1620 (2010)
10. Calimera, A., et al.: Design of a family of sleep transistor cells for a clustered power-gating flow in 65 nm technology. In: Proceedings of the 17th ACM Great Lakes symposium on VLSI, pp. 501–504. ACM (2007)
11. Krause, P.K., et al.: Adaptive voltage over-scaling for resilient applications. In: 2011 Design, Automation Test in Europe, pp. 1–6, March 2011
12. Das, S., et al.: RazorII: in situ error detection and correction for PVT and SER tolerance. IEEE J. Solid-State Circ. 44(1), 32–48 (2009)
13. Kim, S., et al.: Variation-tolerant, ultra-low-voltage microprocessor with a low-overhead, within-a-cycle in-situ timing-error detection and correction technique. IEEE J. Solid-State Circ. 50(6), 1478–1490 (2015)
14. Valadimas, S., et al.: Timing error tolerance in nanometer ICs. In: 2010 IEEE 16th International On-Line Testing Symposium (IOLTS), pp. 283–288. IEEE (2010)
15. Bowman, K.A., et al.: Energy-efficient and metastability-immune resilient circuits for dynamic variation tolerance. IEEE J. Solid-State Circ. 44(1), 49–63 (2009)
16. Bowman, K., et al.: A 45 nm resilient microprocessor core for dynamic variation tolerance. IEEE J. Solid-State Circ. 46(1), 194–208 (2011)
17. Kwon, I., et al.: Razor-lite: a light-weight register for error detection by observing virtual supply rails. IEEE J. Solid-State Circ. 49(9), 2054–2066 (2014)

18. Das, S., et al.: A 1 GHz hardware loop-accelerator with razor-based dynamic adaptation for energy-efficient operation. IEEE Trans. Circ. Syst. I: Regul. Pap. **61**(8), 2290–2298 (2014)
19. Yang, Y.-M., et al.: PushPull: short-path padding for timing error resilient circuits. IEEE Trans. Comput. Aided Des. Integr. Circuits Syst. **33**(4), 558–570 (2014)
20. Ghosh, S., Bhunia, S., Roy, K.: CRISTA: a new paradigm for low-power, variation-tolerant, and adaptive circuit synthesis using critical path isolation. IEEE Trans. Comput. Aided Des. Integr. Circuits Syst. **26**(11), 1947–1956 (2007)
21. Kahng, A.B., et al.: Slack redistribution for graceful degradation under voltage overscaling. In: Proceedings of the 2010 Asia and South Pacific Design Automation Conference, pp. 825–831. IEEE Press (2010)
22. Karakonstantis, G., Roy, K.: Voltage over-scaling: a cross-layer design perspective for energy efficient systems. In: 2011 20th European Conference on Circuit Theory and Design (ECCTD), pp. 548–551. IEEE (2011)
23. Ernst, D., et al.: Razor: circuit-level correction of timing errors for low-power operation. IEEE Micro **24**(6), 10–20 (2004)
24. Ramasubramanian, S.G., Venkataramani, S., Parandhaman, A., Raghunathan, A.: Relax-and-retime: a methodology for energy-efficient recovery based design. In: Proceedings of the 50th Annual Design Automation Conference, p. 111. ACM (2013)
25. Wan, L., Chen, D.: DynaTune: circuit-level optimization for timing speculation considering dynamic path behavior. In: Proceedings of the 2009 International Conference on Computer-Aided Design, pp. 172–179. ACM (2009)
26. Greskamp, B., et al.: Blueshift: designing processors for timing speculation from the ground up. In: IEEE 15th International Symposium on High Performance Computer Architecture, HPCA 2009, pp. 213–224. IEEE (2009)
27. Wan, L., Chen, D.: CCP: common case promotion for improved timing error resilience with energy efficiency. In: Proceedings of the 2012 ACM/IEEE International Symposium on Low Power Electronics and Design, pp. 135–140. ACM (2012)
28. Mohapatra, D., Karakonstantis, G., Roy, K.: Low-power process-variation tolerant arithmetic units using input-based elastic clocking. In: Proceedings of the 2007 International Symposium on Low Power Electronics and Design, pp. 74–79. ACM (2007)
29. Carmona, J., Cortadella, J., Kishinevsky, M., Taubin, A.: Elastic circuits. IEEE Trans. Comput.-Aided Des. Integr. Circuits Syst. **28**(10), 1437–1455 (2009)
30. Shim, B., Sridhara, S.R., Shanbhag, N.R.: Reliable low-power digital signal processing via reduced precision redundancy. IEEE Transactions on Very Large Scale Integration (VLSI) Systems **12**(5), 497–510 (2004)
31. Pagliari, D.J., Calimera, A., Macii, E., Poncino, M.: An automated design flow for approximate circuits based on reduced precision redundancy. In: 2015 33rd IEEE International Conference on Computer Design (ICCD), pp. 86–93. IEEE (2015)
32. Zhou, J., et al.: HEPP: a new in-situ timing-error prediction and prevention technique for variation-tolerant ultra-low-voltage designs. In: 2013 IEEE Asian Solid-State Circuits Conference (A-SSCC), pp. 129–132. IEEE (2013)
33. Chakraborty, A., et al.: Dynamic thermal clock skew compensation using tunable delay buffers. IEEE Transactions on Very Large Scale Integration (VLSI) Systems **16**(6), 639–649 (2008)

Integrating Simulink, OpenVX, and ROS for Model-Based Design of Embedded Vision Applications

Stefano Aldegheri and Nicola Bombieri[(✉)]

Department of Computer Science, University of Verona, Verona, Italy
{stefano.aldegheri,nicola.bombieri}@univr.it

Abstract. OpenVX is increasingly gaining consensus as standard platform to develop portable, optimized and power-efficient embedded vision applications. Nevertheless, adopting OpenVX for rapid prototyping, early algorithm parametrization and validation of complex embedded applications is a very challenging task. This paper presents a comprehensive framework that integrates Simulink, OpenVX, and ROS for model-based design of embedded vision applications. The framework allows applying Matlab-Simulink for the model-based design, parametrization, and validation of computer vision applications. Then, it allows for the automatic synthesis of the application model into an OpenVX description for the hardware and constraints-aware application tuning. Finally, the methodology allows integrating the OpenVX application with Robot Operating System (ROS), which is the de-facto reference standard for developing robotic software applications. The OpenVX-ROS interface allows co-simulating and parametrizing the application by considering the actual robotic environment and the application reuse in any ROS-compliant system. Experimental results have been conducted with two real case studies: An application for digital image stabilization and the ORB descriptor for simultaneous localization and mapping (SLAM), which have been developed through Simulink and, then, automatically synthesized into OpenVX-VisionWorks code for an NVIDIA Jetson TX2 board.

1   Introduction

Computer vision has gained an increasing interest as an efficient way to automatically extract of meaning from images and video. It has been an active field of research for decades, but until recently has had few major commercial applications. However, with the advent of high-performance, low-cost, energy efficient processors, it has quickly become largely applied in a wide range of applications for embedded systems [1].

The term *embedded vision* refers to this new wave of widely deployed, practical computer vision applications properly optimized for a target embedded

© IFIP International Federation for Information Processing 2019
Published by Springer Nature Switzerland AG 2019
M. Maniatakos et al. (Eds.): VLSI-SoC 2017, IFIP AICT 500, pp. 178–197, 2019.
https://doi.org/10.1007/978-3-030-15663-3_9

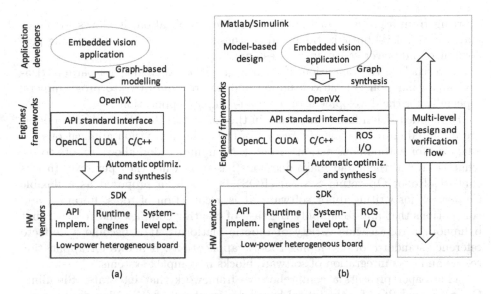

Fig. 1. The embedded vision application design flow: the standard (a), and the extended with the model-based design paradigm (b)

system by considering a set of design constraints. The target embedded systems usually consist of heterogeneous, multi-/many-core, low power embedded devices, while the design constraints, beside functional correctness, include performance, energy efficiency, dependability, real-time response, resiliency, fault tolerance, and certifiability.

Developing and optimizing a computer vision application for an embedded processor can be a non-trivial task. Considering an application as a set of communicating and interacting kernels, the effort for such application optimization goes over two dimensions: the single kernel-level optimization and the system-level optimization. Kernel-level optimizations have traditionally revolved around one-off or single function acceleration. This typically means that a developer rewrites a computer vision function (e.g., any filter, image arithmetic, geometric transform function) with a more efficient algorithm or offloads its execution to accelerators such as a GPU by using languages such as OpenCL or CUDA [2].

On the other hand, system-level optimizations pay close attention to the overall power consumption, memory bandwidth loading, low-latency functional computing, and Inter-Processor Communication overhead. These issues are typically addressed via frameworks [3], as the parameters of interest cannot be tuned with compilers or operating systems.

In this context, OpenVX [4] has gained wide consensus in the embedded vision community and has become the de-facto reference standard and API library for system-level optimization. OpenVX is designed to maximize functional and performance portability across different hardware platforms, providing a computer vision framework that efficiently addresses current and future hardware architectures with minimal impact on software applications.

Starting from a graph model of the embedded application, it allows for automatic system-level optimizations and synthesis on the HW board targeting performance and power consumption design constraints [5–7].

Nevertheless, the definition of such a graph-based model, its parametrization and validation is time consuming and far from intuitive to programmers, especially for the development of medium-complex applications.

Embedded vision finds a large use in the context of Robotics, where cameras are mounted on robots and the results of the embedded vision applications are analysed for autonomous actions. Indeed, Computer vision allows robots to see what is around them and make decisions based on what they perceive. In this context, Robot Operating System (ROS) [8] has been proposed as a flexible framework for writing robot software. It is a collection of tools, libraries, and conventions that aim to simplify the task of creating complex and robust robot behaviour across a wide variety of robotic platforms. It is become a de-facto reference standard for developing robotic applications. It allows for application re-use and easy integration of software blocks in complex systems.

This paper presents a comprehensive framework that integrates Simulink, OpenVX, and ROS for the model-based design of embedded vision applications (see Fig. 1). Differently from the standard approaches at the state of the art that require designers to manually model the algorithm through OpenVX code (see Fig. 1(a)), the proposed approach allows for a rapid prototyping, algorithm validation and parametrization in a model-based design environment (i.e., Matlab/Simulink). The framework relies on a multi-level design and verification flow (see Fig. 1(b)) by which the high-level model is then semi-automatically refined towards the final automatic synthesis into OpenVX code. The integration with ROS has two main goals: first, to allow co-simulating and parametrizing the application by considering the actual robotic environment, and then, to allow for application reuse in ROS-compliant systems.

The paper presents the results obtained by applying the proposed methodology for developing and tuning two real-case applications. The first is an algorithm for digital image stabilization for two different application contexts. The second is the application implementing the oriented fast and rotated brief (ORB) descriptor for simultaneous localization and mapping (SLAM). The paper presents the Simulink toolbox developed to support the NVIDIA OpenVX-VisionWorks library, and how it has been used in the design flow to synthesize OpenVX code for an NVIDIA Jetson TX2 embedded system board.

The paper is organized as follows. Section 2 presents the background and the related work. Section 3 explains in details the model-based design methodology. Section 4 presents the experimental results, while Sect. 5 is devoted to the conclusions.

2   Background and Related Work

OpenVX relies on a graph-based software architecture to enable efficient computation on heterogeneous computing platforms, including those with GPU accelerators. It provides a set of primitives (or kernels) that are commonly used in computer vision algorithms. It also provides a set of data objects like scalars, arrays, matrices and images, as well as high-level data objects like histograms, image pyramids, and look-up tables. It supports customized user-defined kernels for implementing customized application features.

The programmer defines a computer vision algorithm by instantiating kernels as nodes and data objects as parameters. Since each node may use the mix of the processing units in the heterogeneous platform, a single graph may be executed across CPUs, GPUs, DSPs, etc. Figure 2 and Listing 1.1 give an example of computer vision application and its OpenVX code, respectively. The programming flow starts by creating an OpenVX *context* to manage references to all used objects (line 1, Listing 1.1). Based on this context, the code builds the graph (line 2) and generates all required data objects (lines 4 to 11). Then, it instantiates the kernel as graph nodes and generates their connections (lines 15 to 18). The graph integrity and correctness is checked in line 20 (e.g., checking of data type coherence between nodes and absence of cycles). Finally, the graph is processed by the OpenVX framework (line 23). At the end of the code execution, all created data objects, the graph, and the context are released.

The definition of algorithms through primitives has two benefits: First, it allows defining the application in an abstract way while preserving an efficient implementation. Then, it allows enabling system-level optimizations, like inter-node memory transfers, pipelining, concurrent and overlapped node execution. To utilize the different accelerators on the board, data transfer management needs to be addressed. Each operation requires time and power resources, and this has to be considered in the mapping process. Pipelining and tiling techniques can be efficiently utilized together to achieve better memory locality. This greatly reduces the data transfer overhead between global and scratchpad memory [9].

Different works have been presented to analyse the use of OpenVX for embedded vision [5–7, 11]. In [6], the authors present a new implementation of OpenVX targeting CPUs and GPU-based devices by leveraging different analytical optimization techniques. In [7], the authors examine how OpenVX responds to different data access patterns, by testing three different OpenVX optimizations: kernels merge, data tiling and parallelization via OpenMP. In [5], the authors introduce ADRENALINE, a novel framework for fast prototyping and optimization of OpenVX applications for heterogeneous SoCs with many-core accelerators. The authors in [10] implemented a graphic interface that allows computer vision developers to create visual algorithms in OpenVX. The framework then automatically generates the corresponding OpenVX code, with a translation back-end that creates all the glue code needed to correctly run the OpenVX environment. This work extends the preliminary implementation of the model-based design presented in [11] by including the interface towards ROS. This allows co-simulating the OpenVX application with the external application environment (e.g., input streams, concurrent interactive systems, etc.) and, as a consequence, tuning more efficiently the SW parametrization. Results on a more advanced Robotic application (ORB descriptor) underlines that making any application ROS-compliant is strategic for IP-reuse.

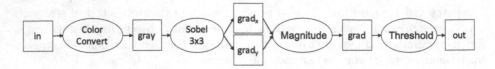

Fig. 2. OpenVX sample application (graph diagram)

```
1  vx_context c = vxCreateContext();
2  vx_graph g = vxCreateGraph(context);
3  vx_enum type = VX_DF_IMAGE_VIRT;
4  /* create data structures */
5  vx_image in = vxCreateImage(c, w, h, VX_DF_IMAGE_RGBX);
6  vx_image gray   = vxCreateVirtualImage(g, 0, 0, type);
7  vx_image grad_x = vxCreateVirtualImage(g, 0, 0, type);
8  vx_image grad_y = vxCreateVirtualImage(g, 0, 0, type);
9  vx_image grad   = vxCreateVirtualImage(g, 0, 0, type);
10 vx_image out = vxCreateImage(c, w, h, VX_DF_IMAGE_U8);
11 vx_threshold threshold = vxCreateThreshold(c, VX_THRESHOLD_TYPE_BINARY,
       VX_TYPE_FLOAT32);
12 /* read input image and copy it into "in" data object */
13 ...
14 /* construct the graph */
15 vxColorConvertNode(g, in, gray);
16 vxSobel3x3Node(g, gray, grad_x, grad_y);
17 vxMagnitudeNode(g, grad_x, grad_y, grad);
18 vxThresholdNode(g, grad, threshold, out);
19 /*verify the graph*/
20 status = vxVerifyGraph(g);
21 /*execute the graph*/
22 if (status == VX_SUCCESS)
23   status = vxProcessGraph(g);
```

Listing 1.1. OpenVX code of the example of Fig. 2

Differently from all the work of the literature, this paper presents an extension of the OpenvX environment to the model-based design paradigm. Such an extension aims at exploiting the model-based approach for the fast prototyping of any computer vision algorithm through a Matlab/Simulink model, its parametrization, validation, and automatic synthesis into an equivalent OpenVX code representation.

3   The Model-Based Design Approach

Figure 3 depicts the overview of the proposed design flow. The computer vision application is firstly developed in Matlab/Simulink, by exploiting a computer vision oriented toolbox of Simulink[1]. Such a block library allows developers to define the application algorithms through Simulink blocks and to quickly simulate and validate the application at system level. The platform allows specific

---

[1] In this work, we selected the *Simulink Computer Vision* toolbox (CVT), as it represents the most widespread and used toolbox in the computer vision community. The methodology, however, is general and can be extended to other Simulink toolboxes.

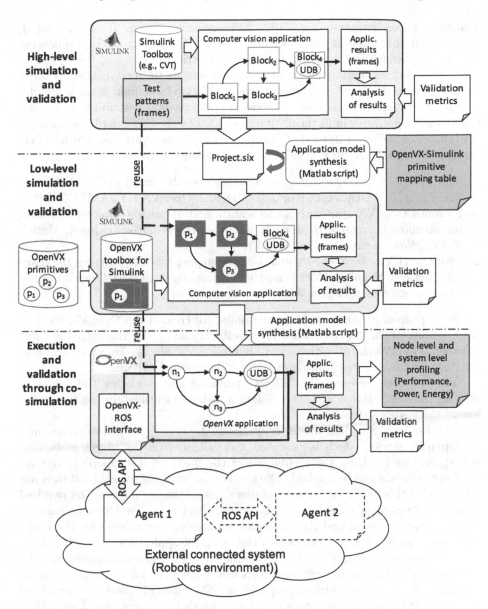

Fig. 3. Methodology overview

and embedded application primitives to be defined by the user if not included in the toolbox through the Simulink *S-Function* construct [12] (e.g., user-defined block UDB *Block₄* in Fig. 3). Streams of frames are given as input stimuli to the application model and the results (generally represented by frames or streams of frames) are evaluated by adopting any ad-hoc validation metrics from the computer vision literature (e.g., [13]). Efficient test patterns are extrapolated, by using any technique of the literature, to assess the quality of the application results by considering the adopted validation metrics.

The high-level application model is then automatically synthesized for a low-level simulation and validation through Matlab/Simulink. Such a simulation aims at validating the computer vision application at system-level by using the OpenVX primitive implementations provided by the HW board vendor (e.g., NVIDIA VisionWorks) instead of Simulink blocks. The synthesis, which is performed through e Matlab routine, relies on two key components:

1. *The OpenVX toolbox for Simulink.* Starting from the library of OpenVX primitives (e.g., NVIDIA VisionWorks [14], INTEL OpenVX [15], AMDOVX [16], Khronos OpenVX standard implementation [17]), such a toolbox of blocks for Simulink is created by properly wrapping the primitives through Matlab *S-Function*, as explained in Sect. 3.1.
2. *The OpenVX primitives-Simulink blocks mapping table.* It provides the mapping between Simulink blocks and the functionally equivalent OpenVX primitives, as explained in Sect. 3.2.

As explained in the experimental results, we created the OpenVX toolbox for Simulink of the NVIDIA VisionWorks library as well as the mapping table between VisionWorks primitives and Simulink CVT blocks. They are available for download from https://profs.sci.univr.it/bombieri/VW4Sim.

The low-level representation allows simulating and validating the model by reusing the test patterns and the validation metrics identified during the higher level (and faster) simulation.

The low-level Simulink model is synthesized, through a Matlab script, into an OpenVX model, which is executed and validated on the target embedded board. At this level, all the techniques of the literature for OpenVX system-level optimization can be applied. The synthesis is straightforward (and thus not addressed in this paper for the sake of space), as all the key information required to build a stand-alone OpenVX code is contained in the low-level Simulink model. Both the test patterns and the validation metrics can be re-used for the node-level and system-level optimization of the OpenVX application.

The proposed design flow also allows the embedded vision application to be refined by considering the external Robotics system, which is supposed to be implemented as ROS-compliant application. The OpenVX model is interfaced to ROS through a set of interface templates, which implement the OpenV-ROS communication based on message passing. A lightweight *target* I/O module is responsible to handle the information sent by the system (e.g., sensors, controllers, etc.) and to translate it into an OpenVX data structure. A similar I/O module implements the *initiator* interface, which allows sending information from OpenVX (generally the results of a computation) to the ROS system. By relying on the ROS communication protocol, the embedded vision application can easily interact with multiple external actors, allowing an easy integration and reuse into real Robotics systems.

```
1  function s_colorConvert(block)
2    setup(block);
3
4    function setup(block)
5      % Number of ports and parameters
6      block.NumInputPorts  = 1;
7      block.NumOutputPorts = 1;
8
9      block.RegBlockMethod('Start', @Begin);
10     block.RegBlockMethod('Stop', @End);
11     block.RegBlockMethod('Outputs', @Outputs);
12   function begin(block)
13     %create vx_image
14     gray = m_vxCreateImage();
15   function end(block)
16     %destroy vx_image
17     m_vxReleaseImage(gray);
18   function outputs(block) //computation phase:
19     in = block.InputPort(1).Data;
20     ret_val = m_vxColorConvert(in, gray);
21     block.OutputPort(1).Data = gray;
```

Listing 1.2. Matlab S-function code for the color converter node

3.1   OpenVX Toolbox for Simulink

The generation of the OpenVX toolbox for Simulink relies on the *S-function* construct, which allows describing any Simulink block functionality through C/C++ code. The code is compiled as *mex file* by using the Matlab *mex utility* [18]. As with other *mex* files, *S-functions* are dynamically linked subroutines that the Matlab execution engine can automatically load and execute. *S-functions* use a special calling syntax (i.e., *S-function API*) that enables the interaction between the block and the Simulink engine. This interaction is very similar to the interaction that takes place between the engine and built-in Simulink blocks.

We defined a *S-function* template to build OpenVX blocks for Simulink that, as for the construct specifications, consists of four main phases (see the example in Listing 1.2, which represents the *Color Converter* node of Fig. 2):

– *Setup phase* (lines 4–11): it defines the I/O block interface in terms of number of input and output ports and the block internal state (e.g., point list for tracking primitives).
– *Begin phase* (lines 12–14): It allocates data structure in the Simulink memory space for saving the results of the block execution. Since the block executes OpenVX code, this phase implementation relies on a *data wrapper* for the OpenVX-Simulink data exchange and conversion.
– *End phase* (lines 15–17): It deallocates the created data structures at the end of the simulation (after the computation phase).
– *Computation phase* (lines 18–20): it reads the input data and executes the code implementing the block functionality. It makes use of a *primitive wrapper* to execute OpenVX code.

Three different wrappers have been defined to allow communication and synchronization between the Simulink and the OpenVX environments. They are

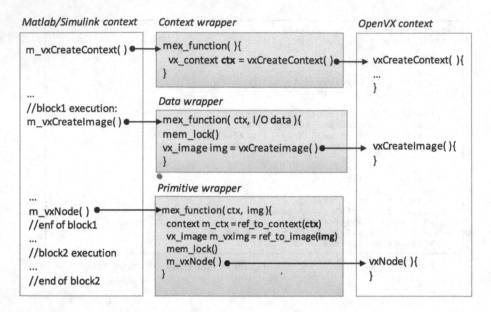

Fig. 4. Overview of the Simulink-OpenVX communication

summarized in Fig. 4. The *context wrapper* allows creating the OpenVX context (see line 1 of Listing 1.1), which is mandatory for any OpenVX primitive execution. It is run once for the whole system application. The *data wrapper* allows creating the OpenVX data structures for the primitive communication (see *in, gray, grad$_x$, grad$_y$, grad,* and *out* in the example of Fig. 2 and lines 4–11 of Listing 1.1). It is run once for each application block. The *primitive wrapper* allows executing, in the Simulink context, each primitive functionality implemented in OpenVX. To speed up the simulation, the wrapped primitives work through references to data structures, which are passed as function parameters during the primitive invocations to the OpenVX context. To do that, the wrappers implement memory locking mechanisms (i.e., through the Matlab *mem_lock()/mem_unlock()* constructs) to prevent data objects to be released automatically by the Matlab engine between primitive invocations.

3.2 Mapping Table Between OpenVX Primitives and Simulink Blocks

To enable the application model synthesis from the high-level to the low-level representation, mapping information is required to put in correspondence the built-in Simulink blocks and the corresponding OpenVX primitives. In this work, we defined such a mapping table between the Simulink CVT Toolbox and the NVIDIA OpenVX-VisionWorks library. The table, which consists of 58 entries in the current release, includes primitives for image arithmetic, flow and depth, geometric transforms, filters, feature and analysis operations. Table 1 shows, as an example, a representative subset of the mapped entries.

Table 1. Representative subset of the mapping table between Simulink CVT and NVIDIA OpenVX-VisionWorks

Simulink block	Visionworks primitive	Notes to the developer
CVT/AnalysisAnd -Enhancement/ EdgeDetection	vxuCannyEdgeDetector	If Simulink EdgeDetection set as Canny
CVT/AnalysisAnd -Enhancement/ EdgeDetection	vxuSobel3x3	If Simulink EdgeDetection set as Sobel
CVT/AnalysisAnd -Enhancement/ EdgeDetection	vxuConvolve	If filter size different from 3x3
CVT/Morphological operation/Opening	vxuErode3x3 + vxuDilate3x3	
CVT/Filtering/Median Filter	vxuMedianFilter3x3	
CVT/Filtering/Median Filter	vxuNonLinearFilter	If filter size different from 3x3
Math Op./Subtract + Math Op./Abs	vxuAbsoluteDifference	
CVT/Conversion/Color space conversion	vxuColorConvert	
CVT/Statistics/2D Mean	vxuMeanStdDev	Only mean and standard deviation of the entire image supported
CVT/Statistics/2D StandardDev		
Simulink/Math operations/Real/ComplexTo -Imag	vxuMagnitude	Gradient magnitude computed through complex numbers
Simulink/Math operations/Real/Imag to Magnitude		

We implemented three possible mapping strategies:

1. 1-to-1: the Simulink block is mapped to a single OpenVX primitive (e.g., color converter image arithmetic).
2. 1-to-n: the Simulink block functionality is implemented by a concatenation of multiple OpenVX primitives (e.g., the opening morphological operation).
3. n-to-1: a concatenation of multiple Simulink blocks are needed to implement a single OpenVX primitive (e.g., subtract + absolute blocks).

For some entry, the mapping also depends on the Simulink block setting. As an example, the OpenVX primitive for edge detection is selected depending on the setting of the corresponding CVT block. The setting includes the choice of the filter algorithm (i.e., Canny or Sobel) and the filter size.

The blocks listed in the left-most column of the table form the OpenVX toolbox for Simulink. Any Simulink model built from them can undergo the proposed automatic refinement flow. In addition, user-defined Simulink blocks implemented in C/C++ are supported and translated into OpenVX user kernels. They are eventually loaded and included in the OpenVX representation as graph nodes. To do that, we defined the wrapper represented in Listing 1.3, which follows the node implementation directives required by the standard OpenVX for importing user kernels[2]. The wrapper invocation (i.e., $vx\_userNode()$) is

---

[2] www.khronos.org/registry/openVX/specs/1.0/html/da/d83/group_group_user_kernels.html.

```
1  vx_userNode(){
2    vx_status processingOpenVX(vx_node node, const vx_reference *parameters,
         vx_uint32 num)
3    {
4      //convert data in internal representation
5      SimulinkBlockFunctionality(); //C/C++ code of the UDB functionality
6      return VX_SUCCESS;
7    }
8    vx_status validationOpenVX(vx_node node, const vx_reference parameters
       [], vx_uint32 num,  vx_meta_format metas[]))
9    {
10     //insert parameter validation
11     return VX_SUCCESS;
12   }
13
14   vx_status singleShotProcessing(vx_context context, parameters)
15   {
16     //create graph and execute it
17   }
18
19   vx_status registerCustomKernel(vx_context context)
20   {
21     vx_status = vxAddUserKernel(context, ...);//register kernel in context
22     return VX_SUCCESS;
23   }
24 }
```

Listing 1.3. Overview of wrapper for user-defined Simulink block implementations

similar to the invocation of any built-in OpenVX node (i.e., $vxNode()$) in the OpenVX context through the previously presented *context wrapper* (see the righmost side of Fig. 4).

Finally, some restrictions on the Simulink block interfaces are required to allow the Simulink/OpenVX communication as well as the model synthesis. The set of data types and data structures available for the high-level model is reduced to the subset supported by OpenVX, whereby each I/O port of the Simulink blocks consists of:

- *Dimension* $d \in \{1D, 2D, 3D, 3D + AlphaChannel\}$, e.g., greyscale, RGB or YUV, and alpha channel for transparency.
- *Size* $s \in \{N \times M \times 1, N \times M \times 3, N \times M \times 4\}$.
- *Type* $t \in \{uint8, float\}$, where $uint8$ is generally used for representing data (pixels, colours, etc.) while $float$ is generally used for representing interpolation data.

3.3 ROS Integration

The adoption of ROS provides different advantages. First, it allows the platform to model and simulate blocks running on different target devices. Then, it implements the inter-node communication in a modular way and by adopting a standard and widespread protocol, thus guaranteeing code portability.

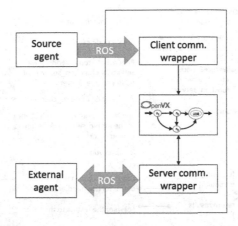

Fig. 5. The OpenVX-ROS communication through the server and client models

```
1  bool function_service(
2      ServerType::Request  &req,
3      ServerType::Response &res  )
4  {
5    // compute the results
6    res.output1 = openvx2ros(
7      wrapper_openvx
8      (ros2openvx(req.input1),
9       ros2openvx(req.input2))
10       );
11   if(errors) return false;
12   else        return true;
13 }
14
15 int process_init()
16 {
17   ros::init(0, [],
18       "service_server");
19   ros::NodeHandle n;
20   // Inform that this server is up
21   ros::ServiceServer service =
22       n.advertiseService(
23       "topic_service",
24       function_service
25       );
26   ros::spin();
27 }
```
(a)

```
1  int process_init()
2  {
3    ros::init(0, [],
4        "service_client");
5    ros::NodeHandle n;
6
7    ros::ServiceClient client =
8        n.serviceClient<ServerType>(
9        "topic_service"
10       );
11   ros::Publisher pub =
12       n.advertise<DataType>("
13       topic_out", 10);
13   ServerType srv;
14   //fill input data(opt. parameter)
15   srv.req.input1 = ...;
16   if (client.call(srv))
17   {
18     // processing went good
19     n.publish(
20       openvx2ros(wrapper_openvx(
21       ros2openvx(srv.res.output1)
22     )));
23   }
24   else
25   {
26     // processing fails
27   }
28 }
```
(b)

Fig. 6. Skeleton implementation for the (a) server model and the (b) client model

ROS implements the messages passing among nodes by providing a publish-subscribe communication model. Every message sent through ROS has a topic, which is a unique string known by all the communicating nodes. An initiator node assigns a topic to publish a message, and the receiving nodes subscribe to the topic.

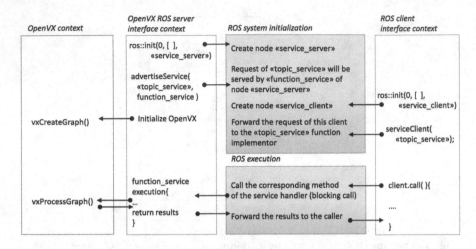

Fig. 7. Server model time evolution

Based on such a message passing interface, the proposed design flow relies on two communication models:

- *Client model:* The OpenVX application actively fetches inputs from a particular ROS node. It relies on a client communication wrapper, as shown in the upper side of Fig. 5. It is particularly suited for intensive yet synchronous communication (e.g., data acquisition of the OpenVX application from an input sensor).
- *Server model:* It allows the OpenVX application to be run on-demand. The external environment, which is implemented as ROS node, sends an execution request through an input data structure. The OpenVX application executes and returns the result as a response packet. It relies on a server communication wrapper, as shown in the bottom side of Fig. 5. It is well suited to implement sporadic communication (e.g., interpretation of the map built by a SLAM application by an external agent).

Figure 6(a) shows the skeleton implementation of the server interface. The *process_init* function is responsible to perform the node initialization in the ROS framework. It adds the current process to the ROS node list in the master server (lines 17–18). This node is sensitive to the topic specified in line 23. Line 24 specifies the function that will be called on the server invocation. Lines 1–13 provide the invocation of the OpenVX application. Two parameters are necessary to the function: the request, which contains the input data, and the response, which will be updated by the computing function. Conversion functions are defined to convert the data format between ROS and OpenVX. Finally, line 26 implements the busy waiting until the ROS framework shuts down all the nodes. Figure 7 shows the temporal evolution of the OpenVX-ROS communication based on the server model of Fig. 6(a).

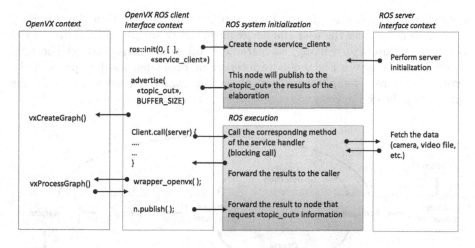

Fig. 8. Client model time evolution

Figure 6(b) depicts the skeleton for the client interface. After adding the process to the list of ROS nodes (lines 3–4), the system informs the ROS framework that the client requests need to be forwarded to the *topic_service* listener (lines 7–10). The wrapper creates the object to write the results of the computation (lines 11–12). Parameters are filled in line 15, and the call to request data is performed in line 16. In case of positive message receiving, the OpenVX computation is called (lines 20–21), through ad-hoc functions to convert the data format between ROS and OpenVX. The system publishes the results back to the network (line 19). Figure 8 shows the temporal evolution of such a client model process.

4   Experimental Results

We applied the proposed model-based design flow for the development of two embedded software: the first one implements a digital image stabilization algorithm for camera streams, while the latter calculate the ORB descriptor.

4.1   Image Stabilization

Figure 9 shows an overview of the algorithm, which is represented through a dependency graph. The input stream (i.e., sequence of frames) is taken from a high-definition camera, and each frame is converted to the grayscale format to improve the algorithm efficiency without compromising the quality of the result. A *remapping* operation is then applied to the resulting frames to remove fisheye distortions. A sparse optical flow is applied to the points detected in the previous frame by using a feature detector (e.g., Harris or Fast detector). The resulting points are then compared to the original point to find the homography matrix. The last N matrices are then combined by using a Gaussian filtering, where N is defined by the user (higher N means more smoothed trajectory a the cost of more latency). Finally, each frame is inversely warped to get the final result. Dashed lines in Fig. 9 denote inter-frame dependencies, i.e., parts of the algorithm where a temporal window of several frames is used to calculate the camera translation.

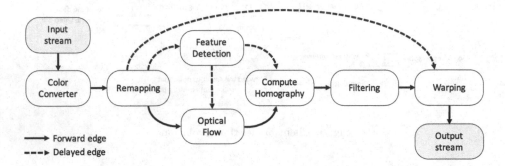

Fig. 9. Digital image stabilization algorithm

We firstly modelled the algorithm application in Simulink (CVT toolbox). The nodes *Optical flow* and *Filtering* have been inserted as user-defined blocks, since they implement customized functionality and are not present in the CVT toolbox. We conducted two different parametrizations of the algorithm, and in particular of the feature detection phase: For an indoor and for an outdoor application context. The first targets a system for indoor navigation of an Unmanned aerial vehicle (UAV), while the second targets a system for outdoor navigation of an Autonomous Surface Crafts (ASCs) [19].

We validated the two algorithm configurations starting from input streams registered by different cameras at 60 FPS with 1280×720 (1080P) and 1920×1080 wide angle resolution, respectively. Table 2 reports the characteristics of the input streams (columns *Video real time* and *#Frames*) and the time spent for simulating the high-level model on such video streams in Simulink (*Model simulation time*). Starting from the original video streams, we extrapolated a subset of test patterns, which consist of the minimal selection of video streams necessary to validate the model correctness by adopting the Smith et al. validation metrics for light field video stabilization [13]. The table reports the characteristics of such selected test patterns (sequences of frames).

We then applied the Matlab synthesis script to translate the high-level model into the low-level model by using the OpenVX toolbox for Simulink generated from the NVIDIA VisionWorks v1.6 [14] and the corresponding Simulink CVT-NVIDIA OpenVX/VisionWorks mapping table, as described in Sects. 3.1 and 3.2, respectively. In particular, the low level simulation in Simulink allowed us to validate the computer vision application implemented through the primitives

Table 2. Experimental results: High-level simulation time in Simulink

Context	Original input stream			Selected test patterns		
	Video real time (min)	Model simulation time (min)	Frames (#)	Video real time (min)	Model simulation time (min)	Frames (#)
Indoor	364	492	1.296.278	20.5	30.5	72.112
Outdoor	192	263	648.644	11.0	13.0	36.935

provided by the HW board vendor (e.g., NVIDIA OpenVX-VisionWorks) instead of Simulink blocks.

Finally, we synthesized the low-level model into pure OpenVX code, by which we run the real time analysis and validation on the target embedded board (NVIDIA Jetson TX1). Table 3 reports a comparison among the different simulation time (real execution time for the OpenVX code) spent to validate the embedded software application at each level of the design flow. At each refinement step, we reused the selected test patterns to verify the code over the adopted validation metrics [13] for both the contexts and by assuming a maximum deviation of 5%. The results underline that the higher level model simulation is faster as it mostly relies on built-in Simulink blocks. It is recommended for functional validation, algorithm parametrization, and test pattern selection. It provides all the benefits of the model-based design paradigm, while it cannot be used for accurate timing analysis, power, and energy measurements. The low level model simulation is much slower since it relies on actual primitive implementation and many wrapper invocations. However, it represents a fundamental step as it allows verifying the functional equivalence between the system-level model implemented through blocks and the system-level model implemented through primitives. Finally, the validation through execution on the target real device allows for accurate timing and power analysis, in which all the techniques at the state of the art for system-level optimization can be applied.

Table 3. Experimental results: Comparison of the simulation time spent to validate the software application at different levels of the design flow. The board level validation time refers to real execution time on the target board

Validation level	Sim./Exec. time (min)	
	Indoor	Outdoor
Simulink high-level model	30.5	13.0
Simulink low level model	59.0	26.5
Software application on target embedded system device	20.5	11.0

4.2   ORB Descriptor

In computer vision, *visual descriptors* or *image descriptors* represent visual features of image or video contents captured by an input video sensor. One of the most adopted is ORB [20], which is generally integrated in complex localization and mapping systems (i.e., ORB-SLAM [21]). The ORB-SLAM algorithm performs ORB computation at different levels, to detect both fine and coarse features of images. The inputs generally consists of a gray-scale image, the number of such levels, and the number of features to be analysed per level.

We applied the proposed model-based design flow to define the ORB algorithm, which is depicted in Fig. 10. For the sake of space, the figure shows the implementation of a single level in the Simulink environment. The data-flow oriented algorithm consists of 5 main steps: The input image is resized according to the scale level with the nearest-neighbors interpolation. The interesting points are detected by using the FAST corner detection algorithm with a specified threshold. Then, the computed keypoints are divided into a regular grid where a pruning is applied to each cell by using an higher threshold. This step is applied only to the cells where the results are non-empty (i.e., there exist at least one keypoint for each cell). The algorithm organizes the keypoints in a *quadtree data structure*, which allows achieving a uniform sampling of the keypoints in the image, carrying out the final pruning, and obtaining final keypoints, where as a result, an angle is computed (i.e., since FAST detector is not oriented). The algorithm applies a gaussian blur operation to the resized image, in order to improve the descriptor quality and to avoid artifacts that can be introduced by the nearest neighbor interpolation. Finally, the ORB descriptor is computed for each keypoint. The final coordinates of the keypoints are rescaled to the corresponding location in the original image.

Along the design flow, we measured the execution time of the algorithm implementations at different refinement steps, by using the KITTI dataset [22], which is a standard set of benchmarks for SLAM and computer vision applications. We also adopted the ROS interfaces described in Sect. 3.3 to receive the video stream (i.e., based on the slave model) and to integrate an external agent that reads the ORB result (i.e., based on the server model).

Table 4 reports the execution time we obtained by running the application on the input sequence 11 of the KITTI dataset at different refinement levels. We applied the semi-automatic translation process from Simulink to the final implementation as explained in Sect. 4.1, targeting an NVIDIA Jetson TX2 embedded board. We observed a slightly reduced execution time for the Simulink low-level model execution with respect to the high-level model despite the wrapper usage. This is due the fact that the algorithm implementation in Simulink required specialized MATLAB code that was not available with Simulink CVT library as native blocks. As a consequence, we developed custom code in MATLAB to meet the requirements, and imported such a code as user-defined Simulink blocks using the level-2 S-functions. As for the model-based design flow, the main focus of the Simulink implementation was to target the functional verification of the embedded application, with little effort on performance optimizations. On the

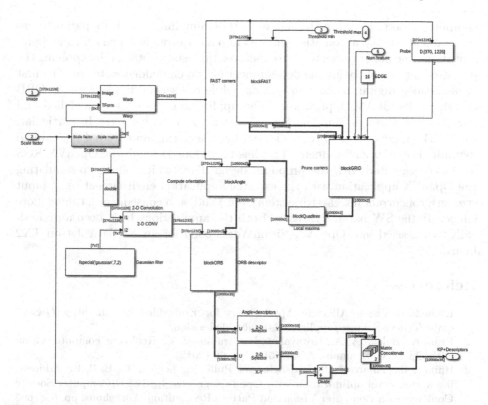

Fig. 10. ORB design in Simulink

Table 4. Experimental results: Comparison of the simulation time spent to validate the software application at different levels of the design flow. The board level validation time refers to real execution time on the target board including the ROS communication overhead

Validation level	Sim./Exec. time (seconds)
Simulink high-level model	804.0
Simulink low level model	762.0
Software application on target embedded system device (with accelerators) and ROS interface overhead	30.0

other hand, such user-defined blocks were available in the OpenVX-Vision Works library thorough GPU-accelerated primitives.

5   Conclusion

This paper presented a methodology to integrate model-based design to OpenVX. It showed how such a design flow allows for fast prototyping of any computer vision algorithm through a Matlab/Simulink model, its parametrization, validation, and automatic synthesis into an equivalent OpenVX code representation. The paper presented the experimental results obtained by applying the proposed methodology for the development of two embedded software. The first implements a digital image stabilization, while the second implements an ORB descriptor for SLAM applications. The applications have been modelled and parametrized through Simulink for different application contexts. In particular, the ORB application has been validated by considering an external typical and dynamic Robotics environment. This has been done through the OpenVX-ROS interface generated with the proposed design flow, which allows co-simulating the OpenVX application with the external application environment (e.g., input streams, concurrent interactive systems, etc.) and, as a consequence, tuning more efficiently the SW parametrization. Both the applications have been automatically synthesized into OpenVX-VisionWorks code for an NVIDIA Jetson TX2 board.

References

1. Embedded Vision Alliance: Applications for Embedded Vision. https://www.embedded-vision.com/applications-embedded-vision
2. Pulli, K., Baksheev, A., Kornyakov, K., Eruhimov, V.: Real-time computer vision with OpenCV. Commun. ACM **55**(6), 61–69 (2012)
3. Rainey, E., Villarreal, J., Dedeoglu, G., Pulli, K., Lepley, T., Brill, F.: Addressing system-level optimization with OpenVX graphs. In: IEEE Computer Society Conference on Computer Vision and Pattern Recognition Workshops, pp. 658–663 (2014)
4. Khronos Group: OpenVX: Portable, Power-efficient Vision Processing. https://www.khronos.org/openvx
5. Tagliavini, G., Haugou, G., Marongiu, A., Benini, L.: Adrenaline: an OpenVX environment to optimize embedded vision applications on many-core accelerators. In: International Symposium on Embedded Multicore/Many-core Systems-on-Chip, pp. 289–296 (2015)
6. Yang, K., Elliott, G.A., Anderson, J.H.: Analysis for supporting real-time computer vision workloads using OpenVX on multicore+GPU platforms. In: Proceedings of the 23rd International Conference on Real Time and Networks Systems, RTNS 2015, pp. 77–86 (2015)
7. Dekkiche, D., Vincke, B., Merigot, A.: Investigation and performance analysis of OpenVX optimizations on computer vision applications. In: 14th International Conference on Control, Robotics and Vision, Automation, pp. 1–6 (2016)
8. Open Source Robotics Foundation: Robot Operating System. http://www.ros.org/
9. Popp, M., van Son, S., Moreira, O.: Automatic control flow generation for OpenVX graphs. In: 2017 Euromicro Conference on Digital System Design (DSD), pp. 198–204, August 2017
10. Syschikov, A., Sedov, B., Nedovodeev, K., Ivanova, V.: OpenVX integration into the visual development environment. Int. J. Embed. Real-Time Commun. Syst. **9**(1), 20–49 (2018). www.scopus.com
11. Aldegheri, S., Bombieri, N.: Extending OpenVX for model-based design of embedded vision applications. In: Proceedings of 2017 IFIP/IEEE International Conference on Very Large Scale Integration (VLSI-SoC), pp. 1–6 (2017)

12. Simulink: S-Functions. https://it.mathworks.com/help/simulink/s-function-basics.html
13. Smith, B.M., Zhang, L., Jin, H., Agarwala, A.: Light field video stabilization. In: International Conference on Computer Vision, pp. 341–348 (2009)
14. NVIDIA Inc.: VisionWorks. https://developer.nvidia.com/embedded/visionworks
15. INTEL: Intel Computer Vision SDK. https://software.intel.com/en-us/computer-vision-sdk
16. AMD: AMD OpenVX - AMDOVX. http://gpuopen.com/compute-product/amd-openvx/
17. Khronos: OpenVX lib. https://www.khronos.org/openvx
18. Matlab: MEX functions. https://it.mathworks.com/matlabcentral/fileexchange/26825-utilities-for-mex-files
19. Aldegheri, S., Bloisi, D.D., Blum, J.J., Bombieri, N., Farinelli, A.: Fast and power-efficient embedded software implementation of digital image stabilization for low-cost autonomous boats. In: Hutter, M., Siegwart, R. (eds.) Field and Service Robotics. SPAR, vol. 5, pp. 129–144. Springer, Cham (2018). https://doi.org/10.1007/978-3-319-67361-5_9
20. Rublee, E., Rabaud, V., Konolige, K., Bradski, G.: ORB: an efficient alternative to SIFT or SURF. In: 2011 International Conference on Computer Vision, pp. 2564–2571, November 2011
21. Mur-Artal, R., Montiel, J.M.M., Tardós, J.D.: ORB-SLAM: a versatile and accurate monocular SLAM system. IEEE Trans. Rob. **31**(5), 1147–1163 (2015)
22. Geiger, A., Lenz, P., Stiller, C., Urtasun, R.: Vision meets robotics: the KITTI dataset. Int. J. Rob. Res. (IJRR) **32**, 1231–1237 (2013)

Modeling and Evaluation of Application-Aware Dynamic Thermal Control in HPC Nodes

Daniele Cesarini[1]([✉]), Andrea Bartolini[1], and Luca Benini[1,2]

[1] DEI, University of Bologna, 40136 Bologna, Italy
{daniele.cesarini,a.bartolini}@unibo.it
[2] IIS, Swiss Federal Institute of Technology, 8092 Zurich, Switzerland
lbenini@iis.ee.ethz.ch

Abstract. As side effects of the end of Dennard's scaling, power and thermal technological walls stand in front of the evolution of supercomputers towards the exaflops era. Energy and temperature walls are big challenges to face for assuring a constant grow of performance in future. New generation architectures for HPC systems implement HW and SW components to address energy and thermal issues for increasing power and efficient computing in scientific workload. In thermal-bound HPC machines, workload-aware runtimes can leverage hardware knobs to guarantee the best operating point in term of performance and power saving without violating thermal constraints.

In this paper, we present an integer-linear programming formulation for job mapping and frequency selection for thermal-bound HPC nodes. We use a fast solver and workload traces extracted from a real supercomputer to test our methodology. Our runtime is integrated into the MPI library, and it is capable of assigning high-performance cores to performance-critical processes. Critical processes are identified at execution time through a mathematical formulation, which relies on the characterization of the application workload and on the global synchronization barriers. We demonstrate that by combining long and short horizon predictions with information on the critical processes retrieved from the programming model, we can drastically improve the performance of the target application w.r.t. state-of-the-art DTM solutions.

Keywords: HPC · Thermal model · Power model · Workload model · Energy saving · Thermal constraint · DTM · MPI · Runtime · ILP · Quantum ESPRESSO

1 Introduction

Driven by Moore's law, the trend in increasing performance of CPUs has seen as collateral effects the rapid increase of power consumption and power density

© IFIP International Federation for Information Processing 2019
Published by Springer Nature Switzerland AG 2019
M. Maniatakos et al. (Eds.): VLSI-SoC 2017, IFIP AICT 500, pp. 198–219, 2019.
https://doi.org/10.1007/978-3-030-15663-3_10

that in turn have limited the achievable performance and caused an acceleration of chip aging. Cooling and heat generation are rapidly becoming the key limiters for high performance processors, especially for HPC and data centres which typically host clusters of thousands of high-performance processors.

In High-Performance Computing (HPC) nodes the maximum safe temperature at which the processing elements can run depends on the cooling technologies. For instance, Intel Xeon E5-26XX v3 server class processors have specifications on the maximum silicon temperature ranging from 69 °C to 101 °C according to the package thermal resistance (cost) and the nominal thermal design power (TDP)[1]. To enforce these safe working temperatures, HPC nodes use active-cooling solutions which translate in additional power consumption.

Dynamic thermal management (DTM) has been studied to limit the cooling effort by controlling and reducing the heat generation. This is achieved monitoring the HW thermal sensors and the application workload reacting on CPU dynamic voltage and frequency scaling (DVFS) states. New generation multi-core CPUs, which are used in HPC systems, can apply a different voltage and frequency to each core independently [17]. This opens new scenarios for fine-grain DVFS control in DTM solution. Operating Systems use feedback loops between sensors and DVFS states of each core to scale down frequency states to avoid thermal hazards. Indeed, several solutions explore proactive techniques for DTM strategies to improve performance in thermal-bound systems [2,12,20,21]. DTM strategies take advantages of the heterogeneity in the thermal dissipation of cores, which is related to chip and board design, and manufacture, to maximize the performance. However, these approaches often results in a performance unbalance between the cores. Coldest cores run faster than hottest cores.

Applications in HPC take advantage of the parallel architecture to speed up the execution of large scale simulations and workloads. The message passing interface (MPI) programming model is the de facto standard in HPC programs for splitting the workload in tasks that execute in parallel in the HPC machine. During the execution of an MPI-based application, the tasks alternate phases of computation on local data with phases of data exchange and synchronization. A critical design parameter in MPI applications is the balancing of the workload between the tasks, and the minimization of the waiting time for each tasks in the synchronization points [19,25]. Critical tasks, in a specific code segment, are the ones which carry on the most workload and arrive late at a synchronization point. In practice, they limit the application speed in the specific code segment. Application developers and users in HPC systems parameterize the application configuration to balance the workload between the tasks. This intended to limit the slowdown induced by critical tasks. As previously seen, DTM techniques can create local unbalance between cores to maximize processor's throughput. This can be significantly detrimental for application performance as it may slow down critical tasks in parallel applications. However, this can be translated into an advantage for DTM strategies. Indeed, critical tasks could be assigned to the coldest cores at the application start-up phase and could reward critical tasks

---

[1] Intel Xeon®Processor E5 v3 Family Thermal Guide.

slowing down the less critical ones. In this chapter we focus on this problem, creating an application-aware dynamic thermal management runtime for HPC processors.

We present a DTM solution for HPC systems to increase performance of thermal-bound HPC systems exploiting thermal capacitances. We first propose a novel thermal model description derived from state-space representation of a real HPC node. We study the sensitivity of the application walltime to frequency changes in the communication phases. Our exploration reveals that the penalty in the application walltime caused by the frequency reduction decreases proportionally with time spent in the MPI library. After that, we focus our work on the workload distribution of a real supercomputer's application. We identify the presence of critical tasks, which will be prioritized w.r.t. the other MPI tasks. Secondly, we present two novel ILP formulations for thermal-aware task mapping and frequency selection for large parallel heterogeneous many-core. We propose a task criticality model which relies on a mathematical formulation; this model considers application workload and synchronization constraints to reduce the slack times. We use the thermal characteristics of the compute node to formulate both the ILP problems. In this context we explore the impact of the time horizons at which future temperatures are predicted in the efficacy of the proposed DTM solution. We then show that our optimization models can significantly improve the performance in supercomputer environments without inducing significant overhead in time-to-solution.

This chapter is an extension of the conference paper [8]. We extend the previous work by: (1) A detailed analysis of the power consumed by the main components (core and uncore) in supercomputer's node under different DVFS operational states. (2) A detailed analysis of the workload distribution in our target HPC application among the MPI tasks, and of the task criticality in periods of tens seconds. (3) Proposing new module that we implement the proposed thermal controller called "Task Criticality Generator". This module is responsible to profile, calculate the MPI activity using a new proposed mathematical formulation, and identify the task criticality of each task in each time period. (4) Evaluating the performance trade-offs given by the "Task Criticality Generator".

The chapter is organized as follows. Section 2, presents state-of-the-art works on thermal management. Section 3 characterizes thermal proprieties of a scientific computing node and reports a study on workload unbalance in a target scientific application. Section 4 shows our DTM solution for thermal-aware mapping and control based on ILP formulation and task criticality generator. Section 5 reports experimental results. While Sect. 6 describes the conclusions of this work.

2   Related Work

Several works were focused on thermal-aware workload allocation based on DVFS strategies. Those techniques include: (i) on-line optimization policies [4,10,11,32], which are based on predictive models and embedded sensors to read the current temperatures on the system; (ii) scheduling approaches for off-line allocation [24,26] which rely on simplified thermal models, usually embedded in the target platform [4] or simulating chip temperature [31].

Today's thermal management works range from mobile to large scale parallel machine, like supercomputer and HPC systems. Xie et al. [30] show that mobile systems are thermally constraint. Interestingly, thermal constraints, come from user experience and not from silicon limits. Conficoni et al. [9] show that the power cost of HPC cooling depends on several factors, for instance IT power consumption, the cooling control policies, and the ambient temperature. On the other hand, the power consumption is intertwined with workload execution and computation phases [7,23], which can produce high thermal heterogeneity between nodes and CPUs. For this reason, over-provisioning cooling design can causes severe inefficiencies.

Wang et al. [29] show that fan power can account for up to 23% of typical server power and scales super-linearly with node utilization. Authors in [6] extract a predictive thermal model directly from the multicore device correlating power, performance and thermal sensors implemented in HW. They show that the thermal evolution of a multicore device can be modeled with a linear state-space representation. The leakage-power dependency from temperature can be modeled as a perturbation of the state matrix of the thermal model. Due to different materials present in the heat dissipation path, the thermal transient is multi-modal with time constants that vary from ms to tens of seconds. Beneventi et al. [5] shows in an Intel based computing nodes with 36 physical cores, that the increased number of processors integrated in the same die generates significant thermal gradients and this thermal heterogeneity can be exploited by thermal/aware MPI task allocation to reduce the fan speed and power without impacting the application performance.

To find a close form solution of the fast mapping problem under thermal constraint, Hanumaiah [18] assumes the absence of direct thermal exchange from the hot to the cold cores of the same die. Mutapcic et al. [24] formulate a convex optimization problem to control the speed of the processor, which is subject to environment thermal constraints. They solve it with a specialized algorithm. However, their optimization algorithm does not cover the case of an higher number of cores than the number of tasks (some cores remain in idle state).

Predictive controls are often based on thermal and optimization models which can guarantee a safe-working condition applying performance constraints to the systems. Rudi et al. [28] have developed an Integer Linear Programing (ILP) model for task allocation and frequency selection to avoid thermal hazards in many-core architectures. This thermal control is able to leverage on the idleness of the cores when tasks are less than the number of available cores allocating tasks on the coldest cores and leaving hottest ones in idle states. The limit of [28] is the task allocation, which is not handled by the systems.

There are even significant works on energy-aware MPI library. Rountree et al. [27] use DVFS mechanism to reduce the frequency when there are no critical tasks running on the CPU. Adagio is not only one that use predictions to improve energy efficiency with DVFS techniques [14,15,22]. Instead, Eastep et al. [13] improve performance in power-constraint system balancing node's power budget to speed up critical tasks. However, these solutions do not consider thermal constraint systems where CPU performance are limited to respect the safe-working temperature.

3   Workload and Thermal Modelling of HPC

Dynamic thermal management policies aim to reduce the cooling effort and power by adapting the processing element's performance to ensure a safe working temperature. In this section, we first introduce the nomenclature and the thermal properties of HPC nodes with direct measurements. Then, we extract from real scientific parallel workload a model linking the performance knob to the real performance of the final application. Finally, we analyze how the application workload is distributed among all the cores.

We took as a target machine an HPC system based on an IBM NeXtScale cluster. Each node of the cluster is equipped with two Intel Haswell E5-2630 v3 CPUs, with 8 cores with 2.4 GHz clock speed and 85 W Thermal Design Power (TDP, [17]). This supercomputer is ranked in the Top500 supercomputer list [1].

3.1   Thermal Model

We focus our attention on a single node of the cluster as the rack is constructed by replication of the same node. To understand the thermal properties of a computing node, we have executed three main stress tests on which we have: (i) Kept the system in idle and measured the total power and the temperature for each core after ten minutes; (ii) We then have executed a stressmark[2] in sequence on each core of each socket in the node, leaving idle the remaining ones. We maintained the workload constant for ten minutes and measured the power consumption and the temperature, we used this test to extract the maximum steady state temperature gradient. Finally, (iii) we have simultaneously executed the stressmark for ten minutes in all the cores of the node and measured the temperature and the power consumption. In all the previous tests the temperature and power values are measured using an infrastructure similar to the one presented in [3], the Turbo mode was disabled to avoid power consumption to workload dependency. The results of our analysis are reported in Table 1.

As we will see in the experimental results section, we used the extracted characteristics to create a thermal model using a distributed RC approach [4], with one tuned RC per core to have similar thermal characteristics as the measured ones.

---

[2] cpuburn stressmark by Robert Redelmeier: it is a single-threaded application which takes advantage of the superscalar architecture to load the CPU.

Table 1. Thermal model

AVG temperature - Idle cores	15.93 °C
AVG temperature - Active cores	33.39 °C
Gradient - Idle cores	4.47 °C
Gradient - Active cores	4.79 °C
Gradient - Active core vs idle cores	8.05 °C
Stady-state time	120 s

3.2 Power Model

To model the impact of DVFS states on the target system, we have re-executed the stressmark in each core while scaling down the frequency for each core in all the available speed steps. We maintained each configuration for ten minutes and we measured the power consumed by each CPU. We collected these measurements in a lookup-tables (LUTs), one for each CPU. We then used the LUTs to compute the power dissipated by each CPU on each available frequency. We measured a total power of 17.86 W when all cores in a computing node are idle. The total power raises to 92.44 W when all the cores are active. We then

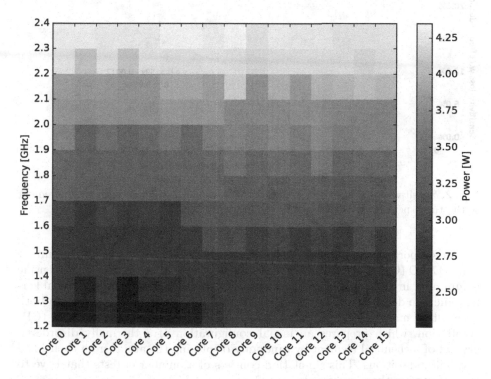

Fig. 1. Average power consumption of cores at all available frequency levels.

extracted the power consumed by each core at each DVFS level with an average standard deviation in between cores of 0.1 W. The average uncore region of the CPUs contribute for 11.84 W and 17.85 W respectively when idle or active. The Fig. 1 shows the average power consumption for each core of the system at all available frequency levels.

3.3 Workload Model

A HPC application can be seen as the composition of several tasks executed in a distributed environment, interconnected with a low-latency high-bandwidth network. HPC communications happen by sending explicit messages through a standard MPI programming model which takes advantage of the high-performance interconnect sub-system. Usually, tasks are composed by computational intensive phases on independent data segments interrupted by synchronization points and communications. This characteristic impacts the sensitivity of the application to each core's performance as computational imbalance can lead to longer synchronization phases.

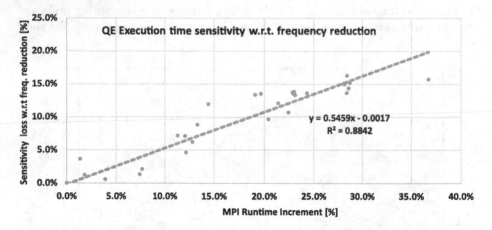

Fig. 2. Sensitivity loss w.r.t the reduction of frequency compared with the increment of the time spent into MPI library

As support to this statement, in this work we use as benchmark Quantum ESPRESSO (QE) [16], which is a real application widely used from the scientific community in high-end supercomputers. Moreover, QE main computational kernels include dense parallel linear algebra and 3D parallel FFT, which are both relevant in many HPC applications. In our test we use a Car-Parrinello (CP) simulation, which prepares an initial configuration of a thermally disordered crystal of a chemical element by randomly displacing the atoms from their ideal crystalline positions. This simulation consists of a number of tests that have to be executed in the correct order.

In the following experiment, we have explored how the different ratio of active code and MPI library for each QE task changes the impact of frequency scaling on the overall application execution time. We computed QE-CP on two computing nodes with 32 MPI tasks to increase the number of results respect to a run on a single node. We run QE-CP 32 times. At each run we configured sequentially one core of the 32 at minimum frequency while the other are maintained at the maximum. We compared it with the run in which all the cores are at the nominal frequency. We then correlated the overall QE-CP slow down and the MPI percentage of the slowed down task. Figure 2 shows that the impact of frequency reduction increases with percentage of MPI library present in each task. This result is in line with what was shown in [27]. We can use it for extracting on-line the sensitivity to frequency for each MPI task. In this work, we take advantage of this information to address energy saving at execution time.

3.4 Workload Distribution

While Fig. 2 shows the workload unbalance for the entire application run, it does not show how this unbalance is distributed in time -at a finer granularity-. In this section we explore how the workload is spread among all the MPI tasks and in time. We computed QE-CP on a single compute node with 16 MPI tasks. For each MPI task, we extract the time spent in the application and we compare it with the time spent in the MPI library. Every 10 s, we calculate the ratio between application time and MPI time, we plot this result in Fig. 3. We can see that the MPI task 0 spends more time in the application with respects to the others. In our benchmark, the core that slows down the application execution

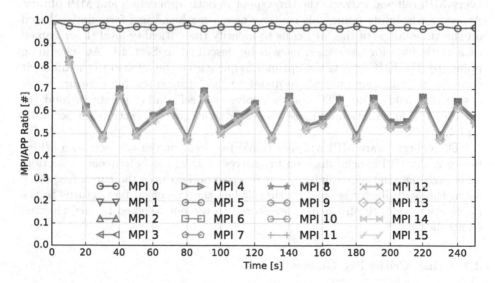

Fig. 3. Ratio of the time spent in application phases and MPI phases for each core and every 10 s.

mostly is the core that runs the MPI task 0. If we slow down this core, we will have the highest penalty in the total execution time.

In the next section, we will see how this information can be extracted and considered in the thermal management problem.

4   HPC Optimal Thermal Control

In this section, we present a Dynamic and Thermal Management (DTM) ILP formulation, namely the Optimal Thermal Controller (OTC), which matches all the requirements of HPC systems and proactive thermal control: (i) limiting the future temperature of all the cores below a critical threshold by selecting the proper frequency for each core; (ii) maximizing the application performance (frequency of all the cores); (iii) identifying cores that host critical tasks to promote their performance; (iv) slowing down the cores' frequency during communication.

As shown in Fig. 4, the OTC operates at node level and it is composed of two main components: the thermal-aware task mapper and controller and the energy-aware MPI wrapper.

The thermal-aware task mapper and controller (TMC) is triggered: (a) after the job scheduler has deployed the parallel application on the reserved portion of the HPC machine for its execution; (b) periodically, with period T_s, and (c) at the start/end of every MPI call. At scheduling point (a) the TMC specifies the task to core mapping which will be maintained until the application completion. Clearly, if a critical task is mapped to a thermally inefficient core this will more likely cause a severe degradation of the final application performance. To capture the task criticality, we use a task criticality generation module, which intercepts every MPI call and extracts the time spent in both application and MPI library. At every scheduling point, this runtime uses a mathematical formulation based on the timestamps of the MPI calls to identify the criticality level (later named task criticality) for each task, as will be described in Sect. 4.1. At scheduling point (b), the TMC selects the optimal frequencies to be applied to the different cores for the following interval (to maintain the future cores' temperature below a safe threshold). Our OTC solution solves the scheduling points (a) and (b) with an ILP formulation and custom solver strategies as described in Sects. 4.2 and 4.3.

The energy-aware MPI wrapper (EAW) is event-driven and acts as a bridge between the MPI synchronization primitives and the core's frequency selection. This programming model interface is reactive and reduces the core's frequency when the MPI library is busy waiting. When the execution flow returns to the application code, the frequency is restored to the one selected by the Thermal Controller.

4.1   Task Criticality Generator

The per-task criticality level is calculated based on the time spent by the task in the application and waiting in the global synchronization points for each time interval. It is not sufficient to consider only the total time spent in the application during the last interval to compute a criticality level. We need to consider each global synchronization point independently and for each of them compute the waiting time of each task.

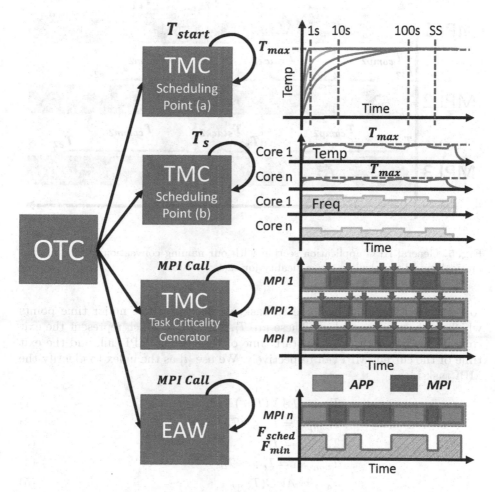

Fig. 4. Optimal thermal controller at node level

We use a mathematical model to extract the per-task criticality level between two global synchronization points and we calculate the criticality of each task for all the global synchronization points in an interval. We define the criticality level for each task in this interval time as the average of the criticality levels weighted by the time which lasts between each pair of global synchronization points.

Figure 5 shows a general HPC application section enclosed by two global synchronization points where all the MPI tasks are involved. Every time that a MPI task encounters a global synchronization point, it must wait all other tasks

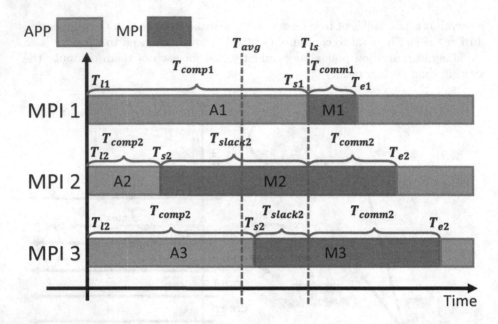

Fig. 5. General HPC application section with our naming convention for the mathematical model to calculate the criticality for each MPI task.

to continue its execution. For each task, we identify three major time points which we base our model on. These are T_l, T_s, and T_e which represent the exit time of the last MPI call, the start time of the current MPI call, and the exit time of the current MPI call respectively. We use $[i]$ as the index to identify the MPI task id.

$$T_{ls} = MAX(T_{s[i]}) \tag{1}$$

$$T_{comp[i]} = T_{s[i]} - T_{l[i]} \tag{2}$$

$$T_{slack[i]} = T_{ls} - T_{s[i]} \tag{3}$$

$$T_{comm[i]} = T_{e[i]} - T_{ls} \tag{4}$$

$$T_{avg} = AVG(T_{s[i]}) \tag{5}$$

$$\delta_i = \frac{T_{comp[i]}}{T_{avg} - T_{l[i]}} = \frac{T_{s[i]} - T_{l[1]}}{T_{avg} - T_{l[i]}} \tag{6}$$

The last task that enters the global synchronization point unlocks all the waiting tasks which can now continue their execution. T_{ls} in Eq. (1), identifies the time at which the last task enters in the synchronization point. For each application section and for each task $[i]$ we define as computation time $T_{comp[i]}$ in Eq. (2) the time spent in the application code and MPI time the time spent in the MPI library. The latter is composed by two factors: (i) $T_{slack[i]}$ in Eq. (3), which represents the time that a task spends in the MPI library waiting the last task reaching the synchronization point, (ii) $T_{comm[i]}$ in Eq. (4), which identifies the time spent to exchange data. T_{avg} in Eq. (5) is the average of all the $T_{comp[i]}$. We compute the task criticality level δ_i in Eq. (6) as the ratio between the $T_{comp[i]}$ and the T_{avg}. This metrics is proportional to the unbalance between the tasks in each application section.

4.2   The First Step Problem - FSP

This optimization problem is solved during the initialization of the application. Its purpose is to allocate the application tasks on the available cores and selecting for each of them the maximum frequency which meets the thermal constraint T_{max} in the prediction interval (PI_{FSP}). As we will see in the experimental results, the prediction interval (i.e. the time horizon) plays an important role. Indeed, if it is too short, the TMC cannot predict the impact of a task allocation on long term core's temperature as its effect is hidden by the thermal capacitance, making the problem trivial. On the contrary if the time horizon is too long the TMC cannot take advantage of the thermal capacitance for sustaining short time power burst.

In addition, not all tasks have the same criticality. This is captured by the optimization model which maximizes the frequency of the highest critical task penalizing the frequencies of other ones in case a thermal limit is reached. The optimization model considers K tasks to be assigned to N cores where the number of tasks is lower or equal to the cores i.e., $K \leq N$. Each core can be configured with a frequency in a set of M level of frequencies. The Objective Function (O.F.) maximizes the sum of frequencies of all active cores γ_{jf} weighted by the criticality δ_i of the task assigned on that core. To model the problem, we use two sets of binary decision variables:

$$x^i_{jf} = \begin{cases} 1 & \text{if core } j(j=1,\ldots,N) \text{ works at frequency} \\ & \quad f(f=1,\ldots,M) \text{ executing task } i(i=1,\ldots,K) \\ 0 & \text{otherwise.} \end{cases} \quad (7)$$

$$y_j = \begin{cases} 1 & \text{if core } j(j=1,\ldots,N) \text{ is idle,} \\ 0 & \text{otherwise, i.e., if it is working.} \end{cases} \quad (8)$$

We can formulate the following ILP model with three constraints to model the assignments and the thermal bounds:

$$O.F. = max \sum_{i=1}^{K} \sum_{f=1}^{M} \sum_{j=1}^{N} \delta_i \gamma_{jf} x^i_{jf} \quad (9)$$

$$\sum_{j=1}^{N} \sum_{f=1}^{M} x^i_{jf} = 1 \quad (10)$$
$$(i = 1,\ldots,K)$$

$$\sum_{i=1}^{K}\sum_{f=1}^{M} x_{jf}^{i} + y_j = 1 \tag{11}$$

$$(j = 1, \ldots, N)$$

$$\sum_{j=1}^{N} GS_{jl} \left(\boldsymbol{p}_j y_j + \sum_{i=1}^{K}\sum_{f=1}^{M} p_{jf} x_{jf}^{i} \right) + T_l^0 + T^a \leq T_{MAX} \tag{12}$$

$$(l = 1, \ldots, N)$$

The constraint (10) specifies that a task must be assigned only on a single core, which works at a given frequency. In addition, it specifies that all the N tasks must be assigned. Constraint (11) is needed to determine the y decision variables which represent the idle cores. These variables are used in constraint (12) in case there are less tasks than cores i.e., $K \leq Mn$. Finally, constraints (12) guarantee that the temperature of each core does not exceed T_{max} over the prediction interval (PI_{FSP}). In the last constraint (12), GS is a gain matrix with dimension $N \times N$. This matrix is used to calculate the increment of temperature of all the cores when a core is subjected to a constant power input for PI_{FSP} seconds. T_0^l represents the dependency of the future temperature(@ PI_{FSP}) from the current core's temperature. These values can be derived from a state-space thermal model as described by [28]. T_a is the ambient temperature. When tasks are less than cores the decision variable y_i is used in conjunction with the vector of idle powers $\bar{p}$, to add the idle power components.

4.3   The i-th Step Problem - ISP

After the tasks have been assigned to the cores in the FSP the TMC has to periodically solve, at a finer time scale, the assignment problem of frequencies to cores only. The ISP has the same objective function as FSP Sect. 4.2 as well as the same thermal model formulation. However the prediction interval for the ISP (PI_{ISP}) can be generally different from the FSP.

Differently from the previous case, the model considers only active cores (T) because the thermal constraints cannot be broken by an idle core. This reduces the overall complexity. As tasks have been already allocated in FPS in this model, tasks and core do not need separate variables, thus a criticality is referred to a core.

$$x_{rf} = \begin{cases} 1 & \text{if core } r(r = 1, \ldots, T) \text{ works at frequency} \\ & \quad f(f = 1, \ldots, M), \\ 0 & \text{otherwise.} \end{cases}$$

The ISP model has fewer constraints than FSP due the lower number of variables.

$$O.F. = max \sum_{a \in A} \sum_{f=1}^{M} \delta_a \gamma_{af} x_{af} \tag{13}$$

$$\sum_{f=1}^{M} x_{af} = 1 \tag{14}$$

$$(\forall a \in A)$$

$$\sum_{a \in A} \sum_{f=1}^{M} GS_{la} p_{af} x_{af} + \sum_{i \in I} GS_{li} p_i + T_l^0 + T^a \leq T_{MAX} \tag{15}$$

$$(\forall l \in A)$$

The constraint (14) bounds each core to a selected frequency. The constraint (15) guarantees the thermal limits imposed on the model. Where the set $A = a_i$ contains the index of the active cores and the set $I = i_i$ contains the index of idle cores directly defined from the solution of FSP. Where $A \cap I$ is empty. In general, the ISP problem is computationally simpler than the FSP problem due to the much lower number of decision variables and constraints.

In the next section we will evaluate the performance of the proposed TMC in a realistic scenario and under different trade-offs in between the predicted horizons of the FSP and ISP problems.

5   Experimental Results

In this section, we first describe the emulation framework we have created, starting from the results of the characterization of computing nodes and real scientific workload conducted in Sect. 3. We use this emulation framework to study the implication of the prediction interval/horizon and the task criticality generator in the thermal-aware task mapping and control of supercomputer nodes.

5.1   Emulation Framework

Our emulation framework is composed by the following components:

(i) The workload traces. The traces have been extracted using a commercial tracing and profiling tool called Intel Trace Analyzer and Collector. The traces contain all the MPI activities (MPI call, data transfer, source/destination MPI task) with time instants. These have been extracted for the QE-CP running on a computing node.

(ii) The thermal simulator. We have created a first order discrete state-space model matched with the computing node as described in Sect. 3.1. The model has a sample time of 10ms (Ts_{TM}), and as state variables has the temperature of each core of the node. Each core's power is computed with the power model presented in Sect. 3.2. Workload traces which have resolution than the 10 ms have been averaged on this period to produce the percentage of time in which each task was in the MPI library for each (Ts_{TM}) interval. We use this value to model the energy-aware MPI wrapper impacts on core's power consumption.

(iii) The thermal-aware task mapping and control problem. The TMC optimization problem proposed in Sect. 3 has been solved using IBM Ilog CPLEX 12.6.1. The emulator calls CPLEX each time there is a new TMC problem to be solved. This happens once at the application start (FSP) and periodically each ISP interval Ts_{ISP} which matches the prediction interval in the ISP problem (PI_{ISP}).

At each CPLEX call, the emulator builds a new instance of the problem with the new thermal parameters and the criticality of the tasks and it waits for CPLEX results. During the waiting time the emulator is frozen, in this way the overhead time does not impact on the chronological MPI events. CPLEX has been executed on the same machine of the emulation framework, which is our HPC node, therefore the time overheads reflect real measurement.

5.2 Evaluation of Prediction Horizons

In this section, we will explore how change the frequency level for high and low critical tasks using different prediction horizon for FSP and ISP problem. We conducted the following experiments with different prediction intervals for both FSP and ISP problems. We considered $PI_{FSP} = 1$s, 10s, 100s, steady state (SS) and $PI_{ISP} = 1$s, 10s, 100s, steady state (SS) because the thermal propagation in our system is in the order of tens of seconds as we reported in Table 1. In the following, we name these tests with the notation $PI_{FSP} - PI_{ISP}$. It must be noted that 1s-1s represent state-of-the-art DTM solutions with no thermal-aware task-to-core mapping, while SS-SS represents state-of-the-art static DTM solutions.

For all the experiments, we set the temperature limit to 65% of maximum temperature which can be reached by the hottest core at the maximum frequency.

Figure 6 shows on the y-axis the temperature evolution of the coldest core (#0) for five cases. Namely no thermal control active, no thermal control active (NoTMC, NoEAW) but energy-aware MPI wrapper active (NoTMC, EAW), TMC active with (1s-1s), (SS-1s), (SS-SS). For the same configurations, the Fig. 7 shows on the y-axis the temperature evolution of the hottest core. Clearly, according to the capability of the FSP problem, to predict the long term thermal evolution the higher critical (HC) task will be mapped on the coldest core. Indeed from Fig. 6, we can notice that if no TMC calls are executed, the coldest core executes a low critical task. When the FSP is empowered with a steady-state thermal predictor instead the TMC allocates the higher critical task on the coldest core and manages to run it always at the maximum frequency. Vertical spikes of the frequency are caused by the energy-aware MPI wrapper, which sets the minimum frequency of the core during the MPI phases. As a consequence,

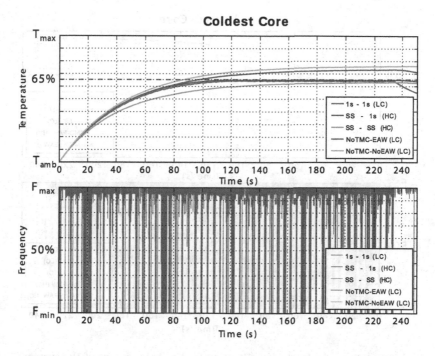

Fig. 6. Temperature and frequency evolution for the coldest core of the system - core #0

the maximum temperature reached by NoTMC-EAW is lower than NoTMC-NoEAW; showing its effectiveness in reducing the power consumption. Differently, short time horizons (1s-1s) in the FSP do not allow the solver to "see" the constraint and thus lead to a sub-optimal task mapping allocation. As a consequence, the high critical task need to be frequency limited to meet the thermal constraint as the thermal capacitance effect vanishes.

5.3 Evaluation of the Task Criticality Generator

As previously introduced, the task criticality is a key parameter for the final application performance. Figure 8 shows the penalty in term of the execution time of application, when we consider equal criticality for each task respected of the one obtained by the TMC task criticality generator presented in Sect. 4.1.

Figure 8 reports on the x-axis the cores where the highest critical task is allocated. We can see when the highest critical task is located on the core #6 or on the core #8 we have the highest and lowest penalty in the execution time, respectively 21.18% and 0.33%. When the root MPI task is located on the core #8, we have a lucky case, this means that it runs on the "coldest" core of the system where the TMC runtime can easily increase the core's frequency without violating the thermal constraint. On the other hand, when the root MPI task is located on the "hottest" core we have a high penalty due the difficult of the runtime to increase the frequency on that core. To conclude, we can evidently

214   D. Cesarini et al.

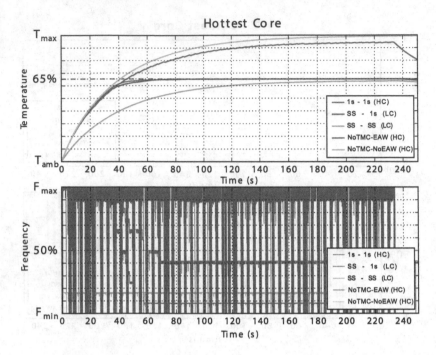

Fig. 7. Temperature and frequency evolution for the hottest core of the system - core #14

see that in all cases the TMC criticality generator outperforms the cases with task with the same criticality.

5.4 Performance Gain

Figure 9 depicts the average frequency of the cores that host the highest critical tasks and the average frequency for all the cores in each configuration. Interestingly, in all the cases the highest critical task never reaches the maximum average frequency. This is the effect of the energy-aware MPI wrapper which reduces the core frequency during MPI calls.

The error bars show the variance for each configuration among different executions of the same QE-CP problem while moving the highest critical task from the MPI root task to another one. This means that if we shift the default position of highest critical task from 0 to 15 in the MPI rank all the configuration with predict interval in the FSP (PI_{FSP}) of 1 and 10 s we have a huge variation. This can be explained by the fact that in both experiments the FSP has a prediction horizon which is too short to see the effect of long term thermal evolution and thus it cannot predict which core will hit the thermal constraint. For this case the allocation FSP problem is trivial and tasks are allocated on the first available core following a simple numerical binding where the task 0 will be allocate to the core 0 and so on. This binding is also the default on the Intel

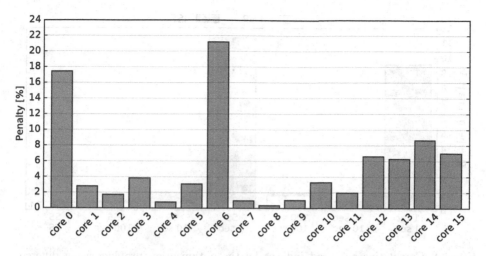

Fig. 8. Execution time penalty in benchmarks with equal per-task criticality level w.r.t. the benchmark with the TMC criticality generator. Every run identify on which core was pinned the highest critical task.

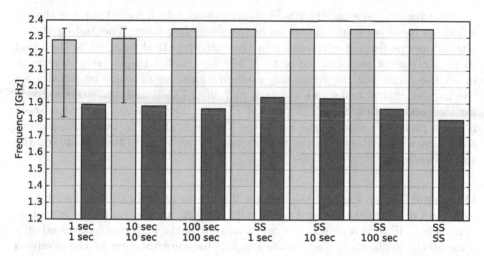

Fig. 9. Comparison between average core frequency and the frequency of the highest critical core using different configuration for the optimization problem.

MPI library. In this particular case, if the highest critical task is lucky, it will be pinned on a "cold" core. Vice versa, if the highest critical task is unlucky, it will be mapped on a "hot" core. At the steady-state the frequency of the core will be limited by the ISP to respect the thermal constraint. On the other cases, the PI_{FSP} is always enough to sense the thermal constraint. The optimization model will avoid the binding of the highest critical task on a "hot" core. In this case the highest critical task will be pinned on a "cold" core allowing the highest critical task to work at maximum frequency.

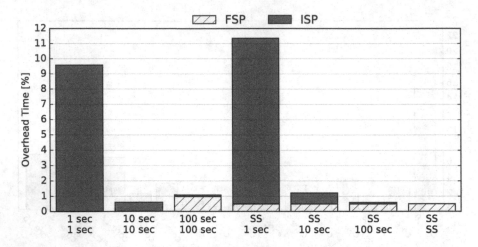

Fig. 10. Cumulative overhead induces by the optimization problem using different configuration for the optimization problem.

We take as a baseline the SS-SS configuration, which model state-of-the-art solutions based on static allocation of tasks and frequency. The 1s-1s and 10s-10s induces performance penalties on the highest critical task, while they lead to an increase of performance of the 4.97% and 4.50% respectively in average in all the cores. For the remaining configurations, we measure no penalty for the highest critical tasks and a gain of to 7.46%, 7.06% and 3.65% respectively for the configuration SS-1s, SS-10s and SS-100s. These results show that short horizon predictive models pay off in the ISP as it allows to take advantage of the thermal capacitance. In the next section, we will add to this conclusion the solver overhead.

Overhead Time. Figure 10 shows cumulative overhead for different configurations and quantify the induced performance loss as it sums up to the execution time. The FSP bars represent the overhead time of the FSP problem solved only once at the application start, while the ISP bars are the sum of the overhead times of all iterations of the ISP solver.

For all the instances and the configurations, the solver is capable of finding the optimal solution. CPLEX allow to bound the solution time by the so called deterministic ticks, we use this approach to limit the solution time in case of harder problem. Authors of [28] show for a 60 core instance that the optimally gap always reduces below the 0.002% with a maximum number of 180 ticks.

We can see that for the 1s-1s and 10s-10s configuration the FSP solver time is negligible. After 1 s or 10 s the thermal transient has not reached the thermal constraint, for this reason the solution is trivial and consequently the solution immediately converge. Instead, all the other configurations have an average overhead time of 0.59% of total execution time.

The total overhead time for the ISP significantly changes when we vary the PT_{ISP} and the Ts_{ISP}. Obviously, the ISP with a prediction interval of 1 s will be called hundred times more than a ISP with a prediction interval of 100 s. The results respect this trend, in particular for 1 s of prediction interval leads to an average penalty of 10.20% of total execution time, which makes this configuration worse than a static allocation (SS-SS) as cause of the solution overhead (7.46% of performance gain - 10.20% of overhead). Interesting the 10 s case (SS-10s) reduces the total penalty to the 0.64% which in conjunction to the 7.06% of performance gain w.r.t. the static-allocation lead to an overall performance gain of the 6%. At 100 s the total overhead penalty decreases to the 0.09%. However, for this case the performance gain in only of the 3.46% making it less performing than the SS-10s case.

6   Conclusion

In this chapter, we propose a thermal-aware mapping and control of thermally-bound HPC nodes. Our system implements a novel ILP formulation for thermal-aware optimization and an exploration analysis on the workload application to address performance promoting critical MPI tasks. Our work is focused on real HPC hardware and workload. We extracted thermal characteristics as well as workload traces to study the workload distribution to identify critical MPI tasks. Our control system relies on these information to optimize the task allocation and the frequency selections in thermal-constraint HPC nodes.

In the experimental section, we compared our system with state-of-the-art DTM solutions which dynamically control only the frequency selection of the cores or can choose a statically task allocation with a specific frequency. Our experimental results show that using a long-time horizon for the task allocation and a short time horizon for selecting DVFS levels at execution time, our solution can lead up to 6% performance gain including overheads. Moreover, our task criticality model embedded in our DTM system can avoid the pinning of critical tasks on hot cores where OTC cannot promote this task with high frequency. This can cause high performance degradation up to 21.18% of the entire application execution.

Acknowledgments. Work supported by the EU FETHPC project ANTAREX (g.a. 671623), EU project ExaNoDe (g.a. 671578), and EU ERC Project MULTITHERMAN (g.a. 291125).

References

1. TOP500 Supercomputer Sites (2017). Top500.org
2. Ayoub, R., Sharifi, S., Rosing, T.S.: GentleCool: cooling aware proactive workload scheduling in multi-machine systems. In: Proceedings of the Conference on Design, Automation and Test in Europe, pp. 295–298. European Design and Automation Association (2010)

3. Bartolini, A., Cacciari, M., Cavazzoni, C., Tecchiolli, G., Benini, L.: Unveiling eurora - thermal and power characterization of the most energy-efficient supercomputer in the world. In: Proceedings of the Conference on Design, Automation & Test in Europe, DATE 2014, 3001, Leuven, Belgium, pp. 277:1–277:6. European Design and Automation Association (2014)
4. Bartolini, A., Cacciari, M., Tilli, A., Benini, L.: A distributed and self-calibrating model-predictive controller for energy and thermal management of high-performance multicores. In: Design, Automation Test in Europe Conference Exhibition (DATE), pp. 1–6, March 2011
5. Beneventi, F., Bartolini, A., Cavazzoni, C., Benini, L.: Cooling-aware node-level task allocation for next-generation green HPC systems. Management 1, 6 (2016)
6. Beneventi, F., Bartolini, A., Tilli, A., Benini, L.: An effective gray-box identification procedure for multicore thermal modeling. IEEE Trans. Comput. 63(5), 1097–1110 (2014)
7. Cesarini, D., Bartolini, A., Benini, L.: Benefits in relaxing the power capping constraint. In: Proceedings of the 1st Workshop on AutotuniNg and aDaptivity AppRoaches for Energy Efficient HPC Systems, ANDARE 2017, pp. 3:1–3:6. ACM, New York (2017)
8. Cesarini, D., Bartolini, A., Benini, L.: Prediction horizon vs. efficiency of optimal dynamic thermal control policies in HPC nodes. In: 2017 IFIP/IEEE International Conference on Very Large Scale Integration (VLSI-SoC), pp. 1–6, October 2017
9. Conficoni, C., Bartolini, A., Tilli, A., Tecchiolli, G., Benini, L.: Energy-aware cooling for hot-water cooled supercomputers. In: Proceedings of the 2015 Design, Automation & Test in Europe Conference & Exhibition, DATE 2015, San Jose, CA, USA, pp. 1353–1358. EDA Consortium (2015)
10. Coskun, A.K., Rosing, T.S., Gross, K.C.: Utilizing predictors for efficient thermal management in multiprocessor socs. IEEE Trans. Comput. Aided Des. Integr. Circ. Syst. 28(10), 1503–1516 (2009)
11. Coskun, A.K., Rosing, T.S., Whisnant, K.: Temperature aware task scheduling in MPSoCs. In: Proceedings of the Conference on Design, Automation and Test in Europe, pp. 1659–1664. EDA Consortium (2007)
12. Coşkun, A.K., Whisnant, K., Gross, K.C., et al.: Static and dynamic temperature-aware scheduling for multiprocessor SoCs. IEEE Trans. Very Large Scale Integr. (VLSI) Syst. 16(9), 1127–1140 (2008)
13. Eastep, J., et al.: Global extensible open power manager: a vehicle for HPC community collaboration toward co-designed energy management solutions (2016)
14. Freeh, V.W., Kappiah, N., Lowenthal, D.K., Bletsch, T.K.: Just-in-time dynamic voltage scaling: exploiting inter-node slack to save energy in MPI programs. J. Parallel Distrib. Comput. 68(9), 1175–1185 (2008)
15. Ge, R., Feng, X., Feng, W.-C., Cameron, K.W.: CPU miser: a performance-directed, run-time system for power-aware clusters. In: 2007 International Conference on Parallel Processing (ICPP 2007), p. 18. IEEE (2007)
16. Giannozzi, P., et al.: QUANTUM ESPRESSO: a modular and open-source software project for quantum simulations of materials. J. Phys.: Condens. Matter 21(39), 395502 (2009)
17. Hammarlund, P., et al.: Haswell: the fourth-generation Intel core processor. IEEE Micro 2, 6–20 (2014)
18. Hanumaiah, V., Vrudhula, S., Chatha, K.S.: Performance optimal speed control of multi-core processors under thermal constraints. In: Design, Automation Test in Europe Conference Exhibition, DATE 2009, pp. 1548–1551, April 2009

19. Huck, K.A., Labarta, J.: Detailed load balance analysis of large scale parallel applications. In: 2010 39th International Conference on Parallel Processing (ICPP), pp. 535–544. IEEE (2010)
20. Khdr, H., Pagani, S., Shafique, M., Henkel, J.: Thermal constrained resource management for mixed ILP-TLP workloads in dark silicon chips. In: Proceedings of the 52nd Annual Design Automation Conference, p. 179. ACM (2015)
21. Khdr, H., et al.: Power density-aware resource management for heterogeneous tiled multicores. IEEE Trans. Comput. **66**(3), 488–501 (2017)
22. Lim, M.Y., Freeh, V.W., Lowenthal, D.K.: Adaptive, transparent frequency and voltage scaling of communication phases in MPI programs. In: SC 2006 Conference, Proceedings of the ACM/IEEE, p. 14. IEEE (2006)
23. Maiterth, M., et al.: Power aware high performance computing: challenges and opportunities for application and system developers—survey tutorial. In: 2017 International Conference on High Performance Computing Simulation (HPCS), pp. 3–10, July 2017
24. Murali, S., Mutapcic, A., Atienza, D., Gupta, R., Boyd, S., Micheli, G.D.: Temperature-aware processor frequency assignment for MPSoCs using convex optimization. In: 2007 5th IEEE/ACM/IFIP International Conference on Hardware/Software Codesign and System Synthesis (CODES+ISSS), pp. 111–116, September 2007
25. Pearce, O., Gamblin, T., de Supinski, B.R., Schulz, M., Amato, N.M.: Quantifying the effectiveness of load balance algorithms. In: Proceedings of the 26th ACM International Conference on Supercomputing, ICS 2012, pp. 185–194. ACM, New York (2012)
26. Puschini, D., Clermidy, F., Benoit, P., Sassatelli, G., Torres, L.: Temperature-aware distributed run-time optimization on MP-SoC using game theory. In: IEEE Computer Society Annual Symposium on VLSI, ISVLSI 2008, pp. 375–380. IEEE (2008)
27. Rountree, B., Lownenthal, D.K., De Supinski, B.R., Schulz, M., Freeh, V.W., Bletsch, T.: Adagio: making DVS practical for complex HPC applications. In: Proceedings of the 23rd International Conference on Supercomputing, pp. 460–469. ACM (2009)
28. Rudi, A., Bartolini, A., Lodi, A., Benini, L.: Optimum: thermal-aware task allocation for heterogeneous many-core devices. In: 2014 International Conference on High Performance Computing Simulation (HPCS), pp. 82–87, July 2014
29. Wang, Z., Bash, C., Tolia, N., Marwah, M., Zhu, X., Ranganathan, P.: Optimal fan speed control for thermal management of servers. In: ASME 2009 InterPACK Conference collocated with the ASME 2009 Summer Heat Transfer Conference and the ASME 2009 3rd International Conference on Energy Sustainability, pp. 709–719. American Society of Mechanical Engineers (2009)
30. Xie, Q., Dousti, M.J., Pedram, M.: Therminator: a thermal simulator for smartphones producing accurate chip and skin temperature maps. In: 2014 IEEE/ACM International Symposium on Low Power Electronics and Design (ISLPED), pp. 117–122, August 2014
31. Xie, Y., Hung, W.-L.: Temperature-aware task allocation and scheduling for embedded multiprocessor systems-on-chip (MPSoC) design. J. VLSI Sig. Process. **45**(3), 177–189 (2006)
32. Zanini, F., Atienza, D., Benini, L., Micheli, G.D.: Thermal-aware system-level modeling and management for multi-processor systems-on-chip. In: 2011 IEEE International Symposium on Circuits and Systems (ISCAS), pp. 2481–2484, May 2011

Pushing the Limits Further:
Sub-Atomic AES

Markus Stefan Wamser[✉] and Georg Sigl

Lehrstuhl für Sicherheit in der Informationstechnik,
Technische Universität München, 80333 Munich, Germany
{wamser,sigl}@tum.de
http://www.sec.ei.tum.de/

Abstract. The recent trend to connect a plethora of sensors, embedded and ubiquitous systems with low computing power, in short the rise of the Internet of Things, has created a great demand for compact, lightweight and cheap to produce implementations of cryptographic primitives.

One approach to meet this demand is the development and standardisation of new tailored primitives, most prominently PRESENT. Yet, the wide proliferation of the Advanced Encryption Standard and the trust it earned through its long history of withstanding cryptanalysis spurred anew the search for small, lightweight implementations of AES.

Among the smallest published architectures is the AtomicAES design by Banik et al., who reported a design size of just over 2000 GE.

Here we present a new 8-bit serial architecture that has been designed from careful observation of the minimum required connections between storage elements to support all dataflows required for execution of the algorithm. While we reach similar conclusions to previous publications, the new architecture enables us to push the area requirement for a fully featured AES primitive further down by more than 8% from the area requirement of AtomicAES while offering more functionality.

Along the way we also answer in the affirmative the open question whether the AES reverse keyschedule can be implemented with negligible hardware overhead based on the forward keyschedule.

Our design sets a new record for an 8-bit serial architecture with full functionality for encryption and decryption including the keyschedule, as well as for a sole encryption architecture. Furthermore our design is flexible enough to allow scaling the S-Box architecture from single-cycle to multi-stage pipelined approaches as are required for high operation frequencies or for protection against side-channel attacks. We demonstrate this by instantiating the design with a serial version of the S-Box to reduce the area requirement even further.

Keywords: AES · Lightweight · 8-bit-serial · ASIC · Block cypher · S-Box

© IFIP International Federation for Information Processing 2019
Published by Springer Nature Switzerland AG 2019
M. Maniatakos et al. (Eds.): VLSI-SoC 2017, IFIP AICT 500, pp. 220–239, 2019.
https://doi.org/10.1007/978-3-030-15663-3_11

1 Introduction

In recent years small and resource-constrained computing platforms and embedded systems became ubiquitously present. With the recent growth of the Internet of Things (IoT), those systems are becoming increasingly connected among each other and with more powerful dedicated servers or applications in the cloud. Along with sensitive data such as firmware or personal data on the devices, all this communication needs cryptographic protection. To solve this problem, many new block cyphers have been conceived, such as NOEKEON [10], PRESENT [6], KATAN [11], PRINTcipher [18], piccolo [24], TWINE [25], LED [15], KLEIN [14], PRINCE [7], SIMON and SPECK [5], RECTANGLE [28] or Midori [2] to name just a few.[1]

While some, such as PRESENT and CLEFIA, have been standardised [17], these new cyphers have not gained as much trust as the well scrutinised Advanced Encryption Standard (AES) nor can they compete with the latter's proliferation. Therefore research on lightweight implementations of AES has gained momentum in the recent years. Moreover, not only interoperability issues, but also the need to defend against side-channel attacks motivates the search for small implementations, because countermeasures against such attacks usually increase the size of the design by a factor, rather than simply adding a constant overhead. The notion of *lightweight* usually denotes low area designs with low energy consumption that "pay" for these optimisations with slightly increased latency. Sometimes the focus is more on (peak) power consumption than on energy consumption. The exact definition of *lightweight* and the ideal tradeoff are usually driven by the actual application scenario. Most of these scenarios, however, have in common that they do not need bulk encryption, but are rather implemented to secure transmission of infrequent small data packages or are used for authentication purposes on SmartCards. In all cases hardware area is at a premium and there is some flexibility in the acceptable latency.

Given the wide range of optimisation targets and the popularity of AES, it is impossible to give a comprehensive account of implementations. Short overviews can be found in [13,22] and [9] (the latter with a focus on FPGA implementations). With respect to compact hardware and a focus on ASICs, some notable publications follow. All these architectures employ serialisation as basic technique of area-runtime tradeoff. The structure of AES suggests a datapath width of 8-bit, given by the S-Box. The S-Box-implementation of [8] is used by all publications unless otherwise noted. Sizes are given in *gate equivalents (GEs)*, the number of 2-input NAND gates from the same cell library that would cover an equivalent area.

Motivated by the column-wise operations of AES, a 32-bit wide serial datapath is used by [23] along with a tower-field approach to the S-Box to achieve a design size of 5389 GE. A better combination of sub-fields for this S-Box-design was subsequently published by [8]. This variant is used in most of the current

---

[1] For a more comprehensive list see e.g. https://www.cryptolux.org/index.php/ Lightweight_Block_Ciphers.

implementations. A significant reduction in area was achieved by [12], who report 3400 GE. The main drawback is the high latency of more than 1000 clock cycles. Improved runtime was reported by [16], who realised the minimum runtime for an 8-bit serial architecture and [21] but for an encryption-only design. The latter design has been extended into an encryption/decryption design by [3,4]. The additional improvement in area is due to a careful selection of the used cell library. The same holds for the design of [20], that was tailored to an Intel 22 nm tri-gate process. While encryption is implemented in less than 2000 GE, no distinct combined implementation, that offers encryption and decryption functionality, is available and the naïve combined implementation weighs in at more than 4000 GE.

Here we discuss in detail the 8-bit serial hardware architecture for encryption and decryption first presented in [27] that is significantly smaller than previously published architectures at the cost of an increase in latency. We show that by carefully designing the datapath we can construct a smaller architecture than by simply extending the architecture of [21] to accommodate decryption as in [4]. Especially we demonstrate that the inverse keyschedule can be realised without significantly increasing the circuit size, something left as an open question in [4]. Beyond that we show how the serial approach to computing the S-Box from [26] integrates nicely into our architecture, giving a further significant reduction in the size of the overall implementation.

The remainder of this chapter is organised in the following way: In Sect. 2 we quickly recapitulate the particulars of AES, before we give the details of our architecture in Sect. 3 through Sect. 6. Section 7 demonstrates how a serial multi-cycle S-Box-implementation can be used with our architecture, before Sect. 8 presents details of actual implementations and lists related results from the literature. Finally we sum up our results in Sect. 9.

2   Background

2.1   The Advanced Encryption Standard

We give a minimal description of AES, focused on its smallest version, AES-128, to keep the chapter somewhat self-contained. For a much better and more complete introduction we suggest the relevant chapter in [19].

AES is a block cypher taking a 128-bit plaintext for encryption and a key of either 128, 192 or 256 bits. The result is a 128-bit cyphertext. The plaintext is mapped to an internal state, then transformed by iterated application of four operations, which are independent of the key-length. These operations are organised in rounds and only the number of rounds depends on the key-length. Finally the state is serialized again to produce the cyphertext. The state is usually envisioned as a square grid of 4 by 4 bytes where the plaintext/cyphertext is mapped in column-major order. For the purpose of this work we will use indexing from top left to bottom right.

Elementary Operations of AES. AES is build from four elementary operations. Three of these are linear operations, e.g. can be implemented in hardware using only xor gates.

ShiftRows is simply a permutation of bytes in the state. From top to bottom the rows of the state are rotated left by 0, 1, 2 and 3 positions respectively. Its purpose is to provide confusion among the columns.

MixColums operates on each of the columns independently. Indexed cyclically, each element is tripled, the double of its predecessor added and the two successors are added unchanged. For these multiplications the byte values are interpreted as elements of a certain finite field. In practice this means that doubling equals a shift left by one bit and in case of a carry out a given constant is added (by xor). Tripling is the same as doubling plus adding the original value. The purpose of MixColumns is to provide confusion among the rows, complementing the ShiftRows operation.

AddRoundkey combines the current roundkey with the current value of the state by a simple bit-wise xor operation. Its purpose is to repeatedly mix in the secret into the state.

Finally there is a single non-linear operation: *SubBytes* replaces each byte with another value, that can either be computed just-in-time by inverting the value in the aforementioned Galois Field and applying an affine transformation, or it can be taken from a lookup-table with precomputed values. Its purpose is to avoid that the cypher can be modelled as a set of linear equations that is easily solvable.

Roundkey Derivation. For each *AddRoundkey* step a new roundkey is used. The input key is used as-is as first roundkey. Each subsequent roundkey is derived from the previous one in chunks of four bytes. A new chunk is generated by adding (xor) the corresponding chunk of the previous roundkey with the last derived chunk. For the first chunk of each roundkey the last chunk of the previous roundkey is taken as previous chunk, but only after applying a three-step transformation on it: First the bytes are cycled by one position in direction of the smaller index, then the *SubBytes* transformation is applied to each of the bytes before a round-specific constant is added to the first byte.

Round Structure. AES-128 encryption starts with a pre-whitening step, where the input key is added as-is. Then nine full rounds, each made up of the sequence SubBytes – ShiftRows – MixColums – AddRoundkey follow. The encryption process finishes with the sequence SubBytes – ShiftRows – AddRoundkey.

Decryption works by applying the inverse operations in reverse order.

It shall be noted here that, due to the byte granularity of the operations, the order of SubBytes and ShiftRows can be swapped.

3   Basic Principles of the Architecture

3.1   Design Rationale

Studying previously published low-area implementations of AES, e.g. [21], we quickly noticed that an 8-bit data-path lends itself nicely to the byte-granularity found in AES. We also noticed that this decision leads to many multiplexers, which the authors of [21] tried to counter by using scan flip flops (scan FFs), which combine a storage element (FF) and a multiplexer in one design unit provided by the cell library used to implement the architecture. In the case of [21] a cell library by UMC was selected. In this library a scan FF uses less area than the two components would require individually, thus saving a considerable amount of area in the implementation.

A significant part of any low-area implementation of a symmetric block cypher is taken by the storage elements. Their number is determined by the algorithm itself, for AES-128 this amounts to at least 128 FFs for the state and 128 FFs for the current roundkey, for a total of 1536 GE, assuming a typical size of 6 GE per FF. To lower this fixed cost, [4] chose a cell library by STM which offers so-called multi-bit FFs, i.e. library cells that offer multiple data I/O ports, but only a single clock port. The internal design of these cells can then be optimised by the library vendor. As a result the *average* area consumption of a FF in [4] is less than 4.5 GE, as can be estimated from the numbers given in [4] and was confirmed by the authors in personal communication.

Those optimisations are specific to a certain technology and therefore not applicable to other cell libraries, e.g. those from TSMC offered to universities through the Europractice[2] program.

We therefore aimed to reduce the area consumption of our implementation through architectural decisions. The aforementioned optimisations may then be applied additionally.

An important insight from this deliberation is that the amount of area available for optimisation through architectural decisions is limited by the difference between the total area consumed by the architecture and the area consumed by the state bits. We will call this the *optimisation gap*. In this work, taking also into account that at least one S-Box is required, it amounts to less than 1000 GE, based on [4].

Our design rationale is therefore an 8-bit datapath that keeps the number of multiplexers low.

We identified two directions of data movement in the square state representation, horizontally to the left and vertically from the bottom up. To reduce multiplexers, we designed each row to rotate one byte per cycle to the left and selected one designated column to also rotate data towards the top. The vertical movement is required for loading and serialisation of the round functions. It can be avoided only at the cost of a 32-bit serial implementation or additional storage and multiplexing, both significantly increasing the required area.

---

[2] http://www.europractice-ic.com/libraries_TSMC.php (last accessed: 30.03.2017).

For the key we identified that movement is either along all key bytes or – in the same direction – among the last four key bytes only. For data that should not move/be updated we used activation signals generated by the control logic.

Finally we kept the architecture flexible enough to accommodate different implementation options for the SubBytes function, from single cycle implementations to pipelined/staged implementations that are required for increased operating frequency, further serialisation or countermeasures against side-channel attacks. We demonstrate this by giving implementation results for two different S-Box architectures in Sect. 8.

3.2 Area-Runtime Tradeoff

Our goal is to push the area-runtime tradeoff significantly towards smaller area, trading a reduction in area for an increase in runtime. Naturally, as we come closer to the minimal possible area, it becomes harder to make progress and the cost (runtime) increases dramatically. Due to practical constraints, there is a point where the additional control logic offsets any gains from serialisation, further reducing the available optimisation gap.

3.3 Serial MixColumns

We chose to implement MixColumns in a serial fashion to avoid duplication of logic. The basic idea of a serial implementation draws from the fact that MixColumns, when written as a matrix operating on a vector over $GF(2^8)$ in Rijndael-representation, is a MDS matrix. Especially all rows/columns are just rotated variants of each other. In practice this can be exploited by keeping the function and rotating the argument. To further ease computation, we use the decomposition

$$(2, 3, 1, 1)(a, b, c, d)^T = [(3, 2, 0, 0) \oplus (1, 1, 1, 1)] (a, b, c, d)^T$$

in the Galois field. This allows to compute the sum of all inputs ahead and only a must be buffered for the computation of the last element. This leads to a total of 6 clock cycles per column for computing the MixColumns operation. More details on serial implementations of MixColumns can be found in [1].

3.4 SubBytes Implementation

A lot of work has gone into finding small implementations of the SubBytes operation. For a long time the architecture published in [8] was considered the smallest. Smaller ones, at the cost of reduced throughput, have been published recently in [26]. We give results for the former one as our main result as it is also used in the referenced publications and therefore facilitates easier comparison of architectures. Nevertheless, as the implementation can be replaced easily with the one from [26], we also give results with a design based on an improved version of the latter and show how it can be integrated tightly into the overall architecture.

4 Our Architecture

4.1 Architecture Overview

The architecture consists of three main modules as depicted in Fig. 1: a data state module implementing storage and all operations exclusive to the state, a keystate module implementing storage for one roundkey and implementing all functions exclusive to the key update and a control module that schedules and synchronises all operations and provides the public interface of the architecture. Some smaller modules implementing shared resources, such as the SubBytes operation, or otherwise lending themselves to encapsulation, such as the generation of the round constants, are also connected and coordinated through the control module.

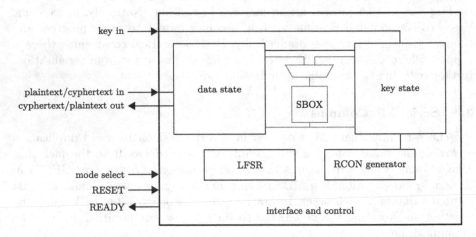

Fig. 1. High level view of the proposed architecture. The control module encapsulates the two state modules and some smaller utility modules. The public interface is described in Subsect. 4.1. The S-Box can be implemented either as a shared module or with a distinct copy for each state.

The public interface has two 8-bit wide ports for inputting data and key, one 8-bit wide port for reading the result, two input bits to select one of the available three modes of operation (see Sect. 5), an input port for the reset signal and an output port to signal availability of the results. Operation details and timings are given in Sect. 6.

4.2 Individual Modules

The **State Module** as shown in Fig. 2a contains all storage elements for the data at its current state of processing along with all logic required for the ShiftRows, MixColumns and AddRoundkey operations. It has two 8-bit wide inputs for data and key, an 8-bit wide output for data and inputs for the relevant control signals. Depending on the implementation of the SubBytes operation (dedicated or shared) another pair of data ports is present.

All data manipulation happens on the rightmost column. Once four bytes have been shifted in from the bottom or fully handled by the round operations, all columns are rotated one position to the left. The control signals can enable/disable shifting per row and individually for each of the bytes in the rightmost column. ShiftRows and its inverse are implemented by selectively activating the rows over the course of three cycles.

The term $3 \cdot [12] \oplus 2 \cdot [13]$ denotes the multiplications in the Galois Field required for a serial implementation of MixColumns. The register ms samples, when enabled, a xor sum of the rightmost column. mb is a register used for buffering during mix columns. Note that key addition can either be chained to MixColumns or computed individually, by virtue of the multiplexer in the input path of mb. To implement AddRoundkey we drew inspiration from the logic description of a multiplexer, with the difference that only the key is gated by the selection signal and combination happens by xor instead of or, hence the $\oplus$ on the multiplexer symbol.

The **Keystate Module** as shown in Fig. 2b contains all storage elements for one roundkey along with all logic required for the key update operations. As with the data state, all manipulation happens on the rightmost column (bytes 12 through 15), with the notable difference that during update the whole keystate gets shifted, since updates of the roundkey can not happen in-place. Rather, each new word is appended to the so far generated key stream. There are two enable signals, one for shifting the whole key by one position and one for only rotating the rightmost column, which is in some cases used to non-destructively read a single word of the key. By properly setting the selectors of the multiplexers, data can either cycle through the whole keystate and from byte 0 back to byte 15 or only in the rightmost column and from byte 12 to byte 15. There is again one multiplexer marked with $\oplus$. This multiplexer has distinct selection signals for each input, so either one or both at the same time can be selected. Combination happens by xor, so we have a dual functionality: In case only one input is selected, it is a regular multiplexer; in case both inputs are active we get the xor required for key updates. As with ShiftRows for the state, the rotation of the last column by one byte can be swapped with the SubBytes operation. This is handled by the multiplexer at the input of the S-Box. SubBytes is applied three times to the value then at byte 13, and after each application the whole keystate is moved by one byte. The remaining byte to be handled can then be found at byte 9. The round constant is added after the S-Box and is delivered by the control unit as required (e.g. it is zero for all but for the first byte). The updated key can either be streamed out at generation time or read back later. It was experimentally verified for our implementation that loading the key into byte 0 instead of byte 15 results in smaller area (by 3 GE) at the cost of an extra cycle.

For the reverse key schedule exactly the same dataflow can be used with the only caveat that after each word the whole key must be cycled by 8 bytes to correctly position the input values. The only additional logic required is found in the control module.

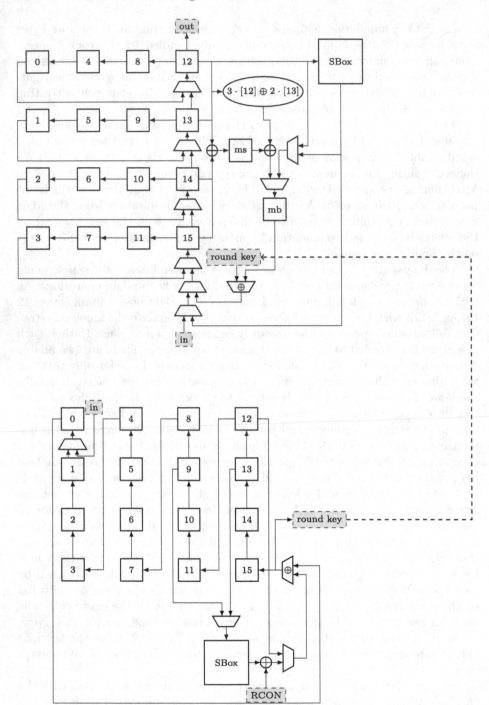

Fig. 2. (a) (upper part) The **state**. All datapaths depicted are 8-bit wide. The S-Box can be implemented as a shared module. (b) (lower part) The **keystate**. All datapaths depicted are 8-bit wide. The S-Box can be implemented as a shared module.

The **Control Module** encapsulates the two modules just presented. It also has three Linear Feedback Shift Registers (LFSRs) and a small 2-bit counter to generate the required control signals. The first LFSR is used during loading and the initial key addition until proper round-operation starts. In the later stages it is used to count the cycles required for the S-Box, which depend on the selected architecture of the latter. The second LFSR coordinates the operations for a single column while the 2-bit counter counts the number of columns. Those counters are coupled, such that a step of a "higher level" counter only occurs when a "lower level" counter wraps or resets itself. The third LFSR generates the round constants required for key scheduling. It is stepped once *during* the round and also serves as round counter for the control module. Once the correct value for the last round is reached and the last round finishes a `ready` signal is generated.

All LFSRs are in Galois configuration, with the one for the round constants being able to enumerate the constants in forward and backward direction.

Control signals are derived from these LFSRs in a straight-forward manner, taking into account the selection of operation mode, namely whether encryption or decryption should occur and in the case of the latter, whether the given key must be expanded or corresponds to the last roundkey of the encryption process and can be directly used for decryption.

Both mode selection signals can be hardwired at design time, allowing for easy synthesis of specialised architectures. The effects for our particular implementations are listed in Sect. 8.

5   Encryption vs. Decryption

The architecture supports encryption and decryption with or without key-expansion, that is for decryption either the same key as for encryption can be given, which is then first expanded before decryption starts, or the last roundkey can be given directly, allowing for flexible application of the architecture. If key-expansion is desired, a regular encryption process is run with a deactivated state. This takes more cycles than actually would be needed for a pure key-expansion, but saves significantly on control logic.

To optimise the architecture, we tried to express the decryption process as much as possible in terms of the encryption process. The inverse to ShiftRows (iSR) is given by swapping the enable signals of row 1 and 3. This is equivalent to three subsequent applications of ShiftRows (SR). As four applications rotate each row by a multiple of four positions, resulting in identity, this results in the inverse operation. Showing that no smaller number of repetitions suffices and that iSR can be expressed in at most three left shifts is trivial.

MixColumns (MC) can be written as a matrix applied to a vector. Computing powers of this matrix resembles repeated application of the MixColumns operation. The fourth power is the smallest power to result in the identity matrix. Therefore the inverse MixColumns (iMC) operation is given by three subsequent applications of MC. AddRoundkey (ARK) is self-inverse and the inverse to Sub-Bytes (SBOX) is given by a dedicated function (iSBOX).

A third step is to align the decryption control flow to the encryption flow. Recall the sequence of operations for encryption:

$$ARK \to (SR \to SBOX \to MC \to ARK)^9 \to SR \to SBOX \to ARK$$

When reversing this sequence, ShiftRows can be swapped with the application of SubBytes, as the latter operates on isolated state bytes. Since the last round does not carry a MixColumns operation, decryption essentially has almost the same sequence of steps as encryption, with all operations replaced by their inverse counterparts and AddRoundkeys *before* inverse MixColumns:

$$ARK \to iSR \to iSBOX \to (ARK \to iMC \to iSR \to iSBOX)^9 \to ARK$$
$$\hat{=} ARK \to (iSR \to iSBOX \to ARK \to iMC)^9 \to iSR \to iSBOX \to ARK$$

For encryption the individual round keys can be derived from the initial key in straightforward order. For decryption, they must be recovered from the last round key and presented to the state in reverse order. A special property of the key schedule is, that no inverse variants of the update operations are required: For each 32-bit word K_i, $i = 0, \ldots, 43$, the update formula for the forward expansion is $K_i = K_{i-4} \oplus f(K_{i-1})$, where $4 < i < 44$ and f is the special key-update transformation for every fourth column and identity otherwise. The update formula for the reverse expansion is then simply $K_i = K_{i+4} \oplus f(K_{i+3})$ with $40 > i > 0$ and f being identity, when $i \neq 0 \mod 4$.

It remains to remark that in both cases all operations aside from ShiftRows and its inverse are restricted to a single column. Thus they can be computed in an interleaved fashion and each column needs to be touched only once per round.

6   Operation and Timing

We first give a rough by-cycle breakdown of the encryption operation, followed by a short enumeration of the differences when the architecture operates in decryption mode.

To prepare the module for encryption of a new block, the RESET input must be activated. All inputs are expected to be available at the input ports once the RESET is deactivated. During the following 16 cycles data is read into the state. Simultaneously the key is loaded into the keystate. The state is subsequently rotated by one column, the key by one byte. During the next 23 cycles the key is added to the state with three cycles to switch between columns. For decryption, this is followed by another 12 cycles to reposition the key for the subsequent key scheduling.

Next, nine regular rounds follow. Each round is subdivided into four repetitions of a column update. The first iteration begins with a ShiftRows operation taking three cycles, in which the rows are gradually disabled to control the amount of shifting. In the remaining column updates, this part of the sub-round is skipped.

The main part of each sub-round starts by computing the SubBytes operation on byte 12, putting the result into byte 15 and cycling the column upwards by one byte. In the next cycle one SubByte operation for the key schedule is computed, the round constant added to the first key byte and the whole key shifted by one position, appending the result to the key state. A total of 8 cycles are needed to compute all SubByte operations for one column.

Following this, MixColumns and AddRoundkey can be computed immediately on this column. This is done in 6 cycles: First the sum of the bytes 12 through 15 is stored in the register ms. Concurrently, byte 12 is copied into the buffer mb. For five cycles the expression $3 \cdot [12] \oplus 2 \cdot [13]$ is evaluated, using hardwired shift-and-adds, the value of ms added and the result stored in mb while the previous value of this register is shifted into byte 15, with the value delivered from the roundkey module added during the last four cycles. The values in the rightmost column of the roundkey are cycled concurrently. A final cycle rotates all columns to the left by one step. Summing up, a total of $3 + 4(8 + 6) = 59$ cycles are required per round, as MixColumns is started while the last S-Box for the keyschedule is evaluated.

In the final round the input multiplexer to mb is set to take the value from byte 12 during the whole MixColumns process, effectively bypassing this operation and implementing a pure AddRoundkey operation.

Along with the last cycle of the last round, a ready signal is raised and the result of the computation is made available one byte per cycle at the output by shifting the last column up and rotating left when necessary. During regular computation the output is gated off to avoid unnecessary toggling at the output. This leads to a total latency of $40 + 10 \cdot 59 + 16 = 646$ cycles per encryption, including 32 cycles for loading/storing results.

The MixColumns of the dedicated encryption architecture can be tweaked a bit more for speed, yielding a slightly bigger design that runs in 606 clock cycles. Instead of computing the value for ms in a dedicated clock cycle, the value is produced by accumulating the outputs of the S-Box as they are produced.

Decryption has an almost identical control flow, with only a few, but important, differences. First, the output of the S-Box is written to mb instead of byte 15, to enable immediate addition of the roundkey. Second, MixColumn is repeated three times to realise the reverse functionality. Finally, after each column, the key must be repositioned to compute the reverse key schedule. This is done concurrently to the MixColumn operation. Altogether, decryption requires an additional 592 cycles compared to encryption for the combined architecture.

Decryption with initial forward key expansion simply runs a full encryption process with deactivated data state, followed by 9 cycles to readjust the key position and switch modes before regular decryption operation commences.

All latencies are listed in Table 1.

Table 1. Area and latency comparison of different architectures. Architectures are annotated with their capability (**E**ncryption/**D**ecryption). If different runtimes apply to combined architectures, they are given as [Encryption]/[Decryption]/[Decryption with full key expansion]. Those marked with * are generated by hardwiring the mode selection inputs of the fully featured architecture.

	Architecture	Technology	Area (GE)	Latency (cycles)
	[12] (**ED**)	Philips 350 nm	3400	1032/1165
	[16] (**E**)	0.13 μm, 1.2 V	3.1k	160
	[21] (**E**)	UMC 180 nm	2400	226
	[20] (**E**)	Intel 22 nm	1947	336
	[20] (**D**)	Intel 22 nm	2090	216
	[4] (**ED**)	STM 90 nm	2060	246/326
	[4] (**ED**)	STM 65 nm	2430	246/326
	[4], re-synth	TSMC 40 nm	2676	246/326
with S-Box from [8]	this (**ED**)	TSMC 40 nm	**2566**	689/1281/1947
	this (**D***) full key-exp	TSMC 40 nm	2569	1947
	this (**D***) rev. key-exp	TSMC 40 nm	2481	1281
	this (**E***)	TSMC 40 nm	2314	689
	this (**E**) (dedicated, small)	TSMC 40 nm	2269	646
	this (**E**) (dedicated, fast)	TSMC 40 nm	2294	606
with S-Box from [26]	this (**ED**)	TSMC 40 nm	**2449**	41419/42011/83407
	this (**D***) full key-exp	TSMC 40 nm	2444	83407
	this (**D***) rev. key-exp	TSMC 40 nm	2350	42011
	this (**E***)	TSMC 40 nm	2279	41419
	this (**E**) (dedicated)	TSMC 40 nm	2244	41326

7 An Even Smaller Variant

To demonstrate the flexibility of our architecture we also instantiate it with S-Box designs following the approach of [26]. This allows us to further reduce the size of the implementation by at least 1.1% up to more than 4.5%, depending on the implemented modes of operation and using the TSMC cell library as detailed in Sect. 8. With other cell libraries (having smaller FFs compared to the respective size of logic gates) the relative savings can be expected to be even more significant.

7.1 The Serial S-Box Architecture

The AES-S-Box is defined as an inversion of elements in a finite field with a given representation, followed by an affine mapping (defined in a different representation of this field). The basic idea of this approach is to serialize the inversion step by exploiting that every element x from the field can uniquely be written as a power g^k of a generating element g. Once the value of g has been selected from the set of admissible values in the field, a bijection $x = g^k$ between x and k is defined. The inverse x^{-1} of x is then indeed given by $x = g^{-k}$, where the exponents are computed modulo a value determined by the field size. The different flavours of serial inversion algorithms given in [26] operate by continually multiplying with either g or its inverse element and comparing to x or a fixed reference value to obtain k resp. $-k$. The result is then computed as g^{-k} or $(g^{-1})^k$.

Since multiplication with a fixed element in a binary extension field can be realised in hardware using a feedback shift-register in Galois configuration, this yields a very small circuit for inversion.

The implementation is based on the two algorithms given hereafter. The first one is a generalised version of Algorithm A from [26], employed to implement the S-Box used in the key scheduling. The other one is a generalised version of Algorithm B2 from the same paper, which can be tightly integrated into the data state.

Algorithm 1.1. S-Box for key scheduling	**Algorithm 1.2.** S-Box for data state
Input: γ	**Input:** γ
Output: $\gamma^{-1}c^2$	**Output:** $\gamma^{-1}c^2$
$r_1 \leftarrow c$;	$r_1 \leftarrow \gamma$;
$r_2 \leftarrow 1$;	$r_2 \leftarrow 1$;
while $(r_1 \neq \gamma) \wedge (r_2 \leq 255)$ **do**	**while** $(r_1 \neq c) \wedge (r_2 \leq 255)$ **do**
$\quad$ $r_1 \leftarrow \alpha r_1$;	$\quad$ $r_1 \leftarrow \alpha^{-1} r_1$;
$\quad$ $r_2 \leftarrow r_2 + 1$;	$\quad$ $r_2 \leftarrow r_2 + 1$;
end	**end**
$r_1 \leftarrow c$;	
while $r_2 \leq 255$ **do**	**while** $r_2 \leq 255$ **do**
$\quad$ $r_1 \leftarrow \alpha r_1$;	$\quad$ $r_1 \leftarrow \alpha r_1$;
$\quad$ $r_2 \leftarrow r_2 + 1$;	$\quad$ $r_2 \leftarrow r_2 + 1$;
end	**end**

Both algorithms have the same constant runtime and the counter r_2 is only required to signal the passing of this timespan. Therefore a simple maximum-length linear feedback shift-register can be used for this purpose. In the actual implementation this was chosen as an 8-bit shift register in Galois-configuration using the Reed-Solomon-Polynomial $x^8 + x^4 + x^3 + x^2 + 1$ as feedback-polynomial

Note that the algorithms run very uniformly and have almost equivalent structure. The only difference between the two is the first phase in Algorithm 1.2 running backwards in comparison to the first phase of Algorithm 1.2, which spares us resetting the register r_1 in between phases. In return the multiplication with the constant g^{-1} has to be implemented along with that for g leading to a second feedback circuit and some multiplexers.

Furthermore, the counter r_2 can be shared across multiple S-Boxes. Therefore, we chose to implement distinct S-Boxes for the data state as well as the keystate. This also makes the multiplexers previously required to multiplex the inputs into a single instance redundant and halves the significant runtime penalty of this serial inversion approach. As this counter can also be used to generate the control signals for loading data and key as well as the control signals for returning the results, since no S-Box is active at the time, the implementation cost is further reduced. The remainder of the implementation can be kept as is without any further modifications.

The algorithms just shown realise only the inversion in the finite field. The constant α can be chosen as any of the 128 generating elements of the Rijndael-field. The constant c can be any element of its multiplicative subgroup. Choosing c to be different from the multiplicative neutral element gives an inversion result that is augmented with a multiplication by c^2. The correcting computation can then be merged with the required affine transformation, which may lead to a computation that is actually less costly to implement. With other words, some computational effort can be split off from the affine transformation and be done more cheaply by encoding it in the choice of the constant.

By exhaustive search (on the standalone S-Boxes) we found that setting α to the element with the canonical bit-representation (written compactly as hexadecimal value) 46 and c to 01 (the neutral element), yielded the smallest implementation for Algorithm 1.1 for our synthesis setup (detailed in Sect. 8). In the same way we determined the choices e9 for α and f1 for c in the context of Algorithm 1.2.

Further area savings can be realised when the S-Boxes are integrated into the overall architecture. Note that the input to Algorithm 1.2 is not used any more once register r_1 has been initialised. This nicely matches the operation of the S-Box in the context of the full AES. Instead of attaching the S-Box to the state byte 12 as in Fig. 2a, this part of the state itself can take the role of this register and the S-Box can operate fully in place. Only the affine transformation is left in the part that is denoted as S-Box in the figure. Unfortunately this optimisation carries not over to the key schedule, where results are only concatenated instead of replaced. Therefore we chose Algorithm 1.1, which is a bit smaller as only one feedback circuit is required, as the inversion core of the S-Box here. On the other hand, this ensures the runtime difference of one cycle between the S-Boxes, so the control logic can work as in the case of a multiplexed single-cycle implementation, if it is halted during S-Box evaluation.

7.2   Runtime Impact

Using the serial S-Box architecture in the implementation adds a latency of 254 cycles per S-Box invocation in the round functions. One more cycle is added per column invocation. The reason is a timing optimisation that can only be applied in the case of the dedicated encryption core with a single-cycle S-Box. This leads to a total of $646 + 160 \cdot 254 + 40 = 41326$ cycles for the dedicated encryption core. For the combined architecture with serial S-Boxes we also decided to spend some idle cycles at the beginning of each column sub-round. This leads to a more uniform execution pattern, matching the execution times of all columns to the first ones (that otherwise take three cycles more to execute the ShiftRows operation). We gain a reduction of 7 GE for a total runtime penalty of 90 cycles. Therefore encryption in case of the fully-functional core with serial S-Boxes takes $689 + 160 \cdot 254 + 90 = 41419$ clock cycles. In case one prefers the reduced latency, the change is easily done by uncommenting a single line in the VHDL source code.

8 Results

We implemented the architecture(s) presented in this work using VHDL. Functional verification of all implementations was done by simulating the VHDL sources directly with *GHDL* and *Synopsys VCS*. The design was compiled, optimised and mapped to a *TSMC* 40 nm *low power* cell library (`tcbn40lpbwp`) using the `compile_ultra` command in *Synopsys DesignCompiler L-2016.03-SP3*. Enabling/disabling of sequential elements was realised through clock gating. The results of manually defining clock-gating structures matched the results of automatic clock gating using the `-gate_clock` option to the `compile_ultra` command. The resulting netlist was simulated with *Synopsys VCS MX* and *Modelsim* using test vectors from the NIST KAT[3] set of test vectors.

Figure 3 shows the area consumption for different variants of our architecture and its relevant competitors, based on the *TSMC* 40 nm *low power* cell library. For each variant also the ratio between combinational and sequential logic is shown. This demonstrates that a significant part of the area is consumed by FFs. All but the pure encryption designs need forward and inverse S-Box implementations and therefore have increased area demands for the combinational part. In case of the serial S-Box variants the share of area used by FFs is even higher.

Finally Table 1 lists our results along with various low-area architectures from the literature, each being one of the smallest designs at the time of publication. A word of caution is needed on the selection of cell libraries: In the UMC 180 nm (and other UMC libraries) the area of a scan-flip-flop cell is 1 GE smaller than the joint areas of a regular flip-flop and a multiplexer cell, therefore in [21] area optimisation was possible by extensive use of scan-flip-flops. The STM 90 nm and STM 65 nm libraries used in [4] offer multibit-flip-flop cells for implementing register banks. Using these the average area consumption of flip-flops can be reduced from 6 GE/bit to roughly 4.5 GE/bit. (This was confirmed through personal communication with one of the authors.) The TSMC libraries used in this work offer none of these features. Therefore we re-synthesized the circuits from [4] based on the VHDL design files given therein. On the contrary we expect our design to significantly benefit from multi-bit cells. Extrapolation from the figures in Table 1 indicate that our design could be the first one to break the 2000 GE-barrier for a fully featured core when synthesized with the STM 90 nm library from [4].

---

[3] http://csrc.nist.gov/groups/STM/cavp/documents/aes/KAT_AES.zip; last accessed: 1st Feb 2017.

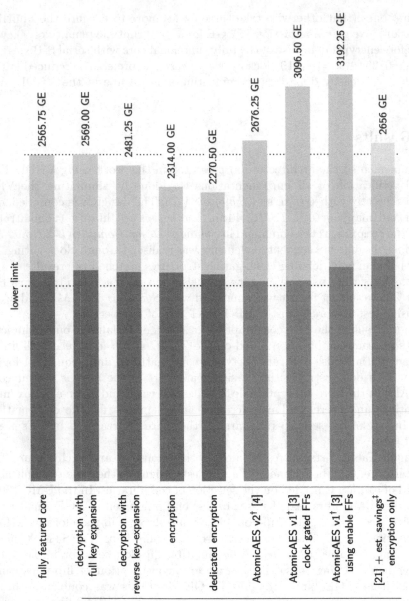

2565.75 GE — fully featured core
2569.00 GE — decryption with full key expansion
2481.25 GE — decryption with reverse key-expansion
2314.00 GE — encryption
2270.50 GE — dedicated encryption
2676.25 GE — AtomicAES v2[†] [4]
3096.50 GE — AtomicAES v1[†] [3] clock gated FFs
3192.25 GE — AtomicAES v1[†] [3] using enable FFs
2656 GE — [21] + est. savings[‡] encryption only

lower limit

[†]re-synthesized with the design flow and cell library of this work
[‡]adjusted for estimated savings of 1 GE per state bit due to
different cell library in original publication

Fig. 3. Comparison of our work with its nearest competitors. The AtomicAES variants were re-synthesized from the source codes linked in [4] using our toolchain and setup. The lower part of each bar signifies the share of sequential elements in the design. Conversely the upper part represents combinational logic. To make a fair comparison we only chose the variant using the S-Box from [8] and conservatively estimated the area saved by using scan-FFs in [21] as 256 GE. The area of 1536 GE required for the state flip-flops is given as a reference lower limit for implementations.

We could not obtain detailed information for the library used in [20], for which it should be noted that the circuit in [20] was designed primarily for energy-efficiency.

Our results show that we can improve the area requirements over [4] for a fully featured AES core by 110 GE, respectively 237 GE with the serial S-Box, which amounts to at least 11%, respectively 23%, of the parts that can be optimised. With other words, everything beyond the inevitable storage for data and key is packed in 1030 GE for the fully featured core and just 734 GE for the dedicated encryption core, less then a third of the total area, when using Canright's S-Box. With the serial S-Boxes this is further reduced to 913 GE (full AES) and 708 GE (encryption only).

Furthermore, by simply fixing the mode selection inputs, optimised circuits can be generated.[4] Modifying the design by hand, also removing unneeded control signals, leads to a very compact dedicated encryption core occupying only 2269 GE, resp. 2244 GE. With the exception of [20], where a proper comparison is not possible due to the differences in the used technologies, these are by far the smallest 8-bit serial implementations of AES reported in the literature.

9   Conclusions

We presented a new 8-bit serial architecture for AES and realised a fully featured implementation and a dedicated encryption variant. Both implementations set new records for low-area consumption at a moderate increase in runtime. For each we also gave results using a different S-Box architecture which further reduced overall area consumption. This makes our architecture especially suited for scenarios where AES needs to be implemented in hardware but is not used for bulk encryption, such as SmartCards, Trusted Platform Modules (TPMs) or IoT nodes.

References

1. Ahmed, E.G., Shaaban, E., Hashem, M.: Lightweight mix columns implementation for AES. In: Proceedings of the 9th WSEAS International Conference on Applied Informatics and Communications, AIC 2009, pp. 253–258. World Scientific and Engineering Academy and Society (WSEAS), Stevens Point, Wisconsin, USA (2009). http://portal.acm.org/citation.cfm?id=1628143
2. Banik, S., et al.: Midori: A block cipher for low energy (extended version). Cryptology ePrint Archive, Report 2015/1142, November 2015. http://eprint.iacr.org/2015/1142
3. Banik, S., Bogdanov, A., Regazzoni, F.: Atomic-AES: a compact implementation of the AES Encryption/Decryption core. Cryptology ePrint Archive, Report 2016/927, September 2016. http://eprint.iacr.org/2016/927

---

[4] The decryption circuit with full key expansion is bigger than the fully featured core, as a FF used to support optimisation in the case of hard-wiring can be removed (manually) from the latter. Keeping this register yields a size of 2573 GE.

4. Banik, S., Bogdanov, A., Regazzoni, F.: Atomic-AES v 2.0. Cryptology ePrint Archive, Report 2016/1005, October 2016. http://eprint.iacr.org/2016/1005
5. Beaulieu, R., Shors, D., Smith, J., Treatman-Clark, S., Weeks, B., Wingers, L.: The SIMON and SPECK families of lightweight block ciphers. Cryptology ePrint Archive, Report 2013/404, June 2013. http://eprint.iacr.org/2013/404
6. Bogdanov, A., et al.: PRESENT: an ultra-lightweight block cipher. In: Paillier, P., Verbauwhede, I. (eds.) CHES 2007. LNCS, vol. 4727, pp. 450–466. Springer, Heidelberg (2007). https://doi.org/10.1007/978-3-540-74735-2_31
7. Borghoff, J., et al.: PRINCE - a low-latency block cipher for pervasive computing applications (full version). Cryptology ePrint Archive, Report 2012/529, September 2012. http://eprint.iacr.org/2012/529
8. Canright, D.: A very compact S-box for AES. In: Rao, J.R., Sunar, B. (eds.) CHES 2005. LNCS, vol. 3659, pp. 441–455. Springer, Heidelberg (2005). https://doi.org/10.1007/11545262_32
9. Chawla, S.S., Aggarwal, S., Kamal, S., Goel, N.: FPGA implementation of an optimized 8-bit AES architecture: a masked S-box and pipelined approach. In: 2015 IEEE International Conference on Electronics, Computing and Communication Technologies (CONECCT), pp. 1–6. IEEE, July 2015. http://dx.doi.org/10.1109/conecct.2015.7383859
10. Daemen, J., Peeters, M., Van Assche, G., Rijmen, V.: The NOEKEON block cipher. Technical report, October 2000. http://gro.noekeon.org/Noekeon-spec.pdf
11. De Cannière, C., Dunkelman, O., Knežević, M.: KATAN and KTANTAN—a family of small and efficient hardware-oriented block ciphers. In: Clavier, C., Gaj, K. (eds.) CHES 2009. LNCS, vol. 5747, pp. 272–288. Springer, Heidelberg (2009). https://doi.org/10.1007/978-3-642-04138-9_20
12. Feldhofer, M., Wolkerstorfer, J., Rijmen, V.: AES implementation on a grain of sand. In: IEE Proceedings - Information Security, vol. 152, no. 1, p. 13+ (2005). http://dx.doi.org/10.1049/ip-ifs:20055006
13. Feldhofer, M., Lemke, K., Oswald, E., Standaert, F.X., Wollinger, T., Wolkerstorfer, J.: State of the art in hardware architectures. Note: deliverable with a special focus on AES hardware architectures. ECRYPT Deliverable No. D.VAM2, September 2005. http://www.iaik.tugraz.at/content/research/krypto/AES/VAM2-IAIK-17-D.VAM2-1_0.pdf
14. Gong, Z., Nikova, S., Law, Y.W.: KLEIN: a new family of lightweight block ciphers. In: Juels, A., Paar, C. (eds.) RFIDSec 2011. LNCS, vol. 7055, pp. 1–18. Springer, Heidelberg (2012). https://doi.org/10.1007/978-3-642-25286-0_1
15. Guo, J., Peyrin, T., Poschmann, A., Robshaw, M.: The LED block cipher. In: Preneel, B., Takagi, T. (eds.) CHES 2011. LNCS, vol. 6917, pp. 326–341. Springer, Heidelberg (2011). https://doi.org/10.1007/978-3-642-23951-9_22
16. Hämäläinen, P., Alho, T., Hännikäinen, M., Hämäläinen, T.D.: Design and implementation of low-area and low-power AES encryption hardware core. In: 9th EUROMICRO Conference on Digital System Design (DSD 2006), pp. 577–583. IEEE (2006). http://dx.doi.org/10.1109/dsd.2006.40
17. ISO/IEC: ISO/IEC 29192-2:2012 - information technology - security techniques - lightweight cryptography - part 2: Block ciphers. Technical report, International Organization for Standardization, January 2012. https://www.iso.org/standard/56552.html
18. Knudsen, L., Leander, G., Poschmann, A., Robshaw, M.J.B.: PRINTCIPHER: a block cipher for IC-printing. In: Mangard, S., Standaert, F.-X. (eds.) CHES 2010. LNCS, vol. 6225, pp. 16–32. Springer, Heidelberg (2010). https://doi.org/10.1007/978-3-642-15031-9_2

19. Knudsen, L.R., Robshaw, M.: The Block Cipher Companion. Springer, Heidelberg (2011). http://link.springer.com/book/10.1007%2F978-3-642-17342-4
20. Mathew, S., et al.: 340 mV-1.1 V, 289 Gbps/W, 2090-gate nanoAES hardware accelerator with area-optimized encrypt/decrypt $GF(2^4)^2$ polynomials in 22 nm tri-gate CMOS. IEEE J. Solid-State Circ. **50**(4), 1048–1058 (2015). http://dx.doi.org/10.1109/jssc.2014.2384039
21. Moradi, A., Poschmann, A., Ling, S., Paar, C., Wang, H.: Pushing the limits: a very compact and a threshold implementation of AES. In: Paterson, K.G. (ed.) EUROCRYPT 2011. LNCS, vol. 6632, pp. 69–88. Springer, Heidelberg (2011). https://doi.org/10.1007/978-3-642-20465-4_6
22. Pramstaller, N., Mangard, S., Dominikus, S., Wolkerstorfer, J.: Efficient AES implementations on ASICs and FPGAs. In: Dobbertin, H., Rijmen, V., Sowa, A. (eds.) AES 2004. LNCS, vol. 3373, pp. 98–112. Springer, Heidelberg (2005). https://doi.org/10.1007/11506447_9
23. Satoh, A., Morioka, S., Takano, K., Munetoh, S.: A compact Rijndael hardware architecture with S-box optimization. In: Boyd, C. (ed.) ASIACRYPT 2001. LNCS, vol. 2248, pp. 239–254. Springer, Heidelberg (2001). https://doi.org/10.1007/3-540-45682-1_15
24. Shibutani, K., Isobe, T., Hiwatari, H., Mitsuda, A., Akishita, T., Shirai, T.: *Piccolo*: an ultra-lightweight blockcipher. In: Preneel, B., Takagi, T. (eds.) CHES 2011. LNCS, vol. 6917, pp. 342–357. Springer, Heidelberg (2011). https://doi.org/10.1007/978-3-642-23951-9_23
25. Suzaki, T., Minematsu, K., Morioka, S., Kobayashi, E.: *TWINE*: a lightweight block cipher for multiple platforms. In: Knudsen, L.R., Wu, H. (eds.) SAC 2012. LNCS, vol. 7707, pp. 339–354. Springer, Heidelberg (2013). https://doi.org/10.1007/978-3-642-35999-6_22
26. Wamser, M.S.: Ultra-small designs for inversion-based S-boxes. In: 17th Euromicro Conference on Digital System Design, pp. 512–519. Department of Computer Science, Università di Verona. IEEE, August 2014. http://dx.doi.org/10.1109/DSD.2014.37
27. Wamser, M.S., Sigl, G.: Pushing the limits further: sub-atomic AES. In: 2017 IFIP/IEEE International Conference on Very Large Scale Integration (VLSI-SoC), pp. 1–6 (2017). http://dx.doi.org/10.1109/VLSI-SoC.2017.8203470
28. Zhang, W., Bao, Z., Lin, D., Rijmen, V., Yang, B., Verbauwhede, I.: RECTANGLE: a bit-slice Ultra-Lightweight block cipher suitable for multiple platforms. Cryptology ePrint Archive, Report 2014/084, February 2014. http://eprint.iacr.org/2014/084

VLSI-SoC: An Enduring Tradition

Ricardo Reis[1(✉)] and Manfred Glesner[2]

[1] PGMicro/PPGC, Instituto de Informática,
Universidade Federal do Rio Grande do Sul, Porto Alegre, Brazil
`reis@inf.ufrgs.br`
[2] Institut für Datentechnik, Mikroelektronische Systeme,
Technische Universität Darmstadt, Darmstadt, Germany
`glesner@mes.tu-darmstadt.de`

Abstract. VLSI-SoC series of conferences started in 1981 and this chapter presents a little bit of its history. Since the beginning, the conference moves around the world, showing recent works in the field of VLSI and Systems-on-Chip design and design automation. The contents of books related to the set of event editions is in some way a witness of the extraordinary evolution of the field in these almost 4 decades.

Keywords: VLSI · SoC · EDA · Test · Microelectronics

1 The Beginning

The year that Lynn Conway and Carver Mead received the "1981 Electronics Award for Creating a Common Design Culture for the LSI ERA" was the year that started the VLSI-SoC (IFIP TC10/WG10.5 International Conference on Very Large Scale Integration) series of conferences (started as VLSI). The first edition was organized in Edinburgh, UK, from August 18 to 21. The General Chair was Sidney Michaelson and the Program Chair was John Gray, both from the University of Edinburgh. Prof. Sidney Michaelson was also the founder of a new Working Group on VLSI for the International Federation for Information Processing, the WG10.5 (http://www.edinburgh.bcs.org/michaelson.htm). The WG10.5 has developed into one of IFIP's most active groups, regularly organizing workshops and conferences. In 1986, Prof. Sidney Michaelson was presented with the IFIP Silver Core award in recognition of his contribution to the work of that organization. At the time of his death he was an active member of the organizing committee for the tenth anniversary conference, VLSI 91, to be held in Edinburgh later that year. Figure 1 shows the cover of the first proceedings, that was published as a book by Academic Press and edited by John Gray. The book includes 35 papers. The first paper of the book has the title "VLSI and Technological Innovations" and the author was Prof. Carver Mead (CALTECH, USA).

The second edition was organized in Trondheim, Norway, August 16–19, 1983, and O. Landsverk from TU Trondheim was the General Chair. The Program Chair was Prof. François Anceau from TIM3/INPG, France. The proceedings were also published as a book, by North-Holland Publishers (Fig. 2).

M. Maniatakos et al. (Eds.): VLSI-SoC 2017, IFIP AICT 500, pp. 240–255, 2019.
https://doi.org/10.1007/978-3-030-15663-3_12

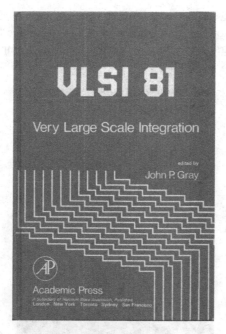

Fig. 1. Cover of the first VLSI conference proceedings published as a book by Academic Press [1].

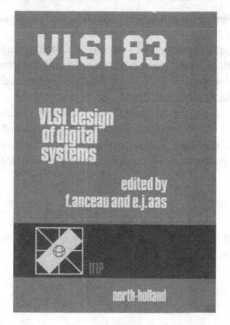

Fig. 2. Cover of the second VLSI conference proceedings published as a book by North Holland [2].

The third edition was organized in Tokyo, Japan, August 26–28, 1985. The General Chair was Prof. T. Moto-Oka from University of Tokyo and the Program Chair was E. Hörbst, from the Central Research Division of Siemens Company in Munich, Germany. The proceedings were again published as a book by North-Holland (Fig. 3).

Fig. 3. Cover of the VLSI 1985 proceedings published as a book by North Holland [3].

The fourth edition was organized in Vancouver, Canada, August 10–12, 1987. The General Chair was D.R. Colton from CMC, Canada and the Program Chair was Prof. C.H. Sequin from University of California, USA. The proceedings were again published as a book by North-Holland (Fig, 4).

The fifth edition was organized in Munich, Germany, August 16–18, 1989. The General Chair was Prof. R. Piloty from Technical University of Darmstadt, Germany and the Program Chair was Prof. Gerald Musgrave from Brunel University, UK. The proceedings with 516 pages were again published by North-Holland (Fig. 4).

Fig. 4. Covers of VLSI 1987 and VLSI 1989 proceedings published by North Holland [4, 5].

Fig. 5. Covers of the VLSI 1991 and VLSI 1993 proceedings published as a book by North Holland [6, 7].

2 Years 90's

The 1991 edition was organized again in Edinburgh, Scotland, August 20–22. The General Chair was I. Barron from InMOS, Uk and the Program Chair was Prof. P.B. Denyer from University of Edinburgh, UK. The proceedings were again published as a book by North-Holland (Fig. 5).

The 1993 edition was organized in Grenoble, France, September 6–9, 1993. The General Chair was J. Monnier from ST Microelectronics, France and the Program Chair was Takayuki Yanagawa from NEC, Japan. The proceedings were published by North-Holland (Fig 5).

In 1995, the conference was again in Tokyo, Japan, August 29 to September 1. The General Chair was Prof. Tatsuo Ohtsuki from Waseda University, Japan and the Program Chair was Prof. Wolfgang Rosenstiel, from University of Tübingen, Germany. This edition was organized together with CHDL 95 (the 12th International Conference on Computer Hardware Description Languages and their Applications) and the first edition of ASP-DAC. The proceedings were published as a joint proceedings of the 3 conferences and published by IEEE (Fig. 6).

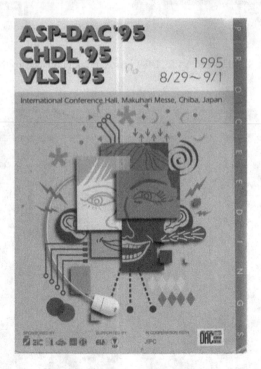

Fig. 6. Cover of the VLSI 1995 proceedings published by IEEE [8].

In 1997, the conference was organized for the first time in South America. The location was Gramado, a small tourist town close to Porto Alegre, South Brazil. It was organized from August 26 to 29. The General Chair was Prof. Ricardo Reis from

Universidade Federal do Rio Grande do Sul (UFRGS), Porto Alegre, Brazil and the Program Chair was Luc Claesen from IMEC, Belgium. The proceedings with 588 pages was published as a book by Chapman&Hall Publishers (now Springer) (Fig. 7).

Fig. 7. Cover of the VLSI 1997 book published by Chapman & Hall and cover of VLSI1999 published by Kluwer Publishers [9, 10].

In 1999, the conference was organized in Lisbon, Portugal. The General Chair was Prof. Luis Miguel Silveira and General Vice-Chair was Prof. José Monteiro both from INESC, Lisbon, Portugal and the Program Chair was Prof. Srinivas Devadas from MIT, USA. There were two Program Co-Chairs, Prof. Peter Ivey from University of Sheffield, UK and Prof. João Marques-Silva from INESC, Portugal. The proceedings were published as a book by Kluwer Publishers (now Springer Nature) (Fig. 7).

3 Years 2000's

In 2001, the conference was organized in Montpellier, France. The General Chair was Prof. Michel Robert, from LIRMM, France and the Program Chairs were Christian Piguet from CSEM, Switzerland and Bruno Rouzeyre, from LIRMM, France. The proceedings were published as a post-conference book by Kluwer Publishers (now Springer Nature). During the conference it was distributed to participant a Digest of Papers (Fig. 8).

Fig. 8. Cover of the VLSI2001 published by Kluwer Publishers [11]

In 2003, the conference was organized in Darmstadt, Germany. The General Chair was Prof. Manfred Glesner, from TU Darmstadt, Germany and the Program Chairs were Hans Eveking from TU Darmstadt, Germany and Prof. Vincent Mooney, Georgia Tech, USA. During the conference, the proceedings were distributed to participants. Then considering also the presentations done during the conference, for the first time a book was assembled with extended versions of conference best papers (with Springer Publishers) (Fig. 9). Leandro Indrusiak (at that time preparing a double PhD between TU Darmstadt, Germany and UFRGS, Brazil) has designed a logo for the VLSI-SoC series, that is being used till today (Fig. 10). It was also proposed by Leandro Indrusiak, a new conference call for papers template, that is being used in most of editions since there (Figs. 11 and 12).

In 2005, the conference was organized in Perth, Australia, October 17–19, 2005. The General Chair was Prof. Adam Osseiran from ECU, Australia. The General Vice-Chair was Stefan Lachowicz, also from ECU. The Program Chairs were Prof. Steve Kang from UC Santa Cruz and Prof. Hans-Joerg Pfleiderer, from University Ulm, Germany. The book with best papers extended versions was again published by Springer (Fig. 13).

From 2005, the conference that was organized each two years, become being organized each year. Prof. Ricardo Reis made the proposal to organize the VLSI-SoC Conference annually. This decision was mainly due to the fact the VLSI-SoC developed as a global conference moving around the world. Being organized each two years as it was, there was a too long time to return to a same region of the world.

Fig. 9. Cover of the VLSI2003 proceedings and cover of the book with extended versions of best papers published by Springer Publishers [12].

Fig. 10. Logo of the VLSI-SoC series developed by Leandro Indrusiak.

In 2006, the conference was organized in Nice, France, October 16–18, 2006. The General Chair was Salvador Mir from TIMA, Grenoble, France. The Program Chair was Prof. Giovanni De Micheli, from EPFL, Switzerland. The book with best papers extended versions was again published by Springer (Fig. 14).

In 2007, the conference was organized in Atlanta, USA, October 15–17, 2007. The General Chair was Prof. Vincent Mooney from Georgia Tech, USA. The Program Chairs were Prof. Yung-Hsiang Lu, from Purdue University, USA and Prof. Paul Hasler, from Georgia Tech, USA. The book with best papers extended versions was again published by Springer (Fig. 14).

In 2008, the conference was organized in Rhodes, Greece, October 13–15, 2008. The General Chair was Prof. Dimitrios Soudris from University of Thrace, Greece. The Program Chairs were Christian Piguet, from CSEM, Switzerland and Prof. Thanos

Fig. 11. VLSI-SoC 2003 CFP, that defined a new CFP template and VLSI-SoC 2009 and VLSI-SoC 2010 CFPs using a template based on the 2003 one.

Fig. 12. Some other CFPs using the CFP template: and VLSI-SoC 2011, VLSI-SoC 2012 and VLSI-SoC 2013.

Stouraitis, from University of Patras, USA. The book with best papers extended versions was again published by Springer (Fig. 15).

In 2009, the conference was organized in Florianópolis, Brazil, October 12–14, 2009. The General Chair was Prof. Ricardo Reis from Universidade do Rio Grande do Sul (UFRGS), Brazil. The Program Chair was Prof. Juergen Becker, from KIT, Germany. The Local Organizing Chair was Prof. José Güntzel from Universidade Federal de Santa Catarina, Brazil. The book with best papers extended versions was again published by Springer (Fig. 15). It was the first time that it was organized a PhD Forum as part of the conference.

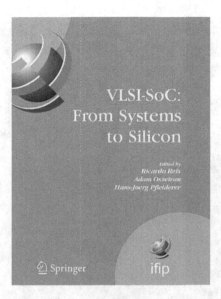

Fig. 13. Cover of the VLSI2005 book with extended versions of best papers published by Springer Publishers [13].

Fig. 14. Covers of the VLSI2006 and VLSI2007 books with extended versions of best papers published by Springer Publishers [14, 15].

Fig. 15. Covers of the VLSI2008 and VLSI2009 books with extended versions of best papers published by Springer Publishers [16, 17].

4   Years 2010's

In 2010, the conference was organized in Madrid, Spain, September 27–29, 2010. The General Chair was David Atienza from EPFL, Switzerland. The Program Chairs were Prof. Rajesh Gupta, from UC San Diego, USA and Prof. Andrea Acquaviva, from Politecnico de Torino, Italy. The book with best papers extended versions was again published by Springer (Fig. 16). In 2011, the event was organized in Hong Kong, October 3–5, 2011. The General Chair was Prof. Chi-Ying Tsui and Program Chair was Salvador Mir from TIMA, INPG, Grenoble.

In 2012, the conference was organized in Santa Cruz, CA, USA, October 7–10, 2012. The General Chair was Prof. Matthew Guthaus from UCSC, USA. The Program Chairs were Prof. Andreas Burg, from EPFL, Switzerland and Prof. Ayse Coskun, from Boston University, USA. The book with best papers extended versions was again published by Springer (Fig. 17). In 2013, the event was organized in Istanbul, Turkey, October 7–9, 2013. The General Chairs were Prof. H. Fatih Ugurdag from Ozyegin University, Turkey, and Prof. Luis Miguel Silveira from Tech. Univ. of Lisbon, Portugal. The Program Chairs were Prof. Alex Orailoglu from UCSD, USA and Prof. Luigi Carro from UFRGS, Porto Alegre, Brazil. The book with best papers extended versions was again published by Springer (Fig. 17).

In 2014, the conference was organized in Playa del Carmen, Mexico, October 6–8, 2014. The General Chairs were Arturo Sarmiento Reyes from INAOE, Puebla, Mexico and Prof. Ricardo Reis from UFRGS, Porto Alegre, Brazil. The Program Chairs were Prof. Luc Claesen, from University of Hasselt, Belgium and María Teresa Sanz, from

Fig. 16. Covers of the VLSI2010 and VLSI2011 books with extended versions of best papers published by Springer Publishers [18, 19].

Fig. 17. Covers of the VLSI2012 and VLSI2013 books with extended versions of best papers published by Springer Publishers [20, 21].

INAOE, México. The book with best papers extended versions was again published by Springer (Fig. 18). In 2015, the event was organized in Daejeon, Korea, October 5–7, 2015. The General Chairs were Naehyuck Chang, from KAIST, Korea and Prof. Kiyoung Choi, from Seoul National Univ, Korea. The Program Chairs were Youngsoo Shin, from KAIST, Korea and Prof. Chi-Ying Tsui, from HKUST, Hong Kong. The book with best papers extended versions was again published by Springer (Fig. 18).

Fig. 18. Covers of the VLSI2014 and VLSI2015 books with extended versions of best papers published by Springer Publishers [22, 23].

In 2016, the conference was organized in Tallin, Estonia, September 7–10, 2015. The General Chairs were Prof. Jaan Raik, from Tallinn UT, Estonia and Prof. Ian O'Connor, from ECL Lyon, France. The Program Chairs were Prof. Thomas Hollstein, from Tallinn UT, Estonia, Germany and Prof. Michael Hübner, from Ruhr-Univ Bochum, Germany. The book with best papers extended versions was again published by Springer (Fig. 19). In 2017, the event was organized in Abu Dhabi, UAE, October 7–10, 2017. The General Chairs were Prof. brahim (Abe) M. Elfadel, from Masdar Institute of Science and Technology, UAE and Prof. Fatih Ugurdag, Ozeyegin University, Turkey. The Program Chairs were Prof. Mihalis Maniatakos, from New York University, Abu Dhabi, UAE and Prof. Matteo Sonza Reorda, from Politecnico di Torino, Italy.

In 2018, VLSI-SoC was organized in Verona, Italy, October 8–10, 2018. The General Chairs were Prof. Graziano Pravadelli from University of Verona, Italy and Prof. Todd Austin from the University of Michigan, USA. The Program Chairs were

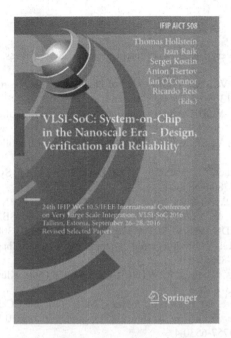

Fig. 19. Cover of the VLSI2016 book with extended versions of best papers published by Springer Publishers [24].

Prof. Nicola Bombieri from University of Verona, Italy and Prof. Masahiro Fujita from University of Tokyo, Japan.

In 2019, the conference is being organized in Cusco, Peru, October 6–9, 2019. The General Chairs are Prof. Carlos Silva-Cardenas, from PUCPeru, and Prof. Ricardo Reis, from UFRGS, Porto Alegre, Brazil. The Program Chairs are Prof. Giovanni De Micheli, from EPFL, Switzerland and Prof. Pierre Emmanuel Gaillardon, from Utah University, USA. In 2020, the conference will be organized in Salt Lake City, USA and in 2021 it will be in Singapore.

5 Conclusions

VLSI-SoC is a real global event in the field of Very Large Scale Integration Systems and Systems on a Chip. Each year it moves around the world, discussing and pre senting the results of researches on state-of-art. The books published during these 38 years are a good witness of the evolution of the VLSI and SoC design technology in the world.

References

1. Grey, J.: VLSI81: Very Large Scale Integration. Academic Press, London (1981). ISBN 9780122968600
2. Anceau, F., Aas, E.: VLSI83: VLSI Design of Digital Systems, North Holland, Amsterdam. ISBN 9780444867513
3. Hörbst, E.: VLSI85: VLSI Design of Digital Systems, North Holland, Amsterdam. ISBN 9780444879202
4. Séquin, C.: VLSI87: VLSI Design of Digital Systems, North Holland, Amsterdam. ISBN 9780444703705
5. Musgrave, G., Lauther, U.: VLSI89: VLSI Design of Digital Systems, North Holland, Amsterdam. ISBN 9780444883445
6. Halaas, A., Denyer, P.: VLSI91, North Holland, Amsterdam. ISBN 0-444-89019-X
7. Yanagawa, T., Yvey, P.: VLSI93, North Holland, Amsterdam. ISBN 0-444-89911-1
8. ASP-DAC 1995/CHDL 1995/VLSI 1995. IEEE Press. ISBN 4-930813-67-0
9. Reis, R., Claesen, L.: VLSI: Integrated Systems on Silicon. Chapman & Hall, London (1997). ISBN 0-412-82370-5
10. Silveira, L., Devadas, S., Reis, R.: VLSI: Systems on a Chip. Kluwer Publishers, Boston (2000). ISBN 0-7923-7731-1
11. Robert, M., Rouzeyre, B., Piguet, C., Flottes, M.-L. (eds.): SOC Design Methodologies. IFIP, vol. 90. Kluwer Publishers, Boston (2001). https://doi.org/10.1007/978-0-387-35597-9_40. ISBN 978-1-4757-6530-4
12. Glesner, M., Reis, R., Indrusiak, L., Mooney, V., Eveking, H. (eds.): VLSI-SOC: From Systems to Chips. IFIP, vol. 200, p. 316. Springer, Boston (2006). https://doi.org/10.1007/0-387-33403-3. ISBN 0-387-33402-5
13. Reis, R., Osseiran, A., Pfleiderer, H.-J. (eds.): VLSI-SoC: From Systems to Silicon. IFIP, vol. 240. Springer, Boston (2007). https://doi.org/10.1007/978-0-387-73661-7. ISBN 978-0-387-73660-0
14. De Micheli, G., Mir, S., Reis, R. (eds.): VLSI-SoC: Research Trends in VLSI and Systems on Chip. IFIP, vol. 249. Springer, Boston (2008). https://doi.org/10.1007/978-0-387-74909-9. ISBN 978-0-387-74908-2
15. Reis, R., Mooney, V., Hasler, P. (eds.): VLSI-SoC: Advanced Topics on Systems on a Chip. IFIP, vol. 291. Springer, Boston (2009). https://doi.org/10.1007/978-0-387-89558-1. ISBN 978-0-387-89557-4
16. Piguet, C., Reis, R., Soudris, D. (eds.): VLSI-SoC: Design Methodologies for SoC and SiP. IFIP AICT, vol. 313. Springer, Heidelberg (2010). https://doi.org/10.1007/978-3-642-12267-5. ISSN 1868-4238
17. Becker, J., Johann, M., Reis, R. (eds.): VLSI-SoC: Technologies for Systems Integration. IFIP AICT, vol. 360. Springer, Heidelberg (2011). https://doi.org/10.1007/978-3-642-23120-9. ISSN 1868-4238
18. Ayala, J.L., Atienza Alonso, D., Reis, R. (eds.): VLSI-SoC: Forward-Looking Trends in IC and Systems Design. IFIP AICT, vol. 373. Springer, Heidelberg (2012). https://doi.org/10.1007/978-3-642-28566-0. ISBN 978-3-642-28565-3, ISSN 1868-4238
19. Mir, S., Tsui, C.-Y., Reis, R., Choy, O.C.S. (eds.): VLSI-SoC: Advanced Research for Systems on Chip. IFIP AICT, vol. 379. Springer, Heidelberg (2012). https://doi.org/10.1007/978-3-642-32770-4. ISSN 1868-4238, ISBN 978-3-642-32769-8
20. Burg, A., Coşkun, A., Guthaus, M., Katkoori, S., Reis, R. (eds.): VLSI-SoC: From Algorithms to Circuits and System-on-Chip Design. IFIP AICT, vol. 418. Springer, Heidelberg (2013). https://doi.org/10.1007/978-3-642-45073-0. ISBN 978-3-642-45072-3

21. Orailoglu, A., Ugurdag, H.F., Silveira, L.M., Margala, M., Reis, R. (eds.): VLSI-SoC: At the Crossroads of Emerging Trends. IFIP AICT, vol. 461. Springer, Cham (2015). https://doi.org/10.1007/978-3-319-23799-2. ISBN 978-3-319-23798-5
22. Claesen, L., Sanz-Pascual, M.-T., Reis, R., Sarmiento-Reyes, A. (eds.): VLSI-SoC: Internet of Things Foundations. IFIP AICT, vol. 464. Springer, Cham (2015). https://doi.org/10.1007/978-3-319-25279-7. ISBN 978-3-319-25278-0
23. Shin, Y., Tsui, C.Y., Kim, J.-J., Choi, K., Reis, R. (eds.): VLSI-SoC: Design for Reliability, Security, and Low Power. IFIP AICT, vol. 483. Springer, Cham (2016). https://doi.org/10.1007/978-3-319-46097-0. ISBN 978-3-319-46096-3
24. Hollstein, T., Raik, J., Kostin, S., Tšertov, A., O'Connor, I., Reis, R. (eds.): VLSI-SoC: System-on-Chip in the Nanoscale Era – Design, Verification and Reliability. IFIP AICT, vol. 508. Springer, Cham (2017). https://doi.org/10.1007/978-3-319-67104-8. ISBN 978-3-319-67103-1

Author Index